RECONSTRUCTION
IN THE
SOUTH

MATERIALS OF AMERICAN HISTORY SERIES

Farrar, Straus & Giroux is preparing a new series of historical materials, primary materials which illustrate the history of every large geographical section and every important historical period in the history of the United States. The series will ultimately include reprints of important historical studies, collections of documents and memoirs, anthologies of classical sources on various historical, economic, and philosophical topics, and important biographies and autobiographies.

RECONSTRUCTION
IN THE
SOUTH

1865-1877
FIRST-HAND ACCOUNTS
OF THE
AMERICAN SOUTHLAND
AFTER THE
CIVIL WAR,
BY
NORTHERNERS & SOUTHERNERS

Edited, with an Introduction by

HARVEY WISH

Professor of History, Western Reserve University

New York

FARRAR, STRAUS AND GIROUX

CONTENTS

IX THE END OF RECONSTRUCTION

Introduction

I Reconstruction North and South: First Phase

Both sides demobilized swiftly, except for small Union detachments which garrisoned the chief Southern towns or policed the uneasy Indian frontier. Northern cities had come through unscathed, homes, factories, and railroads intact, and even the brief, painful postwar depression of 1866 did not slow the amazing growth of 1866-1873 above the Mason and Dixon's Line. The war had stimulated the heavy industries useful for the military; the manufacture of farm machinery exalted King Corn by feeding Europe as well as enabling the undermanned Northern farms to make up for the men who had gone into the Army. Singer and Howe sewing-machine producers were kept busy fulfilling government contracts; the manufacture of both shoes and uniforms became mechanized. Chicago's new Union Stock Yards, largest in the world, had processed cattle for the entire Union, and with Reconstruction came vast new cattle supplies through the Long Drive and the ranch system.

Within one man's lifetime, the rich frontier resources of the Great Plains would be exploited for the nation—silver, gold, lead, farm products, and transcontinental transportation. Alaska, purchased from Russia in 1867, proved no Seward's Folly, for it opened much-needed mineral and timber resources as a new frontier. The planters had, as it happened, deserted Washington in 1861 on the eve of a great economic boom, and Northern congressmen took advantage of the withdrawal of the conservative agrarians to subsidize transcontinental railroads—which naturally took a northern instead of a southern route. They enriched laborers and farmers through the Homestead Act of 1862, allowing "land for the landless," and aided scientific farming in the Morrill College Land Grant Act of the same year by utilizing public-land income for a system of state colleges.

Now in the postwar decades energetic Northern industrial and financial leaders created Carnegie's Age of Steel, Rockefeller's efficient oil-refining empire, the innovative meat-packing regime of Armour, Swift, Morris, and their associates who applied assembly-line techniques to meat-processing, and an army of city-builders to whom even the Great Chicago Fire of 1871 was a stimulant rather than a depressant. Despite the severe 1873-1877 depression, with its Northern railroad riots, the painful deflationary pressures felt by farmers, and the shocking political and speculative scandals of the Grant era, there was no real decline in the sharp upward economic thrust of the industrial states that had begun in the 1850s. Northern capital found outlets in the mines and ranches of the Great Plains and cautiously tapped the South for possibilities in rebuilding railroads, financing plantations, and sponsoring mines and furnaces around Birmingham. While hostile Southerners labeled the Yankee newcomers carpetbaggers, the migration of Northern businessmen and lawyers had been familiar to ante-bellum communities in the South. Long before the end of Reconstruction, reporters spoke of the New South of industry and commerce to which Northern capital was contributing and making the planter and Southern merchant much friendlier to the idea of federal subsidies. While the South did not cease to be rural, it had become so integrated economically and politically that the cry of States' Rights was raised largely upon the race issue and, to a lesser extent, by Southern exporters who wished low tariffs.

For Dixie, the war had taken 250,000 lives and (as the travel reports attest) the defeated people seemed generally plunged into gloom, if not poverty. Sherman's total war had systematically torn up railroad lines, plantations, and crops on the march through Georgia and South Carolina. Mathew Brady's photographs showed Atlanta, Columbia, and Richmond in ruins. The battlefield towns and farms between Washington and Richmond had been wrecked. Everywhere there were reports of closing banks and planters escaping bankruptcy only by the grace of stay laws which prevented foreclosures but endangered credit. The older factories were frequently dismantled and useless. Although the South was too much a farm country to remain devastated very long and would recover her prewar cotton production in a year or two, its large Negro labor force was frequently scattered, confused, or demoralized by the transition from slavery to freedom—although all obviously prized freedom.

Wealthy planters like Wade Hampton of South Carolina, once a millionaire owning some 3000 slaves on various plantations in his state and Mississippi, faced bankruptcy, overwhelmed by personal debts. But the planters did not feel like war criminals, and they angrily resented the imprisonment for two years of Jefferson Davis. They also disliked the old Fire-eaters who had preached secession and war and the "low-down people" who were to improvise the worst of Klan terrorism. In their own way, the planters worked for the return of ante-bellum Whig-style local government by whites and remained suspicious of alleged Negro domination; but they were ready to cooperate economically with Northern capital. While the planters and industrialists were Bourbons only in the sense that they wished to recover their ante-bellum control of race relations, they were "progressive" indeed in their desire to advance economically along modern urban, industrial, and commercial lines.

Before the war the planters had had an open enemy in Hinton Rowan Helper, from the highlands of North Carolina, who had denounced the planter's power and the crippling effects of slavery, cultural as well as economic. His angry *The Impending Crisis* (1857) had gratified antislavery men and shaken both parties in the House of Representatives when conservatives denied the Speakership to anyone who endorsed this dangerous book. Now the virulent Negrophobia that Helper had hitherto concealed burst out, and he proclaimed his purpose to "write the Negro out of America." His postwar books showed the heritage of racism familiar to many nonslaveholding highlanders before the war. While the planters usually tried to avoid racial violence (although some were more than benevolently neutral toward the Klan), they were firm on race policy save where they found it useful to support Negro suffrage as long as they could count upon it to operate in their own interest.

For the postwar Southern Negro, struggling as he was against the poverty and disease which suggested to many observers that the race was dying out, there was great encouragement in the fact of emancipation. The next goal, as seen by both Negro and liberal white supporters, was ultimate social equality. This had been the text of Charles Sumner's noted brief in the 1849 Roberts Case in Massachusetts. He had argued against Boston's school segregation as a violation of the principle of "equality before the law" and proclaimed that the classification of citizens by race violated the Bill of Rights and the Declaration of Independence and was illegal even if good Negro schools existed. Although he lost that case, Sumner and his associates of the Negro clubs led by William C. Nell witnessed shortly the complete desegregation of all Massachusetts schools. This was part of the biracial struggle for social equality that involved Thaddeus Stevens, John A. Bingham, and many other Radicals who had taken part in the ante-bellum reform movement. They saw fulfillment in the Fourteenth Amendment with its "equal protection of the laws"—although the courts tended to restrict its meaning to political and civil (rather than social) rights.

There were many educated Negro leaders during Reconstruction, although too few for the tasks of the Radical legislatures. Some had never been slaves and had entered professions or businesses in the North. Others were acute ex-slaves like Frederick Douglass, whose published work is decidedly realistic in its appraisal of the possibilities and objectives of an equalitarian Reconstruction.[1] Douglass refused to go South and to embark upon racial politics; he accomplished much more as an intelligent journalist and informal racial spokesman. Unfortunately, he agreed to accept the presidency of the ill-fated Freedmen's Bank; but it was not his fault that the bank collapsed. This tragic affair cost the savings of hundreds of thousands of Negroes and destroyed the hope that the race could thus be led along the path of Benjamin Franklin's middle-class virtues of thrift and personal success.

The failure of Reconstruction to provide land for the freedmen reflected the confusion in Congressional objectives and Presidential hostility to the idea. Sumner's 1866 speech "The Equal Rights of All"[2] shows that he had studied the contemporary Czarist precedent of freeing the serfs, giving them civil rights, and establishing many

[1] See pp. 82-89.
[2] See pp. 108-113.

of them on farms of their own. Stevens too had hoped to find confiscated Confederate lands for the freedmen. But various restraints upon the Freedmen's Bureau reduced the small-scale land distribution for Negroes to ineffectiveness, for the new farmers were left stranded after a few months without further support. Besides, President Johnson had no desire to convert Reconstruction into a social revolution, and he hastened to return a good deal of Confederate land seized and to protect the rest from confiscation.

As it turned out, the planters' lack of cash helped fasten the sharecropper system upon farm labor, although some contemporary observers, especially Robert Somers,[3] seemed favorably impressed by its practical effects. What the visitors could not readily see was that sharecropping forbade the Negro to acquire a real stake in the community, since sharecropping did not usually lead to land ownership, as other forms of tenancy might. Besides, dependence upon the fortunes of a single crop determined by the owner or merchant offered no future for the freedmen. It was no social ladder to a higher status; however, hasty observers sometimes concluded that the Negroes, being an irresponsible people, liked the happy ways of the grasshopper.

The surprisingly slow advance of the Negro compared to almost any large immigrant group was attributed by Southern conservatives to his own innate shortcomings. But ahead lay social discriminations, barriers to the entrance of Negroes in many trades they had practiced in slavery days, a ninety-per-cent illiteracy inherited from ante-bellum years and not easily overcome, cheating of the sharecroppers by the land owners without adequate recourse for the victims, shortcomings of justice in local courts and institutions—especially in the local office of sheriff—and the indifference of the "Silent South" described by George Washington Cable of New Orleans. Still, Reconstruction seemed encouraging at first as Negroes left their slave quarters, joined a crusade for mass education as the key to freedom, and even formed independent churches to escape the segregated "nigger pew" of the white churches and to express their own informal and intense religious experiences.

[3] See pp. 198-202.

II Rise and Fall of the Johnson States in the South

Lincoln's assassination on April 15, 1865, left unfulfilled his moderate plan for Reconstruction, but it was clear that he had intended to bring the former Confederate states into the full function of statehood as soon as he could obtain assurances of their loyalty to the Union, the abolition of slavery, and the repeal of the secession ordinances. His amnesty proclamation of December 8, 1863, had offered complete pardons to former Confederates, except for the higher officers and former federal officials who had resigned to join the rebellion. The Lincoln plan permitted seceded states to be readmitted whenever a loyal core amounting to ten per cent of the state's 1860 voters took an oath of loyalty to the Union and established new governments.

But he would not go further. He pocket-vetoed the Radical Republican bill of Senator Benjamin Wade of Ohio and Representative Henry Winter Davis of Maryland which required that a *majority* of enrolled voters take the oath to support the Constitution before organizing state conventions and new governments. In addition, the Wade–Davis bill demanded convention delegates to take an "iron-clad oath" swearing that they had never aided the confederacy or held office under it.

To the Radicals, who feared that the fruits of war would be filched by the unconvinced rebels, the "Lincoln states" were ineligible to take their places in Congress. They hoped for better results from President Andrew Johnson, a man warmly praised by Unionists for his integrity and his bravery as a Southerner in combating wealthy planters, secessionists, and extreme proslavery men. His excellent record as a Union war governor of Tennessee and as a stanch Lincoln supporter and his recent denunciation of rebels as traitors who must be punished seemed reassuring. The fact that he was still a traditional State's-Rights man, a former owner of eight slaves, and a Democrat committed to orthodox Southern racial attitudes was not noted at first. Informally, he threatened to destroy "the social power" of the Confederate leaders and at first even excluded from his amnesty well-to-do Southerners with more than $20,000 in taxable income. Furthermore, he kept Lincoln's cabinet and his general policies.

But before long Johnson was speeding up Lincoln's rate of pardons among Confederate leaders. He sent General Grant and other investigators—usually nonabolitionists—to report upon the temper of the South. Grant, who was never an antislavery man and who usually voted Democrat (when he did vote), reassured the country that "the mass of thinking men of the South accept the present situation of affairs in good faith." Similar assurances came from Benjamin Truman, Johnson's friend and former aide during his governorship of Tennessee.[4] But it was a mistake for the President to send Carl Schurz, a lifelong liberal; he was not at all impressed by the alleged repentance of the South. He angered Johnson by reporting that racial persecution and arrogant attitudes in the South required Negro suffrage as an effective check.[5] These official impressions of the defeated South may be compared with the detailed firsthand observations of socially minded Scottish editor Robert Somers, antislavery novelist John T. Trowbridge, and blunt Major John William De Forest, an able writer who viewed his duties as a minor Freedmen's Bureau official without narrow dogmatism.[6]

The South was obviously happy with the rapid establishment of the new Johnson state governments. Except for Mississippi, they cheerfully complied with the condition that they ratify the Thirteenth Amendment abolishing slavery and repeal the secession resolutions, but they ignored Johnson's mild appeal that some token Negro suffrage be adopted to checkmate the Radicals. The local mores held that the Negro was uneducable and required no training for jobs normally denied him—although, inconsistently, some feared

[4] See pp. 30-38.
[5] See pp. 40-48.
[6] See pp. 66-77.

that education would make the Negro too powerful. The Johnson legislatures were quite willing to adopt the Yankee idea of free public schools so long as they excluded Negroes. They undertook the expensive task of rebuilding the war-torn South, but later critics observed that these state governments had shown their own pattern of fraud and scandal usually ascribed exclusively to the effect of the Carpetbag regimes of 1868-1876.

Northern public opinion, watchful for any signs of the return of slavery in some new guise, flared up at the news of anti-Negro riots during 1866 in Memphis and New Orleans—the latter vouched for in a report by the irrepressible General Philip Sheridan.[7] The Congressional Joint Committee of Fifteen on Reconstruction collected hundreds of pages of testimony on these racial incidents and persecution. They noted that following the speedy demobilization of Union troops, especially Negro soldiers, local terrorists had organized Regulators and Jayhawkers to intimidate the freedmen and their friends. These were the antecedents of the Klan.

Southerners felt deep resentment when the federal government created the Freedmen's Bureau just before the war ended. This unique agency, whose services have been minimized by accusations of wholesale corruption, spent millions to feed and clothe poor whites and Negroes, and protected the freedmen by scrutinizing labor contracts, acting as a court to resolve conflicts affecting the Negroes and their employers, and putting pressure on Southern officials to curb discrimination. Especially significant were the energetic pioneer efforts to set up Negro schools at all levels, including Negro colleges such as Howard University, named for O. O. Howard, the "Christian General" who headed the Bureau.[8] Since most local white teachers feared to lose caste by teaching Negroes, and faced ostracism if they did, the Bureau welcomed the Yankee schoolmarms of both races who were usually detested by the natives as enemies and spies. That the Bureau failed miserably to provide farms for the freedmen was due in great part to the hostile policy of President Johnson, who looked upon the Bureau officials as meddlers and

[7] See pp. 52-58.
[8] See pp. 172-179.

hastened to return confiscated land to former Confederates without finding suitable alternatives for the Negro's future. Soviet historians, looking back at this era in their own history, note that even the Czar, Autocrat of All the Russias, far excelled the American Reconstruction governments in providing land for recently emancipated people.

Northern editors and travelers were incensed by the wave of Black Codes that swept the Johnson legislatures. These codes were intended as an improvement over chattel slavery and they even added some civil rights previously denied. Although they sought to assure stability—and cheap labor—amid an illiterate people, evidence of deep racial prejudice was unmistakable. Negroes, it was pointed out, could now sue in the courts, hold property, and even act as witnesses; but Trowbridge and others noted that the ex-slaves enjoyed limited freedom of movement due to stringent vagrancy laws, severe fines for those who "enticed" laborers away from their employers, and strictly enforced contract obligations. Peace was to be preserved not only by forbidding Negroes weapons and drinking in excess, but also through rigid curfew rules. The caste system was strengthened by making intermarriage between races a felony. While some of the states passed relatively mild codes, others (like Mississippi) tightly hemmed in the freedman.

While the Republicans fumed at the Black Codes and denounced the Dixie legislatures for refusing to pass the Fourteenth Amendment, Southern defenders pointed out that certain Northern states had also rejected the Amendment and discriminated against Negroes. Sumner could only reply[9] that there were too few Negroes in the North for these prejudices to do much harm; besides, the reluctant Northern states did finally approve the Amendment early in 1867.

So long as President Johnson could count on Congressional majorities during 1865-1866, he was able to outmaneuver the Radicals. When Congress tried to extend the Freedmen's Bureau, Johnson emphatically vetoed the bill and was sustained in both Houses. But moderates as well as Radicals were increasingly disturbed by news from the South and feared that the admission of representa-

[9] See pp. 108-113.

tives of the Johnson governments to Congress would mean a greatly strengthened South—with fifteen more congressmen than before—due to the abolition of the old Three Fifths clause that had given planters the right to count three fifths of their slaves as a basis for representation. Thus the recently defeated states, aided by Northern Democrats, could dominate Congress indefinitely. Thaddeus Stevens made this clear in his speeches,[10] arguing that the former Confederacy consisted of "conquered provinces" and that freedom required the "permanent ascendancy of the Union Party." This fear of Southern power provides the context for Sumner's theory that the Southern states had committed suicide by secession. In either case, the Radical solution was the rejection of the Johnson states, Congressional reconstruction of pro-Union governments, and military control.

The Radical Joint Committee of Fifteen, consequently, resolved to refuse admission to the Union of the eleven states of the Confederacy until Congress should decide upon their future. Congress passed Senator Lyman Trumbull's Civil Rights Bill to protect the freedmen's citizenship by permitting the federal government to intervene directly if necessary. This law assured the freedman his right to sue and to share with white citizens the equal protection of the laws. The President, as expected, vetoed the Civil Rights bill on April 9, 1866, pointing out again violations of States' Rights. But his foes were now united, and Congress refused to sustain him. A few weeks later a rebellious Congress not only passed a second Freedmen's Bureau Bill, but promptly overrode Johnson's veto of it.

Apprehensive over any future action by a conservative Democratic Congress to overthrow these gains for the freedmen, the Radical-controlled Joint Committee on Reconstruction pushed through the Fourteenth Amendment. Its vital and varied provisions gave relative permanence to Trumbull's Civil Rights law, defined citizenship, penalized voting discrimination by reducing the state's congressional representation proportionately (a clause never used), and wiped out the Confederate debt. Congressman John A. Bingham of Ohio, a Radical long associated with the antislavery movement, wrote the famous

[10] See pp. 92-98.

clause guaranteeing "the equal protection of the laws" for all citizens and freedom from state discrimination. Hence the Fourteenth Amendment was designed to extend the privileges of the federal Bill of Rights to citizens injured by the states as well as those hurt by the federal government. While business came under the same protections as those reserved for the freedmen, there is little doubt that Congress was thinking primarily of the plight of Negroes.

Historians call 1866 the "critical year" because voters elected an overwhelming majority of Radicals to Congress, thus insuring the equalitarian experiment that followed in the so-called Carpetbag states. In that campaign, President Johnson tried to check the Radicals by backing the new National Union Convention at Philadelphia, in which Massachusetts and South Carolina delegates walked together arm in arm. This conservative convention included not only Northern Democrats but a number of well-known Confederate leaders—including Alexander Stephens, the Vice-President of the Confederacy. Johnson himself attracted national attention by his highly publicized "swing around the circle" to defend his policies in the chief Northern cities; but persistent Radical hecklers, counting upon the President's short temper when crossed, ruined the effect of his appeal. With their two-thirds majority in both Houses, the Radicals prepared to destroy the conservative Johnson state governments and inaugurate Congressional reconstruction.

III *The Radical Experiment*

To replace the Johnson governments, Congress passed the Reconstruction Act of March 2, 1867, and supplementary acts. The ten seceded states (Tennessee had been admitted) were combined into five military districts, each under the rule of a brigadier general (or higher) who initiated elections for state conventions to write new constitutions prescribing the details of state and local government.

A strict test oath eliminated the former Confederate leaders but permitted Negroes to vote, thus allowing the registration of more than 703,000 Negroes and 660,000 whites—the latter figure being about the same as the total white register for 1860. Johnson of course vetoed this bill along with supplementary proposals, denounced the Radical plan as a military dictatorship, and warned that this meant Africanization of the South. Again large Radical majorities overwhelmed him.

The next Radical step was to weaken the President's patronage power and prestige through the Tenure of Office Act, which forbade the Chief Executive to remove his officials appointed with the consent of the Senate unless that body approved. Johnson nevertheless, dismissed Secretary of War Stanton from the cabinet because of his liaison with the Radicals in Congress. Thereupon his opponents had their issue and went to work to draw up a long list of so-called high crimes and misdemeanors based on this violation of the Tenure of Office Act and other more tenuous charges to justify the impeachment and conviction of the President. The House did impeach Johnson, and the Senate, presided over by Chief Justice Salmon P. Chase, sat as a quasi-judicial body to hear the charges and arguments during the spring of 1868. While none could actually impugn the personal integrity of Johnson, the majority apparently felt, as Sumner did in his "Opinion" [11] that the real issue was freedom for the ex-bondsmen of the South. Only a single vote short of the required two thirds saved Johnson from conviction.

But Johnson's prestige and power had been badly shaken and even the Democratic Convention of 1868 decided to pass up his candidacy for re-election in favor of Horatio Seymour of New York. The Republicans almost inevitably chose General Ulysses S. Grant, who was now close to the Radicals and angry with Johnson on personal grounds. Although the general won twenty-six out of thirty-four states, his slim popular majority of 306,000 out of a total of 5,715,000 votes was retained only by the fact that 700,000 Negroes voted. The Republicans decided to press immediately for a Negro

[11] See pp. 114-121.

suffrage amendment—the Fifteenth—to insure the continuance of their program.

Meanwhile the South looked to the Supreme Court for aid, but were thoroughly disappointed. In two cases, *Georgia v. Stanton* and *Mississippi v. Johnson,* Southern states tried to enjoin the Executive from enforcing the Reconstruction Acts, but the Court denied its jurisdiction in such political disputes. In at least one major case, however, *Ex Parte Milligan* (December 1866) the Court did anger the Radicals by holding that even in wartime there was no right to use military law wherever the civil courts were in operation, but this did not discourage the Radicals from requiring military tribunals in administering the Reconstruction Acts.

The Radical state government record of 1868-1876 has been referred to as Black Reconstruction, but this is misleading since Negroes very rarely enjoyed legislative majorities and the majority of actual voters was white. Besides, the Negroes did not press their advantage even on issues that attracted them, such as mixed schools or a revolutionary land program, and their moderate representatives in Congress such as Senator Hiram Revels of Mississippi even urged the removal of civic disabilities from the former Confederates. While there were a good number of educated Negro leaders among the ministers, teachers, and lawyers who held office, the average Negro was illiterate and ignorant of democratic processes— though eager to learn. Still, over two centuries of American residence even under slavery had taken the Negro far from the cultural level of his African ancestors and the charge of "Africanization" made by Johnson and the Southern conservatives had little substance.

Inevitably, in this critical hour of biracial government (it was never "Negro rule"), the freedman looked to the tutelage of friendly and experienced white mentors, many of them undoubtedly concerned with their own political advantage. The northern Union Leagues, organized during the war to promote patriotism, sponsored hundreds of Southern branches which trained the Negroes to become Radical Republicans through political catechisms, oral propaganda, and social pressures. Closely allied to the Union Leagues were the officials and employees of the Freedmen's Bureau, many of them Union officers and uniformed soldiers whose support by the Army made them anathema to Southern conservatives; their biracial educational program and equalitarianism aroused the wrath of the Ku Klux Klan. As the tense early years of Radical rule passed and the occupation troops were greatly reduced, counter-revolutionary groups openly threatened to overthrow the Carpetbag regimes by force. Apparently for this reason the Radicals expanded the state militias and, since Southern whites did not usually care to serve with Negroes (although some did), these forces came to be known as Negro militias.

The contemptuous term *Carpetbaggers* (derived from the low status attributed to those who could put all their possessions in a single bag) has been so invidious that the historian must point out that the migration of ambitious Northerners to the South was quite familiar before the war, that many Union veterans stationed in the South liked that warmer clime as their home, and that the so-called Carpetbag politicians of the North included such well-educated racial idealists as Governor Adelbert Ames of Mississippi and Governor Daniel H. Chamberlain of South Carolina, both of whom were respected among many Southern conservative voters; Chamberlain even leaned backwards in his efforts to be "fair" to the South.[12] True, these men were also interested in economic and professional opportunities for themselves, and some, as in Louisiana, even forged a tight alliance between the Radical governments and monopolistic business interests;[13] in some states these politicos gave overgenerous favors to the railroads. By the middle 1880s, the Supreme Court was using the equal rights clause of the Fourteenth Amendment increasingly to protect corporate "persons" rather than freedmen.

[12] See pp. 255-273.
[13] In the noteworthy Slaughterhouse cases of 1873 in Louisiana, Radicals had given one corporation a monopoly of the entire slaughtering business at the expense of the small butchers. This practice was upheld by the Supreme Court, which rejected the argument that such a monopoly violated the individual rights protected by the Fourteenth Amendment; Justice Miller, speaking for the Court, insisted that this Amendment was primarily intended to protect the Negro.

If the term *carpetbagger* is obviously invidious, the word *scalawag* is even worse, for to the conservative it implied betrayal by disloyal native Southerners. Yet the South had never been altogether of one mind on secession and war, for in 1861 the Southern Unionists came close to blocking the secessionists. Crackers, cajuns, highlanders, and the people of the hill country had often looked upon the Civil War as "a rich man's war and a poor man's fight." Besides, there were many Southern editors between 1868 and 1872 who urged fellow conservatives to collaborate with the new Radical regimes so as to bore from within against prolonged domination; an undetermined number of qualified voters, it is true, chose to abstain from cooperation.

Ante-bellum planters, merchants, and factory owners had commonly voted the Whig ticket and now tended to blame the Democrats for the war and everything else. There was the interesting example of Governor James L. Alcorn, the first Republican governor of Mississippi, a rich Delta planter and former Whig, who was technically a scalawag, ready to associate with Negro politicians so long as he could utilize their voting strength. Only in the early 1870s, when the campaign against alleged Negro rule reached a tense pitch, did he draw the line at the Radical policies. By that time the cooperative conservatives had switched over to overt counter-revolutionary strategy.

Perhaps the factor most disheartening to sincere Radicals like Sumner were the chronic reports of gross Carpetbag corruption and of the freedman's alleged incompetence. Horace Greeley's widely read correspondent James S. Pike, who had been Lincoln's minister to The Hague and an ardent Republican, wrote a shockingly racist book on the "Sambo" legislators of South Carolina in *The Prostrate South* (1874). He pictured them as minstrel types, pompous, arrogant, childlike, and given to inventive types of larceny, embezzlement, and fraud. While it requires no close analysis of the book to discern Pike's crude prejudices, the fact that a Republican of his standing should publish *The Prostrate South* seemed to confer credibility upon the current indictment of the Carpetbaggers and Africanization. By this time too, Carl Schurz as well as Sumner had wearied

of the Radical race experiment, but they offered no practical alternatives.

It may be assumed that there was substance in the repeated
charges of widespread corruption, but historians are coming to agree
that these have either been greatly exaggerated or presented out
of context of the unusual national picture of corruption—such as
"Grantism." It was the speculative era of the Gilded Age, of the ex-
ploits of the Robber Barons, the high-level thievery of top officials
involved in the Whisky Ring, or the robbery of the Indian trading
posts. Jay Gould and Jim Fisk tricked a naïve President into temporarily tolerating the gold corner of Black Friday, and New York's
Tammany Hall bribed multitudes to accept favors for their votes.
Even Louisiana and South Carolina graft paled by comparison with
the feat of William Marcy Tweed and his City Hall ring, who
mulcted New York taxpayers of perhaps one or two hundred million
dollars. Several Northern state governments reported their own in-
genuities in fraud.

While none cared to justify the robbery of a people recently impoverished by war, there were explanations for the scandals. As in
the rapid construction of Northern cities, the giant task of rebuilding the South offered quick profits to unscrupulous contractors and
politicians. Among the wealthy beneficiaries were planters who obtained the official privilege of exploiting convict lease contracts,
which meant very cheap labor indeed. Railroad men bargained with
legislators for special franchises and concessions. Younger historians
tend to minimize the older charge that the Radical governments
burdened the next generation with enormous debts, for the Radical
constitutions (most of them kept by their conservative successors)
often prevented the pledging of state funds and credit for corporate
enterprises. That the New South retained large pockets of poverty
had much to do with the backward technology of its people and the
denial of opportunities to Negroes who were capable of far more
productive tasks than those of sharecroppers and menial workers.

On the favorable side, the Radical legislatures could justify their
heavy expenditures and rising taxes. They continued the expensive
task of rebuilding a wrecked section, replacing public buildings and

broken rail lines, and restoring bridges and impassable roads. Unlike the Johnson governments, they built a public school system for Negroes for the first time; this brought an enthusiastic response from the colored people. To the high cost of providing mass education was added the new burden of providing charitable and welfare institutions for the hitherto-neglected Negroes: orphanages, homes for the aged, hospitals, and other services that had to be financed. The record for probity of high Negro officials like Senators Revels and Blanche K. Bruce was unchallenged, while most of the local Negro officials apparently were no worse—and often better—than the usual run of rural jobholders for that era.

Factionalism and rioting stained the record of Radical governments, especially in Louisiana, where an anti-Grant coalition from both parties fought pro-Grant Republicans for power. Anti-Grant factions attacked Negro parades and homes in 1873 and since nearly all of the deaths were of Negroes, it seemed credible to assume that they were not the aggressors. President Grant decided to back one of the rival governors, Walter P. Kellogg, and sent federal troops to support him. On this occasion former President Johnson, now the Senator from Tennessee, rose to make one of his last speeches to denounce the administration for establishing a military despotism in violation of state and judicial rights.[14]

Some of the worst episodes of the Reconstruction were the handiwork of the Ku Klux Klan, the history of which is illustrated in these documents by both official and informal witnesses representing conservative and Radical viewpoints, including those of the living victims. While the planters deplored the terrorism of the Klan, the Red Shirt leader Wade Hampton defended their motives and tried to get Northern lawyers to take the cases of Klansmen. Too many Southern Democrats liked to think of the Klan as a liberating army bent on curbing the menace of the Negro militia, the Union League, and the Freedmen's Bureau, all symbols of Negro equality. However, it was difficult to be romantic about the nightridings, the beatings, the murders, and the burning of Negro schools.

General Howard was probably correct in his belief that Bureau

[14] See pp. 132-135.

officials and schools were special targets of the Klan, who feared that Negro rule would be strengthened by education. Enthusiastic conservatives liked to wear Klan hats, sing Klan songs, flourish Klan knives, and dance to special Klan tunes. Although the Klan may have originated in Pulaski, Tennessee, during 1866 in the spirit of a lark—a contested interpretation—it soon became a secret underground movement to destroy Radical power in the interest of white supremacy. It had its rivals in the secret Knights of the White Camelia of Louisiana, the Knights of the Rising Sun in Texas, and other local cults of violence. Their depredations of 1869-1871 infuriated Northerners and led Congress to hold intensive hearings into these activities.[15] As a result Congress passed the Ku Klux Klan Acts of 1870-1871 to enforce the guarantees of the Fourteenth and Fifteenth amendments. Heavy fines and imprisonment were provided to keep Klansmen from intimidating voters, while the federal courts and the President were empowered to enforce these laws. Grant, in consequence, declared nine South Carolina counties regions of prevailing terror. Federal troops moved into threatened areas, hundreds were arrested, many trials took place, but too few convictions were won. Radical legislatures passed their own anti-Klan laws, but these were not too effective. When the terrorism of the "low-down people" subsided, the planters supported rifle clubs, saber clubs, artillery clubs, and other counter-revolutionary groups to intimidate the Radicals and their Negro following. Wade Hampton's Red Shirts adopted the colored political shirts of Garibaldi's revolutionary army as their uniform, the precursor of twentieth-century fascist shirts of Italy, Germany, and even the Silver Shirts of the United States.

However, the Northern Republicans seemed so disillusioned with the failures of Radical policies that they allied themselves with Southern Conservatives imbued with the old Whig philosophy of merchants and planters. Conservatives were eager to catch up with the federal subsidies they had missed by a futile war and deserted the Democrats even before the election of 1876. These "Bourbons" needed Northern capital and moved to victory under the banner of

[15] See pp. 153-179.

the three *Rs*—Retrenchment, Reconciliation, and Reform. They were fully prepared for the Wormley Bargain of 1877 (formalized in the Wormley House in Washington) to end the dispute in the Hayes–Tilden election by supporting the Republican candidate in return for the withdrawal of federal troops, Republican votes for federal subsidies to Southern railways, and other concessions.

IV *The End of Reconstruction*

Governor Rutherford B. Hayes of Ohio was an honored Civil War general and a scrupulously honest, if economically conservative, governor of his state. Apparently he felt kindly toward the Negro in a paternalistic way, and he was to spend his years following retirement from the Presidency as an active head of the Slater Fund for Negro education despite his doubts as to Negro educability. (He was to tell a Baltimore audience that the only gift of Negroes was in oratory!) During the 1876 campaign Hayes told anxious Negroes that their rights would be safer in the hands of the South than in those of the federal government. But, as already noted, such intellectual inconsistencies were not uncommon among erstwhile Radicals in the age of expanding corporate power, imperialism, and newer interests divorced from the old antislavery cause.

Thus the Wormley Bargain rescued Hayes from defeat, after Election Day had showed that Tilden had won an overwhelming popular vote and was only one electoral vote short of victory. The miracle of reversal was accomplished by an Electoral Commission of Fifteen (five from the Senate, five from the House, and five from the Supreme Court) that split eight to seven on key questions. They refused "to go behind the returns" and gave the disputed votes of Florida, South Carolina, and Louisiana to Hayes. The Bargain insured that the Tilden men would not rise up in revolution, for the South had been split.

President Hayes' withdrawal of federal troops meant the automatic collapse of the remaining Radical governments and the momentous decision to return the control over race relations to the Southern whites. Northern opinion now veered to the Southern view that Reconstruction had been a terrible mistake and that it had now been "proved" that legislation was impotent against local customs. Not everything the Radicals had done was scrapped, of course. Conservatives retained the Radical constitutions and even the Negro schools, although funds were not overgenerous. Retrenchment, as interpreted by the victorious Bourbons (or Redeemers), also meant the enlargement of the iniquitous convict lease system, the use of chain gangs, and the strengthened vagrancy laws that could be used to keep the Negro in his place and to keep wages down. Furthermore, the Bourbons were even willing to permit the Negro to vote, so long as they controlled that vote. This tolerance might even be extended to cooperative Negro officeholders.

The implications of the Compromise of 1877 became clear in the next two decades with the victory of the discontented small farmers under the self-styled Demagogues, Ben Tillman of South Carolina and James K. Vardaman of Mississippi. After 1885 the Negroes saw the Fifteenth Amendment become a nullity. Jim Crow laws were not only formalized by local laws but also greatly expanded in application until the Fourteenth Amendment lost force as Negroes were denied equal access to public facilities. The Supreme Court in the Civil Rights cases (1883)[16] nullified federal laws that guaranteed to the Negro such social rights as free access to inns, railroad depots, and theaters. Thus the fears of the Radicals regarding the reversal of civil rights were realized. This tendency was emphasized in *Plessy v. Ferguson* (1896), which stated the segregationist principle of "separate and equal" that was to endure until the Earl Warren decision of 1954 in *Brown v. Topeka*. In the Plessy decision the jurists had gone back to a decision of Justice Lemuel Shaw, who had rejected Sumner's pleas in the Roberts case of 1849 for "equality under the law" as irrelevant in considering the legality of racial classification. Another Sumner—William Graham Sumner, the Yale sociologist and

[16] See pp. 146-147.

author of *Folkways*—was to teach the next generation that legislation could not change customs. Thus the basic racial problems of Reconstruction were left to a later generation for a solution.

The events of the 1960s will not leave the student of Reconstruction untouched or detached, regardless of a desire to achieve the fullest objectivity. He can only evaluate the events of a great historical movement by their consequences as well as the expressed intentions of the actors. The arguments of Bingham, Sumner, and their fellows regarding the meaning and necessity of the Fourteenth Amendment are still contemporary and are now implied in the law of the land. But the conservative position of Andrew Johnson, General John G. Gordon, and the disciples of William Graham Sumner is reflected in contemporary resistance to civil rights legislation. Historians have sided with one side or the other. The very titles for books on Reconstruction (such as *The Age of Hate* or *The Tragic Era*) imply that Johnson's solution was the best then and now. Present-day statesmen of each section have revived the debate over Radical centralization versus Johnsonian States' Rights. Can these constitutional issues be resolved without recourse to the much larger issues obviously involved?

Meanwhile, the historical analysis of Reconstruction will continue to suggest controversial present-day implications. The role of Radical ideas and ideals will bog down upon the assumptions of the weakness of human nature that allegedly produced corruption and political despotism in the Radical legislatures. Did the growing Radical disillusionment prove the inherent unworkability of federally directed reforms? Did the experience of Reconstruction bear out the conservative fears of Africanization? Do modern racial theories require a fresh examination of the mind of the post-bellum South, and of the North? For the student, even a limited documentary approach has the great value of visualizing another era in order to understand the emotions of an earlier generation deeply involved in a bitter quarrel.

V *The Rewriting of Reconstruction History*

The controversial story of Reconstruction as told by the chief actors —federal and local statesmen, generals, former Confederates, freedmen, newspaper correspondents, so-called Carpetbaggers and scalawags, and Klan victims—is inescapably contemporary despite major differences in the facts and setting.

The generation of Charles Sumner embarked briefly and indecisively upon an experiment in race relations, but even Sumner was eventually to balk at the slow progress made in civil rights, the continued use of federal troops to occupy the South, and the distressing reports of Carpetbag corruption. Anglo-Saxon ideas of civil rights opposed standing armies for any cause. Radical enthusiasm for equal rights lacked the support of modern theories regarding Negro potentialities and rested largely upon sentiment alone. The anthropologists of that day, generally Southern disciples of Nott and Glidden, were convinced that the Negro was inherently inferior to the white man, and this view was increasingly congenial to global tendencies toward imperialism and the White Man's Burden. It is therefore not surprising that even eminent historians holding antislavery views, like James Ford Rhodes and the members of the Burgess–Dunning group at Columbia University at the turn of the century, were impressed by the Southern idea that Reconstruction meant Africanization.

Foes of the Radicals testify in these documents that the motives for Reconstruction were "hate, revenge, greed, lust for power," to use the words of the former Republican governor of South Carolina, Daniel H. Chamberlain, a disillusioned one-time officer of a Negro regiment during the war and (technically) a Carpetbagger. But he had forgotten the consistently strong record for civil rights of Thaddeus Stevens (whom he hated), Charles Sumner, and John A.

Bingham, and the entire antislavery group which had crusaded before
the war for human equality and were promoting the Reconstruction
amendments (the Thirteenth, Fourteenth, and Fifteenth), whose outstanding features included freeing the slaves, insuring civil rights
against state discrimination, and introducing Negro suffrage. Readers
of these documents will ponder over the question whether the Radical
acts and speeches were part of a coherent pattern or were mere rationalization. Were the Radicals ambitious men concerned primarily with keeping the Republican Party permanently in power by
the use of the race issue? On the other side, readers may wonder
how realistic were the historic veto messages of President Andrew
Johnson and his scruples on violation of States' Rights and fears of
the coming of "Africanization." The so-called "revisionist" historians who agree with Andrew Johnson and D. H. Chamberlain will put
most emphasis on those documents that "prove" that Reconstruction
was a tragic mistake based upon an overestimate of the potentialities of the freedmen. (In this connection, the reader may consider
the documents by Frederick Douglass and other Negro spokesmen
included here.) The case for Radical Reconstruction is strengthened
by the testimony of many brilliant correspondents who visited the
South, among them John T. Trowbridge, Robert Somers, and Charles
Nordhoff (although he was ready in 1875 to call off federal military
forces).

The outlook of the generation that witnessed Southern Reconstruction during 1865-1876 was inevitably affected by their beliefs
concerning the causes of the Civil War. Those moderates like Lincoln and Johnson who believed that the war was primarily concerned
with preserving the Union and abolishing slavery were not ready to
go beyond the limited objectives of the Thirteenth Amendment,
although they would have liked to see some token concessions in
giving the vote to "very intelligent Negroes." Lincoln had hoped
to eliminate slavery by peaceful stages perhaps by 1900, and had
vainly urged slaveholders to accept compensated emancipation. Johnson, as will be noted, shared this gradualist viewpoint despite his
own temperamental vagaries.

One noted conservative historian, Ulrich B. Phillips, who recalled the current opinions of his Georgia neighbors during Reconstruction, came to stress the theme of white-man supremacy as a guiding one for the coming of the Civil War and as the central thread of Southern history. There is much to be said for his argument that the Confederacy fought to keep the South a white man's country. If one ignores his insistence that the abolitionists provoked the war and his racist assumption of Negro inferiority, this argument has high plausibility and also helps explain Southern resistence to Radical equalitarianism as well as the basic motives for the firing on Fort Sumter.

Contemporary observers and later historians have speculated on the reasons why an essentially non-slaveholding population (in 1860 there were 384,000 heads of slaveholding families living amid 8,000,-000 whites) fought so long and so bravely merely to preserve slavery. Why was there so little class antagonism between the wealthy planters and the small white farmers who performed all of their own labor? The hypothesis that seems to fit most of the facts is that both were united, like modern white South Africans, to preserve white supremacy, and believed that slavery and the caste system were the most effective devices to police the Negro. Although there were 8,000,000 whites to 4,000,000 Negroes, there were enormous Negro majorities in ardently secessionist states like Calhoun's South Carolina and Jefferson Davis' Mississippi. All white classes were involved in a common effort to check slave plots, if not actual insurrections, and to support vigilant slave patrols. In that day of rapidly rising slave prices, there could have been only very limited incentives for the non-slaveholder to strive for the status of planter; racial motives seem more powerful than economic motives for the preservation of slavery.

This theory that white supremacy was the leading cause of Southern resistance in 1861 is reinforced by a variety of other factors and helps to explain Southern psychology in 1865-1876. Even great liberals like Jefferson and Washington had hesitated over emancipation because, as they frankly admitted, they feared that race conflicts would emerge out of the long-existent antagonisms; therefore

Jefferson, for one, insisted upon the African colonization of the ex-slaves as part of any plan for freedom. His views of Negro inferiority not only prevailed in the South and much of the North during Reconstruction (see his *Notes on Virginia*), but the ante-bellum South reinforced these ideas (without mentioning emancipation) through the impressive pseudo-science of Nott-Glidden anthropology and the warm acceptance of such European racists as Count Arthur de Gobineau, who had written of the superiority of Aryans.

It is therefore not difficult to understand that the defeated South took the surrender almost philosophically—few joined guerrilla forces —but reacted violently when the Radicals sought to impose racial equalitarianism. With Lee's armies disbanded, there remained only resistance via underground forces—such as the Ku Klux Klan and the White Leagues. Scalawags—white Southerners collaborating with the Radicals—were guilty of racial treason. Noting the large amount of race prejudice existing in the North, evidenced during the debates over the Fourteenth Amendment, Southerners drew the inference that Radicals were either fanatics or hypocrites motivated by a desire to keep themselves in power. They were surprised at Northern resentment over the Black Codes, which seemed to them a logical substitute for the racial policing once done through slavery. These codes assured a cheap labor supply, included strict vagrancy laws (some based on Northern models) to put the idle to work, required apprenticeship for dependent Negro youths, and regularized family relationships while banning intermarriage. As the Klan testimony suggests, the fear of miscegenation operated powerfully in a community where white supremacy played a central psychological role.

Naturally, historians who have discovered a plethora of causes for the Civil War have an equivalent number of explanations for Reconstruction, as the vast literature on the subject reveals. During the Great Depression, when economic interpretations flourished, many historians and teachers were attracted by the theory of Charles Beard in the *Rise of American Civilization* that the Civil War was a conflict between tariff-hungry industrialists and free-trade planters. These industrialists had conspired to write the equal

protection clause of the Fourteenth Amendment to protect corporations (as "persons") from unfriendly state legislative policies on
rate control, burdensome taxes, and reduced corporate-charter privileges. Radicals were pictured as far more concerned with pro-
motional schemes and high tariffs (Stevens as an iron manufacturer
did favor a protective tariff) than with Negro rights.

By the mid-twentieth century those historians who rejected slavery
or Negro rights as the main cause of the war—Revisionists like
James Randall, George Fort Milton, Avery Craven, and many others
—thought of the War as needless, a product of abolitionist fanat-
icism, or a result of the ineptitude of a blundering generation and
parochial statesmen. In this revisionist spirit, the story of Reconstruction was also recast. By as early as 1913, James Schouler
(among others) had converted the crude frontier image of Andrew
Johnson into Lincolnesque terms. Sumner was no longer a great
humanitarian but a pompous, erudite fanatic, and Thaddeus
Stevens (who rarely had a good press) was coarse, abusive, and a
pathological case. Southern conservatives of the Reconstruction era
saw their beliefs become orthodox nationally in 1915, when D. W.
Griffith filmed Thomas Dixon's racist novel *The Clansman* as *The
Birth of a Nation*. One historian, Woodrow Wilson, who gave it a
White House showing, praised it as a wonderful way to teach history.
Liberals and the NAACP protested for more than fifty years
against the repeated exhibitions of this story of the alleged Africanization of the South, the brutality of the Negroes, the fanati-
cism of the Radicals, and the knight-errantry of the Ku Klux Klan
rushing to save outraged white womanhood. Such a Southern conservative view, in more intellectual form, was given in Claude
Bowers' widely read *The Tragic Era* (1929). A spate of pro-Johnson
biographies began to appear.

Behind the extreme revisionist trend was a rising tide of anti-
Negro feeling that accompanied the victory of the demagogic
Tillmans, Vardamans, and other politicians who around 1890 over-
threw the more circumspect Bourbon conservatives—the economically conservative planters and merchants who had held to the prewar
pattern of racial paternalism. There was also, as already noted, the

effect of a new racialism from abroad, fed upon imperialist expansion in Africa and Asia. Jim Crow had become formalized by Southern laws denying public facilities equally to both races, and the Fifteenth Amendment guaranteeing Negro suffrage had been nullified by grandfather clauses, white primaries, literacy tests, and outright intimidation, of which wholesale lynching was one widely adopted method during 1885-1905. In the North even Lincoln's Springfield witnessed a shocking race riot in 1908; just ahead lay the Northern city riots of East St. Louis (1916) and Chicago (1919), and during the Twenties, when antilynching bills failed in the Senate, discouraged Negroes took up Marcus Garvey's "Back to Africa" movement.

In our own time, historians of Reconstruction are far from immune to the impact of the Negro and Civil Rights Revolution of the 1950s and 1960s. These issues, in a world setting of anti-imperialist movements in Africa, Asia, and Latin America, raised directly the question of the role of the colored man in a white man's world. Besides, closer to home, the Negro had impressive strength, far more than in Radical times, in his growing political power in Northern cities where he held the balance of power, even in national elections, as in 1960. Therefore historians could not escape a feeling of participation in the events of Reconstruction because of the obvious analogies with the present. Besides, the new generation of historians, which now included many able Negro scholars directly identified with the basic human issues, were far better equipped than their predecessors in the new social sciences to understand that race and culture were separate entities. Doctrines of racial superiority had become untenable or scientifically obsolete. Hitler's use of racialist doctrine had penetrated Western consciousness too deeply for this lesson to be missed, even by those who had never studied biology. Therefore, readers of the newer histories need not discount the objectivity of this changing image of Reconstruction. Fresh insights and new scientific tools have become available to historians of this generation who are seeking to construct a past that would otherwise remain dead.

Negro historians who feel that they have an immediate stake in Reconstruction history have never been so greatly attracted by

Beard's conspiracy idea of the Fourteenth Amendment as to write off the struggle for freedom as a kind of economic rationalization. Thus one of the more advanced interpretations is held by a convincing Negro scholar, John Hope Franklin, author of *Reconstruction after the War* (1961), as well as by other young scholars of his race. There is considerable modification of the older revisionism in David Donald's rewriting of James Randall's *Civil War and Reconstruction*. Thaddeus Stevens has friendlier biographers than ever in Ralph Korngold and Fawn Brodie, while Andrew Johnson, after enjoying so many ovations from Winston, Stryker, Bowers, Milton, and many more, is critically dealt with by Eric McKitrick's *Andrew Johnson and Reconstruction* (1960) and Kenneth M. Stampp's *The Era of Reconstruction* (1965). While conservative Southerners continue to berate Reconstruction and all its works, Southern-born liberals like C. Vann Woodward add immeasurably to a more convincing and objective interpretation of a highly controversial theme.

EDITORIAL NOTE

All selections have been printed as they appeared in the original sources, except that occasionally punctuation has been silently amended.

Recent Bibliography on Reconstruction

Alexander, Thomas B. *Political Reconstruction in Tennessee* (1950).

Bartlett, Irving H. *Wendell Phillips* (1961); very favorable.

Bentley, George R. *A History of the Freedmen's Bureau* (1955); objective.

Brock, W. R. *An American Crisis: Congress and Reconstruction* (1963).

Brodie, Fawn M. *Thaddeus Stevens* (1959); usually favorable.

Buck, Paul. *Road to Reunion* (1937); stresses social and cultural contacts between sections.

Coulter, E. Merton. *The South During Reconstruction* (1947); a conservative view.

Cox, La Wanda and John. *Politics, Principle, and Prejudice, 1865-66* (1963); anti-Johnson.

Du Bois, W. E. B. *Black Reconstruction* (1935); Marxist, praises Radical record.

Franklin, John H. *Reconstruction after the Civil War* (1961); very acute.

Horn, Stanley F. *Invisible Empire: the KKK* (1939).

Hyman, Harold M. *Era of the Oath* (1954); study of Radical politics.

Korngold, Ralph. *Thaddeus Stevens* (1955); very favorable.

Lewinson, Paul. *Race, Class, and Party: Negro Suffrage and White Politics in the South* (1932); a classic.

McKitrick, Eric L. *Andrew Johnson and Reconstruction* (1960); usually critical.

Morrow, Ralph. *Northern Methodism and Reconstruction* (1956); illuminating.

Quarles, Benjamin. *Lincoln and the Negro* (1962).

Randall, James G. *Lincoln the President* (Vol. IV, 1955); conservative view.

Randall, J. G. and Donald David. *The Civil War and Reconstruction* (1961).

Sharkey, Robert P. *Money, Class, and Party* (1959).

Shugg, Roger W. *Origins of Class Struggle in Louisiana* (1939).

Simkins, Francis B. and Robert H. Woody. *South Carolina During Reconstruction* (1932).

Singletary, Otis. *Negro Militia and Reconstruction* (1957).

Stampp, Kenneth. *The Era of Reconstruction* (1965); raises Radical stock.

Swint, Henry L. *The Northern Teacher in the South, 1862-70* (1941).

Thomas, Benjamin J. and H. M. Hyman. *Stanton* (1962).

Trefousse, Hans L. *Benjamin F. Wade* (1963).

Wharton, Vernon L. *The Negro in Mississippi* (1947); invaluable.

Whyte, James H. *The Uncivil War: Washington During Reconstruction* (1958).

Woodward, C. Vann. *Reunion and Reaction: Compromise of 1877* (1951); original thesis.

Woodward, C. Vann. *The Strange Career of Jim Crow* (1955); brilliant.

PART ONE

THE COLLAPSE OF THE OLD SOUTH

John Townsend Trowbridge: A Critical View of Postwar Georgia and Mississippi by a Popular Novelist

Among the early Northern observers of the wartorn South following closely behind the Northern armies was the Boston journalist, novelist, and editor of boys' adventure books, John T. Trowbridge (1827-1916). He had been born on a farm in Monroe County, New York, and was largely self-taught, gaining valuable experience as a schoolteacher and writer. In a half-century of prolific writing, he turned out some forty volumes of fiction, many of them novels that fascinated an entire generation of boys; in addition he wrote articles for the *Atlantic Monthly*, which was especially interested in the South, and he tried his hand at poetry, plays, and an autobiography.

Like many of the Northern and British visitors of 1865-1866, Trowbridge spoke harshly of the South and its race relations, pointing out the deep prejudices against the Negroes and expressing doubts concerning the reformation of former Confederates. His opinions on such matters as the severe Mississippi Black Code were shared by the Chicago *Tribune* and other Northern papers opposed to the "soft peace" of Lincoln and Johnson.

From Trowbridge's book *A Picture of the Desolated States* (Hartford, Conn., 1868), chaps. 64, 52.

As my first view of Atlanta was had on a dismal night, (if view it could be called), so my last impression of it was received on a foggy morning, which showed me, as I sat in the cars of the Macon train, waiting at the depot, groups of rain-drenched negroes around out-door fires; the dimly seen trees of the Park; tall ruins looming through the mist; Masonic Hall standing alone (having escaped destruction); squat wooden buildings of recent, hasty construction, beside it; wind-rows of bent railroad iron by the track; piles of brick; a small mountain of old bones from the battle-fields, foul and wet with the drizzle; a heavy coffin-box, marked "glass," on the platform; with mud and litter all around.

A tide of negro emigration was at that time flowing westward, from the comparatively barren hills of Northern Georgia to the rich cotton plantations of the Mississippi. Every day anxious planters from the Great Valley were to be met with, inquiring for unemployed freedmen, or returning home with colonies of laborers, who had been persuaded to quit their old haunts by the promise of double wages in a new country. Georgia planters, who raise but a bale of cotton on three, four, or five acres, could not compete with their more wealthy Western neighbors: they higgled at paying their freedmen six or seven dollars a month, while Arkansas and Mississippi men stood ready to give twelve and fifteen dollars, and the expenses of the journey. As it cost no more to transport able-bodied young men and women than the old and the feeble, the former were generally selected and the latter left behind. Thus it happened that an unusually large proportion of poor families remained about Atlanta and other Georgia towns.

There were two such families huddled that morning under the open shed of the depot. They claimed that they had been hired by a planter, who had brought them thus far, and, for some reason, aban-doned them. They had been at the depot a week or more, sleeping in piles of old rags, and subsisting on rations issued to them by the Bureau: stolid-looking mothers, hardened by field-labor, smoking short black pipes; and older children tending younger ones, feeding them out of tin cups, and rocking them to sleep in their arms. It was altogether a pitiful sight,—although, but for the rain which beat in upon them, I might have thought their freely ventilated lodgings preferable to some of the tavern-rooms I had lately slept in. But to me the most noticeable feature of the scene was the spirit manifested towards these poor creatures by spectators of my own color.

"That baby's going to die," said one man. "Half your children will be dead before spring."

"How do you like freedom?" said another.

"Niggers are fated," said a third. "About one out of fifty will take care of himself; the rest are gone up."

"The Southern people are the niggers' best friends," resumed the first speaker. "They feel a great deal of sympathy for them. There are many who give them a heap of good advice when they leave them."

Good advice is cheap; but nobody gave these homeless ones anything else, nor even that,—with a single exception: there was one who gave them kind words and money, but he was a Yankee.

The remarks of the ladies in the car were equally edifying.

"How much better off they were with somebody to take care of 'em!"

"Oh dear, yes! I declare it makes me hate an Abolitionist!"

"The government ought to have given them houses!"—(sneeringly). "If I had seven children to take care of, I'd go back and sell 'em to my old master."

"Do see that little bit of a baby! it's a-kicking and screaming! I declare, it's white! one of the young Federals', I reckon."

From Atlanta, until within about twenty-five miles of Macon, the railroad runs upon a ridge, from which the waters of the country flow each way,—those of the west side, through the Flint River and the Appalachicola to the Gulf; those of the east, through the Ocmulgee and Altamaha to the Atlantic. The soil of this ridge is sandy, with a mixture of red clay; much of it producing little besides oaks and pines. The doorways of the log-huts and shabby framed houses we passed, were crowded with black, yellow, and sallow-white faces,—women, children, and slatternly, barefoot girls, with long, uncombed hair on their shoulders,—staring at the train. The country is better, a little back from the railroad, as is frequently the case in the South.

Macon, at the head of steamboat navigation on the Ocmulgee River, and the most important interior town in the State, is a place of broad, pleasant streets, with a sandy soil which exempts it from mud. It had in 1860 eight thousand inhabitants. As it was a sort of city of refuge, "where everybody was run to," during the latter years of the war, its population had greatly increased. Hundreds of white refugees from other parts of the country were still crowded into it, having no means of returning to their homes, or having no homes to return to. The corporation of Macon showed little disposition to relieve these unfortunate people, and the destitution and suffering among them were very great. They were kept from starvation by the government. "To get rid of feeding them," said Colonel Lambert, Sub-Assistant-Commissioner of the Freedmen's Bureau, "we are now giving them free transportation wherever they wish to go."

By a recent census, taken with a view to catching vagrants and setting them to work, the colored population of Macon was shown to be four thousand two hundred and seventy-three. "All those who are not now employed will soon be taken by the planters. If any will not hire out, they will be set to earning their living on the public streets. I have now on hand applications from Alabama and Mississippi planters for three hundred laborers; I could fill the orders if I chose to, for the negroes are much disposed to emigrate. But all the freedmen in the counties of my district are needed here, and I encourage them to remain."

Colonel Lambert had on hand sixteen cases of murder and felonious shooting by white persons, negroes being the victims. The seventeenth case was reported from Twiggs County, while I was at Macon. A chivalrous sportsman, apparently for the fun of the thing, took a shot at a negro walking peaceably along the street, and killed him. The Colonel sent out twenty-five mounted men to hunt the murderer; but it was almost impossible to make arrests in such cases. There were in every place unprincipled men who approved the crime and helped to shield the criminal. Warned by them of the approach of blue uniforms, he would betake himself to the canebrakes, or to some friendly garret, where he would lie safely concealed until the scouts had given up their search for him and retired from the neighborhood. These negro-shooters and their accomplices were no doubt a small minority of the people, but they were a very dangerous minority, whom the better class did not deem it prudent to offend by assisting the officers of justice.

Crimes of this description were more or less frequent in districts remote from the military posts. In some places the freedmen were shot down in mere wantonness and malice. In others, the very men who had been wishing them all dead or driven out of the country, had become enraged at seeing them emigrate for higher wages than they were willing to pay, and sworn to kill any that attempted to leave the State.

Said Colonel Lambert: "To prevent these outrages, we need a much greater military force than we have. But the force we have is being reduced by the mustering out of more troops. We are thus prevented from carrying out the intentions of the government; and there is danger that before long the continuance of its authority here will be regarded as a mere farce. What we need is cavalry; but our troops are all infantry. I mount them in a case of emergency, where some desperado is to be hunted, by seizing horses at the first livery-stable, which we return after we have got through with them, politely thanking the proprietor in the name of the government."

The southwestern part of Georgia is one of the most fertile sections of the South: it is the region of large plantations and rich planters. The northern half of the State is comparatively unproductive: it is the region of small planters, and of farmers who do their own work with the aid of their sons. Much of the northwestern part is barren. The fertile Southwest suffered little damage from the war; it came out of it with its plantations unimpaired, and a large stock of cotton on hand. Northern and Middle Georgia were ploughed with the furrows of desolation. Sherman's army left nothing in its track but poverty and ruin. Plantations were wasted, provisions taken, stock killed or driven away, buildings and farming implements destroyed. The people were left very poor: they raised no crops in '65, and a famine was very generally anticipated.

In this condition, all the better class of planters recognized the sincere efforts of the Freedmen's Bureau to aid them, and to organize a labor system which should prove beneficial to both employers and employed. They generally spoke of its officers with respect; and many acknowledged that it would be a great injury to the country to have it immediately removed. Others were bitter in their opposition to it; and I often heard such remarks as this: "The idea of a *nigger* having the power of bringing a *white man* before a tribunal! The Southern people a'n't going to stand that."

The negro of Middle Georgia is a creature in whom the emotions entirely predominate over the intellectual faculties. He has little of that shrewdness which town life cultivates in the black race. The agents of the Bureau complained that they had sometimes great difficulty in persuading him to act in accordance with his own interests. If a stranger offered him twelve dollars a month, and a former master in whom he had confidence, appealing to his gratitude and affection, offered him one dollar, he would exclaim impulsively, "I work for you, Mass'r Will!" Sometimes, when he had been induced by his friends to enter a complaint against his master or mistress for wrongs done him, ludicrous and embarrassing scenes occurred in the freedmen's courts. "Now, Thomas," says the good lady, "can you have the heart to speak a word against your old, dear, kind mistress?" "No, missus, I neber will!" blubbers Thomas; and that is all the court can get out of him.

The reverence shown by the colored people toward the officers of the Bureau was often amusing. They looked to them for what they had formerly depended upon their masters for. If they had lost a pig, they seemed to think such great and all-powerful men could find it for them without any trouble. They cheered them in the streets, and paid them at all times the most abject respect.

I was told that the blacks were quite as apt to keep their contracts as the whites; and that often, when they broke them, it was through the persuasion of some planter who lacked laborers. "Look here, Sam,

I'm giving two dollars a month more than this man you are at work for; why don't you come and live with me?" A respectable planter was fined a hundred and fifty dollars for this offence, by the Bureau, whilst I was at Macon. "It is one of the worst offences we have to deal with," said Colonel Lambert, "and one that we punish most severely."

It was the popular belief that the agents of the Bureau had control of funds arising from such fines, and that they appropriated them pretty freely to their own use. On the contrary, they were required at the end of each month to make returns and forward all funds on hand to the chief quartermaster of the State, who alone was authorized to apply them in necessary expenditures.

There were four freedmen's schools in Macon, with eleven teachers and a thousand pupils. There was a night-school of two hundred children and adults, where I saw men of my own age learning their letters (and thought, "What if *I* was now first learning *my* letters?") and gray-haired old men and women forming, with slowness and difficulty, by the aid of spectacles, the first characters in the writing-book. The teachers were furnished by the American Missionary Association, —the freedmen paying for their own books, (an item with the booksellers), and for the necessary fuel and lights.

Mr. Eddy, the superintendent, and an old experienced teacher, said to me: "The children of these schools have made in a given time more progress in the ordinary branches of education than any white schools I ever taught. In mathematics and the higher sciences they are not so forward. The eagerness of the older ones to learn is a continual wonder to me. The men and women say, 'We work all day, but we'll come to you in the evening for learning, and we want you to make us learn; we're dull, but we want you to beat it into us!' "

I was much interested in a class of young clergymen who recited in the evening to the young matron of the "teachers' home." One of them told me with tears of gratitude how kind and faithful all the teachers had been to them.

"Are you not mistaken?" I said. "I have been told a hundred times that the Southern people are your best friends."

He replied: "Georgia passed a law making it a penitentiary offence, punishable with five years' imprisonment, to teach a slave to read.

Now we are no longer slaves, and we are learning to read. They may deceive you, but *we* know who are our best friends."

I was repeatedly assured by earnest secessionists that there were no Union men in Georgia; that, soon or late, all went into the rebellion. But one day I met an old man who denied the charge with indignation.

"I am sixty-five years old. I fought for the spot where Macon now stands, when it was Indian territory. I don't know what they mean by no Union men. If to fight against secession from first to last, and to oppose the war in every way, makes a Union man, I was that. Of course I paid taxes, because I couldn't help it. And when Stoneham raided on us, and every man that could bear arms was pressed, I went with the rest, and was all day behind the breastworks. But I've always spoke my mind, and being an old citizen, I never got hung yet. A majority of the people of Macon were with me, if they had only dared to say so. They hate the secessionists now worse than they hate the Yankees: no comparison! The secessionists now cry, 'No party!' but never a party stuck together closer than they do.

"The Confederates," he went on, "injured us ten times more than the Yankees did. When Wilson came in last April, he put a guard at my house, who stayed with me seven weeks, and did his duty faithfully."

It seemed impossible for the people of Mississippi—and the same may be said of the Southern people generally—to understand the first principle of the free-labor system. Their notions of it were derived from what they had seen of the shiftless poor whites about them, demoralized by an institution that rendered labor disreputable. They could not conceive of a man devoting himself voluntarily to hard manual toil, such as they had never seen performed except under the lash. Some compulsory system seemed to them indispensable. Hence the new black codes passed by the reconstructed legislatures of several States.

Mississippi, like South Carolina, on returning to the fold of the Union, from which those innocent lambs had strayed, made haste to pass apprentice laws, vagrant laws, and laws relating to contracts and labor, designed to bring back the freedmen under the planters' control. "An Act to regulate the Relation of Master and Apprentice," passed in November, 1865, provides that "all freedmen, free negroes, and mulattoes, under the age of eighteen, who are orphans," or are not maintained by their parents, shall be apprenticed "to some competent and suitable person,"—the former owner to "have the preference"; that "the said apprentices shall be bound by indenture, in the case of males until they are twenty-one years old, and in case of females until they are eighteen years old"; that said master or mistress shall have power to inflict "moderate corporal chastisement"; that in case the apprentice leaves them without their consent, he may be committed to jail, and *"punished as provided for the punishment of hired freedmen, as may be from time to time provided for by law,"*—the meaning of which is clear, although the grammatical construction is muddy; and that any person who shall employ, feed, or clothe an apprentice who has deserted his master, "shall be deemed guilty of a high misdemeanor," and so forth.

It will be seen that, by this act, (approved November 2nd, 1865,) not merely children without means of support may be thus bound out under a modified system of slavery, but that young girls, and lads of from fourteen to eighteen, capable not only of supporting themselves, but of earning perhaps the wages of a man or woman, may be taken from the employment of their choice and compelled to serve without wages the master or mistress assigned them by the court.

"An Act to amend the Vagrant Laws of the State" provides that "all freedmen over the age of eighteen years, found on the second Monday in January, 1866, or thereafter, with no lawful employment or business," (as if no man was ever honestly without employment), "or found unlawfully assembling themselves together either in the day or night time, shall be deemed vagrants, and on conviction thereof shall be fined in the sum of not exceeding fifty dollars, and imprisoned at the discretion of the court not exceeding ten days"; provided, however, that in case any freedman "shall fail for five days after the imposition of said fine to pay the same, that it shall be, and is hereby, made the duty of the sheriff of the proper county to hire out said freedman to any person who will for the shortest period of service pay said fine or forfeiture and all costs."

A bill "To confer Civil Rights on Freedmen, and for other Purposes," enacts "That all freedmen, free negroes, and mulattoes may sue and be sued, implead and be impleaded in all the courts of law and equity of this State, and may acquire personal property and choses in action, by descent or purchase, and may dispose of the same, in the same manner, and to the same extent that white persons may: *Provided that the provisions of this section shall not be so construed as to allow any freedman, free negro, or mulatto to rent or lease any lands or tenements, except in incorporated towns and cities.*"

Not to speak of the gross injustice of this last provision, what shall be said of the wisdom of that legislation which prohibits an entire laboring class from acquiring real estate in the country, where their presence and energies are indispensable, and holds out an inducement for them to flock to the towns, which are crowded with them already, but where alone they can hope to become freeholders?

Another section of this bill enacts that freedmen shall be competent witnesses in all cases where freedmen are parties to the suit, or where a crime is alleged to have been committed by a white person upon the person or property of a freedman. But it does not give them the power to testify in cases in which only white persons are concerned. All the negro testimony bills which I have seen, passed by the legislatures of the reconstructed States under gentle pressure from Washington, are marked by this singular inconsistency. If the negro is a competent witness in cases in which his own or his fellow's interests are involved, he is certainly a competent witness in cases involving only the interests of white persons. He is permitted to give evidence when there may exist a temptation for him to swear falsely, and not when there is no such temptation. By the enactment of such laws the whites are in reality legislating against themselves. Even Governor Humphreys— late Rebel general, but now the reconstructed executive of the "loyal" State of Mississippi, elected for his services in the Confederate cause —in his message to this same legislature, favoring the admission of negroes into the courts as an indispensable step towards ridding the State of the military power, and of "that black incubus, the Freedman's Bureau," made this suggestive statement:—

"There are few men living in the South who have not known many white criminals to go 'unwhipt of justice' because negro testimony was not permitted in the courts."

The act "To confer Civil Rights on the Freedmen," proceeds to make the following provisions, which look much more like wrongs: "That every freedman, free negro, and mulatto shall, on the second Monday of January, one thousand eight hundred and sixty-six, and annually thereafter, have a lawful home or employment," (of course on any terms that may be offered him), "and shall have written evidence thereof, as follows, to wit: If living in any incorporated city, town, or village, a license from the Mayor thereof; and if living outside of any incorporated city, town, or village, from the member of the Board of Police of his beat, authorizing him or her to do irregular and job work, or a written contract, as provided in section sixth of this act; which licenses may be revoked for cause, at any time, by the authority granting the same."

Section sixth enacts: "That all contracts for labor made with freedmen, free negroes, and mulattoes, for a longer period than one month, shall be in writing and in duplicate; . . . . and said contracts shall be taken and held as entire contracts; and if the laborer shall quit the service of the employer before expiration of his term of service, without good cause, he shall forfeit his wages for that year up to the time of quitting." But who is to be the judge with regard to the "good cause?" The white man, of course, and not the negro.

"Section 7. Be it further enacted, That every civil officer shall, and every person may, arrest and carry back to his or her legal employer any freedman, free negro, or mulatto, who shall have quit the service of his or her employer before the expiration of his or her term of service."

Section ninth provides that if any person *"shall knowingly employ any such deserting freedman, free negro, or mulatto, or shall knowingly give or sell to any such deserting freedman, free negro, or mulatto any food, raiment, or other thing, he or she shall be guilty of a misdemeanor, and upon conviction, shall be fined not less than twenty-five dollars, and not more than two hundred dollars and the costs."*

These extracts—which I have made verbatim from an authorized copy of the recent State laws, with only such abridgments as were necessary to compress them within reasonable limits—show plainly enough what ideas prevail in the late Slave States on the subject of free labor. The design of all such enactments is simply to place both the labor and the laborer in the power of the employer, and to reorganize slavery under a new name. The fact that they are practically set aside and annulled by the miiltary power and the Freedmen's Bureau, does not set aside or annul the spirit which dictated them. This still animates the people of the South; and I was often plainly told that as soon as the States were fully restored to their rights, just such laws as these would certainly be put in force. I remarked to a Mississippi planter, "Do you not think it was unwise for your Legislature to pass such a code of laws?" "Yes, it was unwise, *at this time*," he replied, not understanding the scope of my question. *"We showed our hand too soon.* We ought to have waited till the troops were withdrawn, and our representatives admitted to Congress; then we could have had everything our own way."

Since the admission of negro testimony in the civil courts of the

State, the freedmen's courts had been discontinued,—greatly to the disadvantage of the colored race. The civil courts could hardly be induced to give the negro's cause a hearing. There were some exceptions; and at Vicksburg I found a judge who seemed inclined to administer justice without regard to the prejudice against color. This was Judge Yerger, an original Union man,—one of the seven (against seventy-eight) who voted No, on the adoption of the ordinance of secession in the Convention of 1861; the same who, when asked by a member what title should be given to that act, replied, "Call it *An Ordinance for the Abolition of Slavery and the Desolation of the South.*"

Yerger was the President of the new Convention that reconstructed the State. That Convention was animated by a very different temper from that shown by the new Legislature. The Convention was composed of the best men in Mississippi, who went prepared to do what the Government at Washington had a right to expect of rebellious States returning to their allegiance; the Legislature was made up of a different class, elected after the people of the South had been encouraged in their animosity and arrogance by the discovery that treason was not to be punished, nor made particularly odious. The Convention was governed by men of large influence and liberal views; the Legislature was controlled by narrow-minded intermeddlers, mostly from the poorer districts of the State, where the inhabitants hated the negroes the more by way of revenge for having owned so few.

It was claimed by the better class that the Legislature did not represent them, and there was talk of calling another State Convention. But the Legislature, although it did not carry out the views of the more enlightened and progressive citizens, nor reflect in any way the sentiments of the great mass of true Union men in the South, namely, the blacks, represented quite faithfully the majority by which it was elected.

I have already alluded to the organizing of the State militia,—an abuse that unfortunately received the sanction of the Administration. The only possible excuse for it was the cry raised regarding anticipated negro insurrections. To guard against danger from a class whose loyalty and good behavior during the war challenged the admiration of the world, arms were put into the hands of Confederate soldiers who had returned to their homes reeking with the blood of the nation. Power was taken from the friends of the government and put into the hands of its enemies. The latter immediately set to work disarming the former. They plundered their houses, under the pretense of searching for weapons; committing robberies, murders, and other atrocities, with authentic reports of which pages might be filled. Neither were white men, known to sympathize with the Union party of the North, safe from their violence. Governor Humphreys himself, startled by the magnitude of the evil that had been called into existence, told Colonel Thomas that he had been obliged to disband several militia companies already organized, "on learning that they were sworn to kill negroes asserting their independence, and to drive off Northern men."

Of what was being done by private parties outside of the militia organizations, a curious glimpse is given in the following "general order," published in the Holmesville (Miss.) "Independent":—

"[General Order No. 1.]"

"SUMMIT, MISS., Nov. 28, 1865."

"In obedience to an order of His Excellency, the Governor of Mississippi, I have this day assumed command of all the militia in this section of the State, with head-quarters at this place. And whereas it has been reported to me that there are various individuals, not belonging to any military organization, either State or Federal, who are engaged in shooting at, and sometimes killing, the freedmen on private account; and whereas there are other white men reported as the attendants of, and participants in, the negro balls, who, after placing themselves upon a social equality with the people of color, raise quarrels with the freedmen, upon questions of social superiority already voluntarily waived and relinquished by them in favor of the negro, by which the peace of the country is broken and the law disregarded; I therefore order the arrest of all such offenders, by the officers and soldiers under my command, and that they be taken before some civil officer having power to commit to the county jail, for the purpose of awaiting the action of the Grand Jury.

"Men must quit blacking themselves, and do everything legally.

"OSCAR J. E. STUART,
"Q. M. G. and Col. Com. Militia."

The objection here seems to be to shooting the freedmen "on private account," or doing anything "illegally," thus taking the proper work of the militia out of its hands.

There were no doubt serious apprehensions in the minds of the people on the subject of negro insurrections. But a great deal that was said about them was mere pretense and cant, with which I have not seen fit to load these pages. There was not, while I was in the South, the slightest danger from a rising of the blacks, nor will there be, unless they are driven to desperation by wrongs.

I remember two very good specimens of formidable negro insurrections. One was reported in Northern Mississippi, and investigated personally by General Fiske, who took pains to visit the spot and learn all the facts concerning it. According to his account, " a colored man hunting squirrels was magnified into a thouand vicious negroes marching upon their old masters with bloody intent."

Sidney Andrews Observes the Demoralization
of the South

Far more acute than John Trowbridge was Sidney Andrews (1835-1880), special correspondent for the Chicago *Tribune* and the Boston *Advertiser,* both strong antislavery papers. Andrews was born and raised in Massachusetts and educated at the University of Michigan. A rover much of his life, an adventurous miner in the gold rush, and a noted journalist, he must have found congenial his assignment of September to November 1865 in the Carolinas and Georgia. His articles, like those of Trowbridge, were critical in tone; they were later combined in a 400-page book, *The South Since the War* (Boston, 1866).

His clear insights into both races, his depiction of the illiterate, prejudiced rural Southern white and the naïve Negro suggests the talents of Frederick Law Olmsted, who had left a classic on the Cotton Kingdom. This selection has considerable human interest and reflects a critical knowledge of the realities behind the rationalizations expressed by the various classes. Andrews found slavery surviving in isolated rural pockets, learned that the freedman was especially concerned over winning the right to testify in the courts, and wondered about the real issues that underlay the new labor relations. Here again a journalist found a state of affairs that could not justify Johnson's desire for the quick restoration of the seceded states.

From Sidney Andrews, *The South Since the War* (Boston, 1866), pp. 180-90.

Summary of Three Weeks' Observations in North Carolina

Wilmington, October 17, 1865.

Spindling of legs, round of shoulders, sunken of chest, lank of body, stooping of posture, narrow of face, retreating of forehead, thin of nose, small of chin, large of mouth,—this is the native North-Carolinian as one sees him outside the cities and large towns. There is insipidity in his face, indecision in his step, and inefficiency in his whole bearing. His house has two rooms and a loft, and is meanly furnished, —one, and possibly two, beds, three or four chairs, half a dozen stools, a cheap pine table, an old spinning-wheel, a water-bucket and drinking gourd, two tin washbasins, half a dozen tin platters, a few cooking utensils, and a dozen odd pieces of crockery. Paint and white-wash and wall-paper and window-curtains are to him needless luxuries. His wife is leaner, more round-shouldered, more sunken of chest, and more pinched of face than her husband. He "chaws" and she "dips." The children of these two are large-eyed, two-headed ur-chins, alike ignorant of the decencies and the possibilities of life. In this house there is often neither book nor newspaper; and, what is infinitely worse, no longing for either. The day begins at sunrise and ends at dark; its duties are alike devoid of dignity and mental or moral compensation. The man has a small farm, and once owned six or eight negroes. How the family now lives, the propping hands of the negroes being taken away, is a mystery, even if one remembers the simple cheapness of mere animal life.

I am not speaking either of the white resident of the cities or of the "poor white," technically so named, but of the common inhabitant of the country,—the man who pays a tax and votes, but never runs for office; who was a private in the Rebel army, but never anything more; who hates the Yankees as a matter of course, but has no personal ill-will toward them; who believes in the Divine right of slavery, but is positive that a free negro cannot be made to work. He is hospitable enough in words and manner, but expects you to pay extravagantly in greenbacks or liberally in silver for a seat at his table and the use of his odd bed. His larder is lean, and his cookery is in the last degree wretched. He tenders "apple-jack," as an evidence of good-will, and wonders in a feeble way how a man can live who don't drink it at least half a dozen times a day. He likes to talk, and rarely has any work that prevents him from hanging on the fence to chat with the chance traveller who asks the road; but his conversation runs in an everlasting circle round the negro, with an occasional pause for the relations of personal adventures in the war. He receives two or three letters per year, perhaps, and wonders why a man should take a daily newspaper. He troubles himself very little about schools or education, but likes to go to meeting, and thinks himself well informed as to matters of theology. He believes the "abolishioners" brought on the war; but he doesn't love Jeff Davis or Governor Vance. He "allers dun hansumly by his niggers," and thinks them the "most ongratefullest creeturs on the face of the yerth."

The complexion of these country residents is noticeable, and suggests many inquiries. If you say that half the men and nearly all the women are very pale, you strike at the matter, but fail to fairly hit it. Their whiteness of skin is simply the whiteness of ordinary tallow. It is sallowness, with a suggestion of clayeyness. Unquestionably soap and water and crash towels would improve the appearance, but I doubt if they would give any bloom to the cheek. The skin seems utterly without vitality, and beyond the action of any restorative stimulants: it has a pitiful and repulsive death-in-life appearance. I am told the climate is in fault, but my judgment says the root of the matter is in the diet of the people. The range of eatables is exceedingly narrow, and swine's flesh constitutes at least half the food of all classes outside the towns and cities; while the consumption of grease —of fat in one form or another—would, I am sure, astonish even an Arctic explorer. The whole economy of life seems radically wrong, and there is no inherent energy which promises reformation.

The amount of tobacco consumed by the people is beyond all calculation. I hardly exaggerate in saying that at least seven tenths of all persons above the age of twelve years use it in some form. Nearly every man and boy smokes or chews, and very many of them do both, while the country women chaw and smoke to some extent, and women of most classes "dip." When I saw old Solon Shingle come into the witness-box to tell the story about his famous "bar'l o' apple sass" I thought the manner in which he disposed of his quid of tobacco the nastiest piece of business I should ever see. I was mistaken. To see a man take it from his mouth and put it in his hat when he goes to breakfast is by no means uncommon. I have even seen men lay it under the edge of their plate at dinner; and one of the leading delegates in the Convention held an immense quid between the thumb and finger of the hand with which he abundantly gesticulated during a ten-minutes speech! Could nastiness go further? And do not these things mark the civilization of a people? In South Carolina, though seeing all classes, I did not once observe a white woman "dipping" snuff; but in this State I have seen scores,—I should scarcely exaggerate if I said hundreds. I saw them in Charlotte, the first town at which I stopped, within an hour after my arrival; and have seen them in every place I have visited since,—"dipping" in the porches of their own houses, on the streets, and twice in the public parlors of hotels. If barbaric life has a filthier and more disgusting custom than this, may I be excused from seeing it.

The labor system of the State is not so badly disorganized as that of South Carolina, but it is thoroughly demoralized. One sees here more white men in trades there almost given up to negroes, but he also sees negroes in trades here from which they are excluded there. The number of grown men, middle-aged men, who have no ostensible business but lounging and whiskey-drinking, is much greater in this State than in that. It is the complaint of papers in all sections of the State, that there never before were so many idle men,—vagrants, consumers, non-producers, non-taxpayers. The chief pity of the matter, however, is, that they seem to have no desire for work. "And who makes so much fuss about the negroes not working as these very white drones who hug the street-corners, lounge about dram-shops, and trust to chance for food and raiment?" asks one of the Raleigh papers, very pertinently. "We trust our law-makers will do all in their power," adds another journal, "to compel the freedmen to work for an honest living; but we consider it equally incumbent on them to take steps to reduce the amount of vagrancy among the whites." These extracts are not from papers edited by Northern or outside men, but the two writers are men who have always lived in the State. The columns of the Wilmington and Newbern papers, edited by new-comers, bear witness, however, to the same state of facts.

It probably never will be settled whether the State did or did not want to go out of the Union in May, 1861. That she did not in December, 1860, nor in February, 1861, is clear enough from the votes cast in those months; but the condition of affairs had greatly changed by the following May. "My situation, and not my will, consents," quoted one delegate of the recent Convention in explanation of North Carolina's course then. I am everywhere urged to believe that the "geographical necessity" forced her out. I have heard that phrase so much since I came into the State, that I should be tempted to consider it a sort of byword if it were not used by sober men of mature years. While many seem anxious that the stranger should believe the State did not voluntarily secede, there are others who insist that it was her matured will to go out in that fatal May. "If she did not believe in the constitutional right of secession, she at least believed the time had come for a revolution," said a gentleman to me here last evening. "The people desired the State to withdraw," said Delegate Ferrebee, who was also delegate in the Secession Convention. "I am convinced that not two fifths of the people ever favored secession in any form," responded Delegate Pool. When doctors disagree, who shall decide? "My calm and deliberate judgment," said a leading lawyer to me in Charlotte, "is, that about five eighths of the people of the State sustained the action of the Secession Convention." On the other hand, Delegate Boyden says, "I don't believe one third of them ever sustained it." How shall an outsider come to a conclusion?

It needs to be continually borne in mind that much of the "Unionism" of the State is mere personal bitterness toward Jeff Davis, or Governor Vance, or some less noted secession leader. Thus, when the outspoken Raleigh *Progress*, says, "it is remarkable that treason has become so rampant and defiant before the State has been readmitted," it is excited because somebody has proposed to ask the President to consider the utter worthlessness of old Governor Vance, and decide if he may not just as well set him free. Yet the *Progress* is quite right when it remarks that "there must be a great change of heart in North Carolina before Andrew Johnson, as a candidate for the Presidency, can carry it against any prominent leader of the Rebellion who may oppose him"; and also quite right again when it says that "the work of restoration in our State has been damaged by attempts to conciliate men who deserve nothing but stripes."

The action of the Convention in respect to the secession ordinance and the war debt pointedly marks the outlines of the situation. Over thirty delegates declared by a solemn vote that the ordinance never had any force whatever, and then turned squarely about and put themselves on records in favor of assuming the debt made in trying to sustain that pretended ordinance! In other words, a large number of gentlemen who consider themselves insulted if called by any other name than "Unionist" desire the State to pay her share of the expense of the war for breaking up the Union. Is there in this action an exhibition of what is technically called "cheek"? There is at least, as I have already said, startling proof that words are very cheap, and that Unionism in name is one thing, and Unionism in fact quite another thing.

The average sentiment of the State is very far from being up to that of the Convention, as shown by its action on the secession ordinance. Of course the declaration that it has always been null and void will be sustained by the vote of next December, but that vote will be smaller even than that just cast in choosing the Convention. That there will be further resistance to the government is not possible. I do not forget that Delegate Phillips declared in debate that "if the North and South ever again come into the position they occupied in 1860-61, blood will be again spilled"; nor do I forget that another delegate said he knew men of position who declared themselves "ready for further trial of the present issue, if England and France would recognize the confederacy"; yet against these signs of the hour I set the declaration of Uncle Nat Boyden, "Neither principalities, nor powers, nor things present, nor things to come, nor life, nor death, nor any other creature, shall hereafter separate us from the sisterhood of States!" That any possible separation may be prevented, we need only to help the Union men of the State. That the average sentiment of her people may be brought up to the best sentiment of the Convention, we need to make haste slowly in the work of construction.

The condition of the negro is in some respects worse and in others better than in South Carolina. He is in such minority here that he cannot enforce his natural rights so easily as he does there; but, on the other hand, because of that same fact, the essential natural rights are generally more readily granted to him here than there. The cold hunkerism of this people, however, stands immovably in his way, and gives him little chance. It is greatly to his credit that he has not been seized by such discontent as prevails below. In the extreme western part of the State he got uneasy and drifted over the line and off toward Charleston; and in the eastern part he must needs go down to Newbern and Wilmington to find freedom. Elsewhere, however, with local exceptions, he is staying on the old place, and working at the old tasks; and I am convinced that, in the main, he has not given serious cause of complaint.

"The chief ambition of a wench seems to be to wear a veil and carry a parasol," said a ladylike-appearing woman at the hotel in Salisbury. The mistress of the hotel in Charlotte, at which chance travellers are fleeced at the rate of four dollars per day regular charges, and another dollar for extras, complained that "the nasty niggers must have a parasol when they ha'n't got no shoes." One of two misses who passed me on the street one day in Raleigh was scolding because her girl had stolen her veil, and she added, finally, "She got so crazy for it that ma had to get her one." A gentleman of this place with whom I spoke this morning professed great amusement at a fact of his observation,—that full-blooded negro wenches carry a parasol and wear a white handkerchief around the neck to protect themselves from the sun. An officer of the Freedmen's Bureau told me the wearing of black veils by the young negro women had given great offence to the young white women, and that there was a time earlier in the season when the latter would not wear them at all. Does this matter of veils and parasols and handkerchiefs seem a small one? Yet it is one of serious import to the bitter, spiteful women whose passionate hearts nursed the Rebellion. I have, one way and another, heard so much about it, that I am not at liberty to suppose it a mere matter of local or temporary grievance. Wretched negro girls, you of sprawling feet and immense lips and retreating foreheads and coal-black color, cease from your vagaries! cease from such sore troubling of the placid and miasmatic waters of good society!

"The nigger is crazy to ride,—to own an old mule and an old cart, and to be seen driving through the streets," said an ex-Rebel colonel to me at Charlotte. "A negro has reached kingdom come," remarked my seat-mate in the wearisome ride last night from Goldsboro, "when he's got on horseback." And it seems to give grave offence to the gentry of the State that the negro likes riding better than walking, that he will insist on buying a poor old mule and a poor old cart and going into business for himself! In this grief is indirect proof that Sambo appreciates the situation, and is anxious to be at work for himself as soon as possible.

To his average good disposition is due the fact that in many counties slavery still exists as a fact even if abolished as a name. I make this assertion only after much inquiry into the condition of things. The State is so large and sparsely settled, and means of communicating with some sections are so unfavorable, that even the Freedmen's Bureau has not yet found all the counties. When the Freedmen's Convention deliberately asks the general commanding the department to give some of its members safe return to their homes, there is such testimony to the existence of the old condition of slavery unconsciously furnished as no amount of negation can overweigh; and when one of the delegates to the Constitutional Convention chuckles over the fact that some of his constituents don't yet know that slavery is abolished, he furnishes proof unquestionable as to the actual situation.

"What my people wants first," said an intelligent colored man to me at Salisbury, "what dey fust wants is de right to be free." He compassed the whole case in few words. In other States, where their number in proportion to the number of whites is greater than it is here, or where the revolution made by the war has been deeper, they assume and hold this first right, to be free,—assume and hold it to their harm, doubtless, in thousands of cases; but here, in many counties, even this primary right is yet denied them. Some of the delegates to the Freedmen's Convention were obliged to sneak off from home in the night, and expected punishment on their return. The negro is no model of virtue, and he delights in laziness and the excitement of the city; but, on the whole, I think he is bearing himself very well in North Carolina,—with credit to himself and to his friends.

So far as I can learn, the intelligent colored men are pleading very little as yet for the right of suffrage, but very much for the right to testify in the courts. "We can live without a vote, but not without the right to speak for ourselves," said one of them to me at Greensboro,— anticipating the sentiment of the lame barber here who observed, as he brushed my hair this morning, and emphasized his words with a thump of my head for which he made a hundred apologies, "To be sure, sah, we wants to vote, but, sah, de great matter is to git into de witness-box." One of the leading lawyers of the western part of the State, a former District Attorney and member of the Legislature, told a friend of mine that he knows no prominent members of the bar who does not favor the admission to the courts of negro evidence. I presume it is true that many leading men of the State occupy this ground; but the distance between these leading men and the common people is very great; and I am sorrowfully certain that the latter are far from being willing to allow the negro to be heard in court in his own behalf.

"We are too poor to educate our own children now," said Delegate Settle; "and much as I wish for the education of the negro, his help will have to come from the North at present." It is something to get a desire that the negro shall be educated,—and Mr. Settle is one of those who want him colonized. The North took Mr. Settle at his spirit before he uttered his word, and this year has in operation, in various parts of the State, about fifty schools under charge of about sixty teachers, and embracing nearly five thousand different pupils. Most of these teachers are ladies, not a few of whom are from Massachusetts. The State Superintendent reports a good degree of progress, and the most indifferent inquiry anywhere among the negroes develops a living and grasping interest.

The labor system, as I have already said, is in better order than in South Carolina. The negroes are not, however, any better paid than there. Where they work for a share of the crop they get from one fourth to one third. Many of them, though, are working for regular wages,—six to eight dollars per month with board, and nine to twelve dollars without board. The planters and farmers rather pride themselves on the liberality of these wages; but they are, of course, utterly insufficient for anything more than bare support. There is less complaint here than below that the negro fails to observe his contract. The local county police does much to keep down disorder, and doubtless is something of a terror to negroes of vicious tendencies who would like to desert their work.

Yet it cannot be denied that there are conflicts between employers and employed, and some careful and observant officers tell me they are increasing because of the injustice of some masters who strive to keep up the old authority of slave days. "It is generally known that the prejudice and bitterness is increasing between the whites and the blacks," says one Raleigh paper; and "clashings between the races are unfortunately becoming more and more frequent," responds Governor Holden's organ. The real question of the hour is neither one of suffrage nor one of giving testimony, but one of establishing the true relations of employer and employed. The true course is luminously indicated by another paper of the State: "If the employers, and especially the late slave-owners, will treat the blacks kindly and justly, these troubles that now annoy us will soon pass away." Will the white man be wise in season? For the negro, strong in his longing for freedom, gropes blindly and passionately, and will not be cheated of what the earth, and the very heavens themselves, assure him is his right.

Benjamin C. Truman's Testimony Supports the Johnson View of the Postwar South

Still another journalist, this time an official emissary and close friend of President Johnson, whom he had served as aide while the latter was military governor of Tennessee, was the energetic Benjamin C. Truman (1835-1916). He came of a pioneer New England family and was born in Providence, Rhode Island. He had been a teacher, a printer, and a Civil War correspondent. In the late summer of 1865, Johnson sent Truman as his confidential agent to report on conditions in the Deep South. From September 1, 1865, to March 15, 1866, he traveled through almost every state of the old Confederacy and, while far from uncritical, he returned to present Congress facts and impressions that encouraged the view that the former slavemasters could be trusted to fulfill their duties to the Union. Later he was sent as a special Treasury agent to South Carolina and Florida. He was to become a vigorous Los Angeles editor and publisher, a very successful correspondent, and even a playwright.

Readers may judge for themselves whether this selection reveals reportorial judgment or stereotyped impressions.

From *Senate Executive Documents*, #43, 39th Cong., 1 Sess. (1865-66), pp. 6-10.

. . . . I record it as my profound conviction, gathered from hundreds of intimate and friendly conversations with leading men in the south, that there are not fifty respectable politicians who still believe in the "constitutional right of secession," though they are exceedingly slow to acknowledge it in public speeches or published articles. Our conversations generally ended with the confession—which to me was entirely satisfactory, as meaning much more than was intended—"Whatever may be said about the *right* of secession, the thing itself may as well be laid aside, for it is certainly *not practicable,* and probably *never will be.*" I believe there is the most charity, and by far the most correctness, in that reasoning which accounts in this way for the extreme reluctance that has been exhibited in most of the conventions against declaring the act of secession null and void from the beginning. They will willingly concede that the *right* of secession *does not now* exist, provided only they are allowed to assert that *it did at that time,* which is simply a petty device of sorely humbled and defeated men to save their wounded pride. Said Governor Hamilton, of Texas, the most nobly and earnestly loyal man I met in all the south, in conversation with me one day: "After all, our people are doing about as well as a reasonable man ought to expect. Politicians must have their 'explanations' and there 'records'; they must be allowed to retreat gracefully, and to fall gently; but the vast majority of them are all right at heart. They must have time." And I will here add that I found in Texas more genuine and honest loyalty and patriotism than in any other of the cotton States. There are 54,000 Germans, 8,000 Norwegians, 9,000 Mexicans, and 70,000 Americans, in that State, who have remained loyal all the time, and they have in Governor Hamilton the noblest leader in any southern State. There were thirty-four men in the Texas convention who voted for the most loyal measures, and in favor of the most enlarged civil rights to the negro, seven of whom favored universal suffrage.

There is a prevalent disposition not to associate too freely with northern men, or to receive them into the circles of society; but it is far from insurmountable. Over southern society, as over every other, woman reigns supreme, and they are more imbittered against those whom they deem the authors of all their calamities than are their brothers, sons and husbands. It is a noteworthy ethnological fact, and one I have often observed, that of the younger generation the southern women are much superior to the southern men both in intellect and energy; and their ascendency over society is correspondingly great. However this disparity is to be accounted for, whether by the enormous wastage of the war among the males, or otherwise, it nevertheless exists, and to its existence is greatly due the exclusiveness of southern society.

But the stories and rumors to the effect that northern men are bitterly persecuted and compelled to abandon the country, I pronounce false. If northern men go south they must expect for a while to be treated with neglect, and sometimes with contempt; but if they refrain from bitter political discussions, and conduct themselves with ordinary discretion, they soon overcome these prejudices and are treated with respect. The accounts that are from time to time flooded over the country in regard to southern cruelty and intolerance toward northerners are mostly false. I could select many districts, however, particularly in northern Texas and portions of Mississippi, where northern men could not at present live with any degree of self-respect. There are also localities in many of the southern States where it would be dangerous for a northern man to live, but they are exceptional, and are about equally unsafe for any man who possesses attractive property. For some unknown cause a large number of persons are engaged in writing and circulating falsehoods. For some unpatriotic purpose or other, reports of an incendiary character concerning the southern people are transmitted north. To learn the falseness of these reports one needs only to obtain the facts. I am personally acquainted with most of the officers of a hundred-odd regiments of volunteers, and out of these I could name thirty regiments one-half of whose officers and many of the men have returned to the south, and as many more that have left large numbers there upon being disbanded. Hundreds, even, of the officers of colored regiments—the most offensive to the south—have remained there and entered into business, the most of them having rented plantations and employing their old soldiers. Large numbers of ex-federal and ex-confederate officers are engaged together in mercantile pursuits and in cotton-planting. Nearly all of the cotton plantations in Florida are being run by such parties. The banks of the Mississippi are lined with plantations being run by such parties. The banks of the Mississippi are lined with plantations which have been leased by northern men and federal officers. Arkansas and White river plantations are generally being run by officers who have served under General Reynolds, while a large number of the Red River plantations have been placed under cultivation by ex-officers of General A. J. Smith's command. Fourteen officers of a colored (Kentucky) regiment are engaged in planting and raising cotton near Victoria, Texas. The First National Bank of Texas, at Galveston, has for president ex-Major General Nichols, of the late Confederate army, and ten of its directors are also ex-rebel officers, while the cashier is ex-Major General Clark, of the Union army, and who formerly commanded a division of colored troops. In all of these connexions the utmost harmony prevails. Notwithstanding the above facts—and I could multiply them—I maintain that in many sections of the south there is a wide-spread hostility to northern men, which, however, in nine cases out of ten, is speedily dispelled by individual contact, and the exercise of a generous regard for private opinions. In fine, I will say that all who can be spared from the industry of the north to go south can readily find places of business where they can live in quiet and prosperity.

I have already alluded to the loyal Germans of Texas. I visited their colony and settlements and was most favorably impressed; they are the most thrifty, industrious, and prosperous citizens of that State, and, now that the rebellion is over, are living in comparative security, though their sufferings during the war were more dreadful than any that the history of this country has before afforded. They were ably represented in the late convention by five men, three of whom favored negro suffrage with certain educational qualifications. The loyal Norwegians and the loyal Americans of the Red River district—men whose loyalty was fearless and unwavering throughout the rebellion—I did not have time to see. Their delegates in the convention, however, were among the ablest as well as the most patriotic in that body, and far superior to those loyalists of North Alabama, who were generally men of moderate capacity. Though there is no district in Florida that can strictly be called loyal in contradistinction to all others, yet I found the feeling of the people in that State much better and more encouraging than in Georgia, which is overrun with politicians, many of whom seem to defy the government and its authority. Alabama is in a much better condition than Georgia, and its state of affairs is extremely encouraging. Mississippi, from one end to the other, of all the States which I visited, is far behindhand in her tokens of loyalty; there is an unmistakable flow of ill feeling in that State, although I witnessed no exhibitions of unmitigated disloyalty; on the whole, the people of that State fear the authority of the United States more than they respect it. In Louisiana there is an encouraging element of loyalty which is experiencing a healthy increase. Tennessee evidenced in a great degree the most flourishings signs of loyalty; I do not think there are ten men in that State at present who could be induced to favor a dissolution of the Union, not even indeed, if such a thing should be peaceably permitted. There is a healthy intercourse between all classes in Arkansas, and it seemed to me to occupy nearly the identical position of Tennessee.

I will now proceed to the second great topic, to wit: "The freedmen and their affairs."

Almost the only key that furnishes a satisfactory solution to the southern question in its relations to the negro, that gives a reasonable explanation to the treatment which he receives and the estimation in which he is held, is found in the fact—too often forgotten in considering this matter—that the people from their earliest days have regarded slavery as his proper estate, and emancipation as a bane to his happiness. That a vast majority of the southern people honestly entertain this opinion no one who travels among them for eight months can doubt.

To one who looks out from this stand-point of theory, and can see no other that is rational, the question presents itself in a different aspect. Every one who conscientiously seeks to know the whole truth should not ignore their beliefs while he censures the resulting practices. Holding that the negro occupies a middle ground between the human race and the animal, they regard it as a real misfortune to him that he should be stripped of a protector, and that the immortal proclamation of President Lincoln was wicked, or at least mistaken, and a scourge to society. The persistency and honesty with which many, even of the greatest men of the south, hold to this opinion, is almost unaccountable to a northern man, and is an element of such magnitude that it cannot well be omitted from the consideration.

Resulting as a proper corollary from these premises, we have seen various laws passed in some of the States, but more particularly in Mississippi—which State, I am bound to say, has displayed the most illiberal spirit toward the freedmen of all the south—imposing heavy taxes on negroes engaged in the various trades, amounting to a virtual prohibition. Petty, unjust, and discriminating licenses are levied in this State upon mechanics, storekeepers, and various artisans. Following the same absurd train of argument that one will hear in the north in regard to the "proper sphere of women," their legislature and their common councils contend that in these pursuits the negro is out of his place; that he is not adapted to such labors, but only the the ruder tasks of the field. What are known as the "poor whites" sustain, in fact originate, this legislation, upon the insane dread they share in common with certain skilled laborers at the north, of competition and an overcrowding of the supply. This folly and injustice on the part of the lawmakers is being corrected in many sections. The negro, however, has not been discouraged, even in Mississippi; his industry and his thrift are overleaping all obstacles, and in Jackson there are at least two colored craftsmen of most kinds to one of the whites.

From the surrender of the rebel armies up to the Christmas holidays, and more especially for a few weeks preceding the latter, there was a nervousness exhibited throughout the south, in relation to their late slaves, that was little consonant to their former professions of trust in them. There were vague and terrible fears of a servile insurrection—a thing which the simple-minded negroes scarcely dreamed of. In consequence of this there were extensive seizures of arms and

ammunition, which the negroes had foolishly collected, and strict precautions were taken to avoid any outbreak. Pistols, old muskets, and
shotguns were taken away from them as such weapons would be
wrested from the hands of lunatics. Since the holidays, however, there
has been a great improvement in this matter; many of the whites
appear to be ashamed of their former distrust, and the negroes are
seldom molested now in carrying the fire-arms of which they make
such a vain display. In one way or another they have procured great
numbers of old army muskets and revolvers, particularly in Texas, and
I have, in a few instances, been amused at the vigor and audacity with
which they have employed them to protect themselves against the robbers and murderers that infest that State.

Another result of the above-mentioned settled belief in the negro's
inferiority, and in the necessity that he should not be left to himself
without a guardian, is that in some sections he is discouraged from
leaving his old master. I have known of planters who considered it an
offence against neighborhood courtesy for another to hire their old
hands, and in two instances that were reported the disputants came to
blows over the breach of etiquette. It is only, however, in the most
remote regions, where our troops have seldom or never penetrated,
that the negroes have not perfect liberty to rove where they choose.
Even when the attempt is made to restrain them by a system of passes
from their employers, or from police patrols, it is of little avail, for the
negroes, in their ignorance and darkness of understanding, are penetrated with a singularly strong conviction that they "are not free so
long as they stay at the old place"; and all last summer and fall they
pretty thoroughly demonstrated their freedom by changing their
places of residence. Such a thorough chaos and commingling of population has seldom been seen since the great barbarian invasion of the
Roman empire. In this general upheaval thousands of long-scattered
families were joyously reunited. It is a strange fact, however, and one
which I have abundantly established by the testimony of hundreds of
the negroes themselves, that a large majority of them have finally
returned voluntarily and settled down in the old cabins of their former
quarters. The negro clings to old associations—it was only a temporary impulse of their new-found freedom to wander away from them;

and at last they returned, generally wearied, hungry, and forlorn. In most cases, or at least in many cases, it was not so much from any affection toward their former masters as it was from a mere instinctive attachment to the homes of their youth—the familiar scenes in the midst of which they were born and reared. When I was in Selma, Alabama, last fall, a constant stream of them, of all ages and conditions, were pouring through that city on their way, as they always told me, to Mississippi or Tennessee. Many were transported free by our government, while many were on foot, trudging hopefully but painfully forward toward their old homes, from which they had been taken to escape our armies.

I believe that in some of the most interior districts, especially in Texas, the substance of slavery still remains, in the form of the bondage of custom, of fear, and of inferiority; but nowhere are there any negroes so ignorant of the great change that has taken place as to submit to the lash. In no place did I hear the slightest allusion to any punishment of this sort having been inflicted since the rebellion ended. In every case it was violent stabbing or shooting, resulting from a personal encounter. The negro was aware of his rights, and was defending them. His friends need never fear his re-enslavement; it never can, never will take place. His head is filled with the idea of freedom, and anything but the most insidious and blandishing encroachments upon his freedom he will perceive and resist. The planters everywhere complain of his "demoralization" in this respect.

As to the personal treatment received by the negro at the hands of the southern people there is wide-spread misapprehension. It is not his former master, as a general thing, that is his worst enemy, but quite the contrary. I have talked earnestly with hundreds of old slave-owners, and seen them move among their former "chattels," and I am not mistaken. The feeling with which a very large majority of them regard the negro is one of genuine commiseration, although it is not a sentiment much elevated above that with which they would look upon a suffering animal for which they had formed an attachment. Last summer the negroes, exulting in their new-found freedom, as was to have been expected, were gay, thoughtless, and improvident; and, as a consequence, when the winter came hundreds of them felt the pinchings of want, and many perished. The old planters have often pointed out to me numerous instances of calamity that had come under their own observation in the case of their former slaves and others.

It was one of the most pernicious effects of slavery that it confined the attention of the owner entirely to the present bodily condition of his slaves, and ignored all calculations upon his future mental or moral growth; it gave him that mean opinion of the negroes' capacity that he still retains. The planter reasoned only from the actual facts, and never from possibilities. Inheriting his slaves, and finding them always brutish, stupid, and slow of understanding, he committed the logical inaccuracy of preventing them from ever becoming anything else, and proceeded to argue that they never could become so. To a certain extent it is true, as has been forcibly said, that "those who have seen most of the negro know least of him," though the assertion should be reduced to this—that they know far less of him as a human being than we of the north, but much more respecting his mere animal characteristics. Notwithstanding all this, I insist that there was in most cases a real attachment between master and slave, and still is, especially between the family and house servants.

It is the former slave-owners who are the best friends the negro has in the south—those who, heretofore, have provided for his mere physical comfort, generally with sufficient means, though entirely neglecting his better nature, while it is the "poor whites" that are his enemies. It is from these he suffers most. In a state of slavery they hated him; and, now that he is free, there is no striking abatement of this sentiment, and the former master no longer feels called by the instincts of interest to extend that protection that he once did. On the streets, by the roadside, in his wretched hut, in the field of labor—everywhere, the inoffensive negro is exposed to their petty and contemptible persecutions; while, on the other hand, I have known instances where the respectable, substantial people of a community have united together to keep guard over a house in which the negroes were taking their amusement, and from which, a few nights before, they had been rudely driven by white vagabonds, who found pleasure in their fright and suffering. I reiterate, that the former owners, as a class, are the negroes' best friends in the south, although many of this class diligently strive to discourage the freedmen from any earnest efforts to promote their higher welfare. When one believes that a certain race of beings are incapable of advancement, he is very prone to withhold the means of that advancement. And it is in this form that a species of slavery will longest be perpetuated—it is in these strongholds that it will last die out. I am pretty sure that there is not a single negro in the whole south who is not receiving pay for his labor according to his own contract; but, as a general thing, the freedmen are encouraged to collect about the old mansion in their little quarters, labor for their former master for set terms, receiving, besides their pay, food, quarters, and medical attendance, and thus continuing on in their former state of dependence. The cruelties of slavery, and all of its outward forms, have entirely passed away; but, as might have been expected, glimmerings of its vassalage, its subserviency, and its helplessness, linger.

It is the result of my observation, also, not only that the planters, generally, are far better friends to the negro than the poor whites, but also better than a majority of northern men who go south to rent plantations—at least, they show more patience in dealing with him. The northerner is practical, energetic, economical, and thrifty—the negro is slow, awkward, wasteful, and slovenly; he causes his new employer to lose his patience, to seize hold and attempt to perform, himself, what he sees so badly executed. The southerner is accustomed to the ways of slaves from his youth up; hence he is languidly and good-naturedly indifferent; or, at most, vents his displeasure in empty fuming. The northern employer is accustomed to see laborers who are vigorous and industrious; he knows the extent of a full day's labor, and he expects all to perform the amount; the southern man has always been compelled to employ two or three to do the work of one, and is more indulgent. It is the almost universal testimony of the negroes themselves, who have been under the supervision of both classes —and I have talked with many with a view to this point—that they prefer to labor for a southern employer. This is not by any means to be construed to mean that they desire to return to slavery—not by any consideration, for the thought of freedom is dearer to their hearts than to any other people. . . .

Carl Schurz Rejects the Johnson Image of the Conquered South

President Johnson regretted his decision to send the liberal German-born Forty-Eighter Carl Schurz (1829-1906) to report on the South during July–September 1865. Schurz had once been a candidate for a history Ph.D. at the University of Bonn, but forfeited a probable brilliant career as a professor to join the German revolutionary movement of 1848. He became a friend of the liberal revolutionaries Joseph Mazzini and Louis Kossuth and decided to embark upon a career in the United States, where he arrived in 1852. In Watertown, Wisconsin, where he came under the influence of the antislavery movement, his wife, a Jewish girl who was a disciple of the progressive Froebel, introduced the first kindergarten in the United States. During the fifties he campaigned energetically for the Republican cause, especially for Frémont and later for Lincoln, and influenced German-American opinion for the antislavery cause. He tried law, but decided to stay in politics and to fight the current bigotry of the so-called Know-Nothing movement that was aimed at foreigners. When the Civil War began, he became an able general, although critics assailed some of his military decisions and reverses. In 1864, he campaigned for the re-election of Lincoln and urged the President from the very beginning to make abolition the primary aim of the war rather than the Union issue alone.

The Schurz report given here plainly reveals its author's distrust of the Southern leaders and the realistic considerations for giving the Negro the right to vote bolstered by the federal government as a means of survival in a hostile area. However, Schurz became one of the many disillusioned antislavery men of 1872 like his friend Horace Greeley, who supported the Liberal Republicans in their effort to end federal intervention in Reconstruction and in effect to leave race relations to the white South.

From Carl Schurz, "Condition of the South," *Senate Executive Documents* #2, 39th Cong., 1st Sess. (1865-66), pp. 42-46.

. . . The continuance of the national control in the south, although it may be for a short period only, will cause some inconvenience and expense; but if thereby destructive collisions and anarchical disorders can be prevented, justice secured to all men, and the return of peace and prosperity to all parts of this country hastened, it will be a paying investment. For the future of the republic, it is far less important that this business of reconstruction be done quickly than that it be well done. The matter well taken in hand, there is reason for hope that it will be well done, and quickly too. In days like these great changes are apt to operate themselves rapidly. At present the southern people assume that free negro labor will not work, and therefore they are not inclined to give it a fair trial. As soon as they find out that they must give it a fair trial, and that their whole future power and prosperity depend upon its success, they will also find out that it will work, at least far better than they have anticipated. Then their hostility to it will gradually disappear. This great result accomplished, posterity will not find fault with this administration for having delayed complete "reconstruction" one, two, or more years.

Although I am not called upon to discuss in this report the constitutional aspects of this question, I may be pardoned for one remark. The interference of the national government in the local concerns of the States lately in rebellion is argued against by many as inconsistent with the spirit of our federal institutions. Nothing is more foreign to my ways of thinking in political matters than a fondness for centralization or military government. Nobody can value the blessings of local self-government more highly than I do. But we are living under exceptional circumstances which require us, above all, to look at things from a practical point of view; and I believe it will prove far more dangerous for the integrity of local self-government if the national control in the south be discontinued—while by discontinuing it too soon, it may be rendered necessary again in the future—than if it be continued, when by continuing it but a limited time all such future necessity may be obviated. At present these acts of interference are but a part of that exceptional policy brought forth by the necessities into which the rebellion has plunged us. Although there will be some modifications in the relations between the States and the national government, yet these acts of direct interference in the details of State concerns will pass away with the exceptional circumstances which called them forth. But if the social revolution in the south be now abandoned in an unfinished state, and at some future period produce events provoking new and repeated acts of direct practical interference—and the contingency would by no means be unlikely to arise—such new and repeated acts would not pass over without most seriously affecting the political organism of the republic.

NEGRO SUFFRAGE

It would seem that the interference of the national authority in the home concerns of the southern States would be rendered less necessary, and the whole problem of political and social reconstruction be much simplified, if, while the masses lately arrayed against the government are permitted to vote, the large majority of those who were always loyal, and are naturally anxious to see the free labor problem successfully solved, were not excluded from all influence upon legislation. In all questions concerning the Union, the national debt, and the future social organization of the south, the feelings of the colored man are naturally in sympathy with the views and aims of the national government. While the southern white fought against the Union, the negro did all he could to aid it; while the southern white sees in the national government his conqueror, the negro sees in it his protector; while the white owes to the national debt his defeat, the negro owes to it his deliverance; while the white considers himself robbed and ruined by the emancipation of the slaves, the negro finds in it the assurance of future prosperity and happiness. In all the important issues the negro would be led by natural impulse to forward the ends of the government, and by making his influence, as part of the voting body, tell upon the legislation of the States, render the interference of the national authority less necessary.

At the most difficult of the pending questions are intimately connected with the status of the negro in southern society, it is obvious that a correct solution can be more easily obtained if he has a voice in the matter. In the right to vote he would find the best permanent protection against oppressive class-legislation, as well as against individual persecution. The relations between the white and black races, even if improved by the gradual wearing off of the present animosities, are likely to remain long under the troubling influence of prejudice. It is a notorious fact that the rights of a man of some political power are far less exposed to violation than those of one who is, in matters of public interest, completely subject to the will of others. A voter is a man of influence; small as that influence may be in the single individual, it becomes larger when that individual belongs to a numerous class of voters who are ready to make common cause with him for the protection of his rights. Such an individual is an object of interest to the political parties that desire to have the benefit of his ballot. It is true, the bringing face to face at the ballot-box of the white and black races may here and there lead to an outbreak of feeling, and the first trials ought certainly to be made while the national power is still there to prevent or repress disturbances; but the practice once successfully inaugurated under the protection of that power, it would probably be more apt than anything else to obliterate old antagonisms, especially if the colored people—which is probable, as soon as their own rights are sufficiently secured—divide their votes between the different political parties.

The effect of the extension of the franchise to the colored people upon the development of free labor and upon the security of human rights in the south being the principal object in view, the objections raised on the ground of the ignorance of the freedmen become unimportant. Practical liberty is a good school, and, besides, if any qualification can be found, applicable to both races, which does not interfere with the attainment of the main object, such qualification would in that respect be unobjectionable. But it is idle to say that it will be time to speak of negro suffrage when the whole colored race will be educated, for the ballot may be necessary to him to secure his education. It is also idle to say that ignorance is the principal ground upon which southern men object to negro suffrage, for if it were, that numerous class of colored people in Louisiana who are as highly educated, as intelligent, and as wealthy as any corresponding class of whites, would have been enfranchised long ago.

It has been asserted that the negro would be but a voting machine in the hand of his employer. On this point opinions seem to differ. I have heard it said in the south that the freedmen are more likely to be influenced by their schoolmasters and preachers. But even if we suppose the employer to control to a certain extent the negro laborer's vote, two things are to be taken into consideration: 1. The class of employers, of landed proprietors, will in a few years be very different from what it was heretofore in consequence of the general breaking up, a great many of the old slaveholders will be obliged to give up their lands and new men will step into their places; and 2. The employer will hardly control the vote of the negro laborer so far as to make him vote against his own liberty. The beneficial effect of an extension of suffrage does not always depend upon the intelligence with which the newly admitted voters exercise their right, but sometimes upon the circumstances in which they are placed; and the circumstances in which the freedmen of the south are placed are such that, when they only vote for their own liberty and rights, they vote for the rights of free labor, for the success of an immediate important reform, for the prosperity of the country, and for the general interests of mankind. If, therefore, in order to control the colored vote, the employer, or whoever he may be, is first obliged to concede to the freedman the great point of his own rights as a man and a free laborer, the great social reform is completed, the most difficult problem is solved, and all other questions it will be compartively easy to settle.

In discussing the matter of negro suffrage I deemed it my duty to confine myself strictly to the practical aspects of the subject. I have, therefore, not touched its moral merits nor discussed the question whether the national government is competent to enlarge the elective franchise in the States lately in rebellion by its own act; I deem it proper, however, to offer a few remarks on the assertion frequently put forth, that the franchise is likely to be extended to the colored man by the voluntary action of the southern whites themselves. My observation leads me to a contrary opinion. Aside from a very few enlightened men, I found but one class of people in favor of the enfranchisement of the blacks: it was the class of Unionists who found themselves politically ostracised and looked upon the enfranchisement of the loyal negroes as the salvation of the whole loyal element. But their numbers and influence are sadly insufficient to secure such a result. The masses are strongly opposed to colored suffrage; anybody that dares to advocate it is stigmatized as a dangerous fanatic; nor do I deem it probable that in the ordinary course of things prejudices will wear off to such an extent as to make it a popular measure. Outside of Louisiana only one gentleman who occupied a prominent political position in the south expressed to me an opinion favorable to it. He declared himself ready to vote for an amendment to the constitution of his State bestowing the right of suffrage upon all male citizens without distinction of color who could furnish evidence of their ability to read and write, without, however, disfranchising those who are now voters and are not able to fulfill that condition. This gentleman is now a member of one of the State conventions, but I presume he will not risk his political standing in the south by moving such an amendment in that body.

The only manner in which, in my opinion, the southern people can be induced to grant to the freedman some measure of self-protecting power in the form of suffrage, is to make it a condition precedent to "readmission."

DEPORTATION OF THE FREEDMEN

I have to notice one pretended remedy for the disorders now agitating the south, which seems to have become the favorite plan of some prominent public men. It is that the whole colored population of the south should be transported to some place where they could live completely separated from the whites. It is hardly necessary to discuss, not only the question of right and justice, but the difficulties and expense necessarily attending the deportation of nearly four millions of people. But it may be asked, what would become of the industry of the south for many years, if the bulk of its laboring population were taken away? The south stands in need of an increase and not of a diminution of its laboring force to repair the losses and disasters of the last four years. Much is said of important European laborers and northern men; this is the favorite idea of many planters who want such immigrants to work on their plantations. But they forget that European and northern men will not come to the south to serve as hired hands on the plantations, but to acquire property for themselves, and that even if the whole European immigration at the rate of 200,-000 a year were turned into the south, leaving not a single man for the north and west, it would require between fifteen and twenty years to fill the vacuum caused by the deportation of the freedmen. Aside from this, the influx of northern men or Europeans will not diminish the demand for hired negro labor; it will, on the contrary, increase it. As Europeans and northern people come in, not only vast quantities of land will pass from the hands of their former owners into those of the immigrants, but a large area of new land will be brought under cultivation; and as the area of cultivation expands, hired labor, such as furnished by the colored people, will be demanded in large quantities. The deportation of the labor so demanded would, therefore, be a very serious injury to the economical interests of the south, and if an attempt were made, this effect would soon be felt.

It is, however, a question worthy of consideration whether it would not be wise to offer attractive inducements and facilities for the voluntary migration of freedmen to some suitable district on the line of the Pacific railroad. It would answer a double object: 1. It would aid in the construction of that road, and 2. If this migration be effected on a large scale it would cause a drain upon the laboring force of the south; it would make the people affected by that drain feel the value of the freedmen's labor, and show them the necessity of keeping that labor at home by treating the laborer well, and by offering him inducements as fair as can be offered elsewhere.

But whatever the efficiency of such expedients may be, the true problem remains, not how to remove the colored man from his present field of labor, but how to make him, where he is, a true freeman and an intelligent and useful citizen. The means are simple: protection by the government until his political and social status enables him to protect himself, offering to his legitimate ambition the stimulant of a perfectly fair chance in life, and granting to him the rights which in every just organization of society are coupled with corresponding duties.

CONCLUSION

I may sum up all I have said in a few words. If nothing were necessary but to restore the machinery of government in the States lately in rebellion in point of form, the movements made to that end by the people of the south might be considered satisfactory. But if it is required that the southern people should also accommodate themselves to the results of the war in point of spirit, those movements fall far short of what must be insisted upon.

The loyalty of the masses and most of the leaders of the southern people, consists in submission to necessity. There is, except in individual instances, an entire absence of that national spirit which forms the basis of true loyalty and patriotism.

The emancipation of the slaves is submitted to only in so far as chattel slavery in the old form could not be kept up. But although the freedman is no longer considered the property of the individual master, he is considered the slave of society, and all independent State legislation will share the tendency to make him such. The ordinances abolishing slavery passed by the conventions under the pressure of circumstances, will not be looked upon as barring the establishment of a new form of servitude.

Practical attempts on the part of the southern people to deprive the negro of his rights as a freeman may result in bloody collisions, and will certainly plunge southern society into restless fluctuations and anarchical confusion. Such evils can be prevented only by continuing the control of the national government in the States lately in rebellion until free labor is fully developed and firmly established, and the advantages and blessings of the new order of things have disclosed themselves. This desirable result will be hastened by a firm declaration on the part of the government, that national control in the south will not cease until such results are secured. Only in this way can that security be established in the south which will render numerous immigration possible, and such immigration would materially aid a favorable development of things.

The solution of the problem would be very much facilitated by enabling all the loyal and free-labor elements in the south to exercise a healthy influence upon legislation. It will hardly be possible to secure the freedman against oppressive class legislation and private persecution, unless he be endowed with a certain measure of political power.

As to the future peace and harmony of the Union, it is of the highest importance that the people lately in rebellion be not permitted to build up another "peculiar institution" whose spirit is in conflict with the fundamental principles of our political system; for as long as they cherish interests peculiar to them in preference to those they have in common with the rest of the American people, their loyalty to the Union will always be uncertain.

I desire not to be understood as saying that there are no well-meaning men among those who were compromised in the rebellion. There are many, but neither their number nor their influence is strong enough to control the manifest tendency of the popular spirit. There are great reasons for hope that a determined policy on the part of the national government will produce innumerable and valuable conversions. This consideration counsels lenity as to persons, such as is demanded by the humane and enlightened spirit of our times, and vigor and firmness in the carrying out of principles, such as is demanded by the national sense of justice and the exigencies of our situation.

In submitting this report I desire to say that I have conscientiously endeavored to see things as they were, and to represent them as I saw them. I have been careful not to use stronger language than was warranted by the thoughts I intended to express. A comparison of the tenor of the annexed documents with that of my report, will convince you that I have studiously avoided overstatements. Certain legislative attempts at present made in the south, and especially in South Carolina, seem to be more than justifying the apprehensions I have expressed.

Conscious though I am of having used my best endeavors to draw, from what I saw and learned, correct general conclusions, yet I am far from placing too great a trust in my own judgment, when interests of such magnitude are at stake. I know that this report is incomplete, although as complete as an observation of a few months could enable me to make it. Additional facts might be elicited, calculated to throw new light upon the subject. Although I see no reason for believing that things have changed for the better since I left for the south, yet such may be the case. Admitting all these possibilities, I would entreat you to take no irretraceable step towards relieving the States lately in rebellion from all national control, until such favorable changes are clearly and unmistakably ascertained.

To that end, and by virtue of the permission you honored me with when sending me out to communicate to you freely and unreservedly my views as to measures of policy proper to be adopted, I would not respectfully suggest that you advise Congress to send one or more "investigating committees" into the southern States, to inquire for themselves into the actual condition of things, before final action is taken upon the readmission of such States to their representation in the legislative branch of the government, and the withdrawal of the national control from that section of the country.

I am, sir, very respectfully, your obedient servant,

CARL SCHURZ.

His Excellency ANDREW JOHNSON,
   President of the United States.

PART TWO

THE FIRST RECONSTRUCTION: JOHNSON'S STATE GOVERNMENTS

General Philip H. Sheridan Blames the New Orleans Riot of 1866 Upon Local Officials and Shakes Confidence in the "Johnson States"

General Philip H. Sheridan (1831-1888), the dashing hero who had closed Grant's trap around Lee's army, was a strong supporter of Radical Reconstruction and an outspoken opponent of Johnson's policies of reconciliation toward the South. During the New Orleans riot of 1866, he was an administrator of the Military Division of the Gulf, entrusted among other major duties with checking the threat of Emperor Maximilian and the French army occupying Mexico. He is credited with forcing Louis Napoleon to withdraw his troops because of Sheridan's material aid to the Mexican liberals of Juarez through American troop demonstrations north of the Rio Grande. When the Reconstruction Acts of 1867 were passed he became military governor of Louisiana and Texas with headquarters at New Orleans. Strongly supported by General Grant, he was able to pen the sharp words of his letters to President Johnson regarding the New Orleans Riot of 1866. The story of his varied career against hostile Indians, Confederates, and unfriendly Louisianans is told in *Personal Memoirs* (2 vols., 1888).

This selection of letters shows the wide disparity between Sheridan's idea of the causes of the New Orleans riot and Johnson's. The newspapers apparently sided with Sheridan's view that local officials and police rather than Negroes were the true aggressors in this incident. The New Orleans riot, following a similar outbreak in Memphis, and the wave of Black Codes built up resentment against Johnson's policy and led to the great Radical Congressional victory of the fall of 1866.

From "Louisiana," *The American Annual Cyclopedia: 1866,* pp. 456-57.

The views of Gen. Sheridan, in military command of the Department, are expressed in the following dispatches:

New Orleans, Aug. 1, 1866.

U. S. Grant, General:

You are doubtless aware of the serious riot which occurred in this city on the 30th. A political body styling itself the Convention of 1864, met on the 30th, for, as it is alleged, the purpose of remodelling the present constitution of the State. The leaders were political agitators and revolutionary men, and the action of the convention was liable to produce breaches of the public peace. I had made up my mind to arrest the head men if the proceedings of the convention were calculated to disturb the tranquillity of the Department, but I had no cause for action until they committed the overt act. In the mean time official duty called me to Texas, and the Mayor of the city, during my absence, suppressed the convention by the use of the police force, and, in so doing, attacked the members of the convention and a party of two hundred negroes with fire-arms, clubs and knives, in a manner so unnecessary and atrocious as to compel me to say that it was murder. About forty whites and blacks were thus killed, and about one hundred and sixty wounded. Every thing is now quiet, but I deem it best to maintain a military supremacy in the city for a few days, until the affair is fully investigated. I believe the sentiment of the general community is great regret at this unnecessary cruelty, and that the police could have made any arrest they saw fit without sacrificing lives.

P. H. SHERIDAN,
Major-General Commanding.

New Orleans, La., August 2, 1866.

U. S. Grant, General, Washington, D. C.:

The more information I obtain of the affair of the 30th, in this city, the more revolting it becomes. It was no riot; it was an absolute massacre by the police, which was not excelled in murderous cruelty by that of Fort Pillow. It was a murder which the Mayor and police of the city perpetrated without the shadow of a necessity; furthermore,

I believe it was premeditated, and every indication points to this. I recommend the removing of this bad man. I believe it would be hailed with the sincerest gratification by two-thirds of the population of the city. There has been a feeling of insecurity on the part of the people here on account of this man, which is now so much increased that the safety of life and property does not rest with the civil authorities, but with the military.

P. H. SHERIDAN,
Major-General Commanding.

New Orleans, La., August 8, 1866.

U. S. Grant, General, Washington, D. C.:

I have the honor to report quiet in the city, but considerable excitement in the public mind. There is no interference on the part of the military with the civil government, which performs all its duties without hindrance.

I have permitted the retention of the military governor appointed during my absence, as it gives confidence and enables the military to know what is occurring in the city. He does not interfere with civil matters.

Unless good judgment is exercised, there will be an exodus of northern capital and Union men which will be injurious to the city and to the whole country. I will remove the military governor in a day or two. I again strongly advise that some disposition be made to change the present mayor, as I believe it would do more to restore confidence than any thing that could be done. If the present Governor could be changed also, it would not be amiss.

P. H. SHERIDAN,
Major-General Commanding.

On August 4th, the President addressed by telegraph the following inquiries to General Sheridan:

Executive Mansion, Washington, D. C., Aug. 4, 1866.

To Major-General Sheridan, commanding, etc., New Orleans, La.:

We have been advised here that, prior to the assembling of the illegal and extinct convention elected in 1864, inflammatory and insurrectionary speeches were made to a mob, composed of white and colored persons, urging them to arm and equip themselves for the purpose of protecting and sustaining the convention in its illegal and unauthorized proceedings, intended and calculated to upturn and supersede the existing State Government of Louisiana, which had been recognized by the Government of the United States. Further, did the mob assemble, and was it armed for the purpose of sustaining the convention in its usurpation and revolutionary proceedings? Have any arms been taken from persons since the 30th ult., who were supposed or known to be connected with this mob? Have not various individuals been assaulted and shot by persons connected with this mob without good cause, and in violation of the public peace and good order? Was not the assembling of this convention and the gathering of the mob for its defence and protection the main cause of the riotous and unlawful proceedings of the civil authorities of New Orleans? Have steps been taken by the civil authorities to arrest and try any and all those who were engaged in this riot, and those who have committed offences in violation of law? Can ample justice be meted by the civil authorities to all offenders against the law? Will General Sheridan please furnish me a brief reply to the above inquiries, with such other information as he may be in possession of?

Please answer by telegraph at your earliest convenience.

ANDREW JOHNSON,
President United States.

The reply of General Sheridan was as follows:

New Orleans, La., August 6, 12 M., 1866.

His Excellency Andrew Johnson, President United States:

I have the honor to make the following reply to your dispatch of August fourth (4th): A very large number of colored people marched in procession on Friday night, July twenty-seventh (27th), and were addressed from the steps of the City Hall by Doctor Dostie, ex-Governor Hahn, and others. The speech of Dostie was intemperate in language and sentiment. The speeches of the others, so far as I can learn, were characterized by moderation. I have not given you the words of Dostie's speech, as the version published was denied; but from what I have learned of the man, I believe they were intemperate.

The convention assembled at twelve (12) M. on the thirtieth (30th), the timid members absenting themselves, because the tone of the general public was ominous of trouble. I think there were but about twenty-six (26) members present. In the front of the Mechanics' Institute, where the meeting was held, there were assembled some colored men, women, and children, perhaps eighteen (18) or twenty (20), and in the institute a number of colored men, probably one hundred and fifty (150). Among those outside and inside there might have been a pistol in the possession of every tenth (10th) man.

About one (1) P.M. a procession of, say from sixty (60) to one hundred and thirty (130) colored men marched up Burgundy Street and across Canal Street toward the convention, carrying the American flag. These men had about one pistol to every ten men, and canes, and clubs in addition. While crossing Canal Street a row occurred. There were many spectators in the streets, and their manner and tone toward the procession unfriendly. A shot was fired, by whom I am not able to state, but believe it to have been by a policeman, or some colored man in the procession. This led to other shots and a rush after the procession. On arrival at the front of the Institute there was some throwing of brickbats by both sides. The police, who had been held well in hand, were vigorously marched to the scene of disorder. The procession entered the Institute with the flag, about six (6) or eight (8) remaining outside. A row occurred between a policeman and one of those colored men, and a shot was again fired by one of the parties, which led to an indiscriminate fire on the building through the windows by the policemen. This had been going on for a short time, when a white flag was displayed from the windows of the Institute, whereupon the firing ceased, and the police rushed into the building.

From the testimony of wounded men and others who were inside the building, the policemen opened an indiscriminate fire upon the audience until they had emptied their revolvers, when they retired, and those inside barricaded the doors. The door was broken in, and the firing again commenced, when many of the colored and white people either escaped through the door or were passed out by the policemen inside; but as they came out, the policemen who formed the circle nearest the building fired upon them, and they were again fired upon by the citizens that formed the outer circle. Many of those wounded and taken prisoners, and others who were prisoners and not wounded, were fired upon by their captors and by citizens. The wounded were stabbed while lying on the ground, and their heads beaten with brickbats in the yard of the building, whither some of the colored men had escaped, and partially secreted themselves. They were fired upon and killed or wounded by policemen. Some men were killed or wounded several squares from the scene. Members of the convention were wounded by the policemen while in their hands as prisoners—some of them mortally.

The immediate cause of this terrible affair was the assemblage of this convention. The remote cause was the bitter and antagonistic feeling that has been growing in this community since the advent of the present Mayor, who, in the organization of his police force selected many desperate men, and some of them known murderers. People of clear views were overawed by want of confidence in the Mayor, and fear of the thugs, many of whom he had selected for his police force. I have frequently been spoken to by prominent citizens upon this subject, and have heard them express fear and want of confidence in Mayor Monroe. Ever since the intimation of this last convention I must condemn the course of several of the city papers for supporting, by their articles, the bitter feeling of bad men. As to the merciless manner in which the convention was broken up, I feel obliged to confess strong repugnance.

It is useless to attempt to disguise the hostility that exists on the part of a great many here toward Northern men, and this unfortunate affair has so precipitated matters that there is now a test of what shall be the *status* of Northern men—whether they can live here without being in constant dread or not; whether they can be protected in life and property, and have justice in the courts. If this matter is permitted to pass over without a thorough and determined prosecution of those engaged in it, we may look out for frequent scenes of the same kind, not only here but in other places. No steps have yet been taken by the civil authorities to arrest citizens who were engaged in this massacre, or policemen who perpetuated such cruelties. The members of the convention have been indicted by the grand jury, and many of them arrested and held to bail. As to whether the civil authorities can mete out ample justice to the guilty parties on both sides, I must say it is my opinion unequivocally that they cannot. Judge Abell, whose course I have closely watched for nearly a year, I now consider one of the most dangerous men we have here to the peace and quiet of the city. The leading men of the convention—King, Cutler, Hahn, and others—have been political agitators, and are bad men. I regret to say that the course of Governor Wells has been vacillating, and that during the late trouble he has shown very little of the man.

P. H. SHERIDAN,
Major-General Commanding.

In answer to General Sheridan the following further dispatch was sent:

War Department,
Washington City, August 7, 1866.

To Maj.-Gen. P. H. Sheridan, Commanding, etc., New Orleans, La.:
The President directs me to acknowledge your telegram of the sixth

(6th), in answer to his inquiries of the fourth (4th) instant. On the third (3d) instant instructions were sent you, by General Grant, in conformity with the President's directions, authorizing you to "continue to enforce martial law so far as might be necessary to preserve the public peace, and ordering you not to allow any of the civil authorities to act if you deem such action dangerous to the public safety, and also that no time be lost in investigating the causes that led to the riot and the facts which occurred." By these instructions the President designed to invest in you, as the chief military commander, full authority for the maintenance of the public peace and safety, as he does not see that anything more is needed pending the investigation with which you are intrusted. But if, in your judgment, your powers are inadequate to preserve the peace until the facts connected with the riot are ascertained, you will please report to this department for the information of the President.

EDWIN M. STANTON,
Secretary of War.

The Lieutenant-Governor, the Attorney-General of the State, and the Mayor of New Orleans made a report to the President on August 7th that the civil authorities took all the precautions possible to prevent the outbreak; that they applied during three days previous to the military to preserve order at the place where the convention was to meet; that the authorities, State and municipal, came to an understanding to act in concert with the military for that purpose; that the citizens no more than the police contemplated preventing the convention from holding their meeting in peace and adjourning and dispersing unmolested; and that the warrant for their arrest would have been submitted to the military as agreed upon, although the President's dispatch to the Lieutenant-Governor, and the subsequent one to the Attorney-General, was imperative that the military must not thwart the convention. The military authorities had been for three days previous to the riot in constant communication with the Attorney-General and the Lieutenant-Governor, with a view to prevent the impending riot. The efforts were unsuccessful and could not counteract the incendiary counsels and appeals of those who, for sinister purposes had in view this very result in order to reap a political harvest. . . .

General Oliver O. Howard and the Freedmen's Bureau's Crusade for Negro Education

Under the remarkable "Christian general" Oliver O. Howard (1830-1909), the Freedmen's Bureau came closer than any other federal agency to fulfilling the hope that Reconstruction might become an experiment in racial equality. Howard, born of a colonial family in Maine, eventually became a heroic if controversial general in various key Civil War battles. He seemed a logical appointee to both Lincoln and Johnson, and on May 12, 1865, the latter chose him Commissioner of the Bureau of Refugees, Freedmen, and Abandoned Lands. His enthusiasm for the freedmen led him to go much further than providing and supervising relief and labor contracts for them; he used his power to put pressure on the South to eliminate racial injustice and, as this selection shows, invoked an educational crusade that went beyond elementary school and into the college level for leadership. Booker T. Washington obtained his educational start in Howard's Hampton Institute, and many leaders won their training in Howard University, named after its chief sponsor. That he failed to solve the problem of land for the rootless Negro was partly due to the hostility of Johnson and local Southern opinion. While his critics argue that Howard was an amazingly poor administrator, he was exonerated in 1874 by Sherman, Grant, and a military court of any concrete charges such as misapplication of public funds, keeping confused records, and alleged embezzlement. They concluded, after thirty-seven days of careful investigation, that Howard "did his whole duty, and [they] believed that he deserved well of his country." The revenge the Klan took on him will be noted later.

From Howard's *Autobiography* (2 vols., 1907), pp. 390-95.

In my earlier interviews with Mr. Stanton in May, 1865, I claimed that the education of the freedmen's children, and of adults, as far as practicable, was *the true relief.*

"Relief from what?" asked Stanton, glancing toward me over his colored glasses.

"Relief from beggary and dependence," I replied.

I had the same opinion with reference to our numerous "white refugees" of the South, though it was believed that they would naturally be incorporated in ordinary schools there without such prejudice to their interests as existed against the negro population.

Very soon all my assistants agreed with me that it would not be long before we must have *negro teachers,* if we hoped to secure a permanent foothold for our schools. This conclusion had become plain from the glimpses already given into Southern society. Naturally enough, the most Christian of the Southern people would prefer to have white teachers from among themselves. Feeling a sympathy for this seeming home prejudice, quite early in 1866, I tried the experiment in one State, in coöperation with the Episcopal Bishop of that State, to put over our school children Southern white teachers, male and female, but the bishop and I found that their faith in negro education was too small, and their ignorance of practical teaching too great, to admit of any reasonable degree of success. After trial and failure it was given up. But faith and enthusiasm combined to give the negro teachers a marvelous progress. Of course, in the outset there were few negroes in the United States who were properly fitted to teach. The most who had a smattering of learning could not speak the English language with a reasonable correctness. It was then a plain necessity to have schools which could prepare teachers. My own sentiment often found vent when I was visited by men of opposite convictions—the one set saying that *no* high schools or colleges were wanted for the freedmen, and the other declaring their immediate and pressing necessity. My own thought favored the latter, but not with haste. It was given in this form: "You cannot keep up the lower grades unless you have the higher." Academies and colleges, universities and normal schools, had long been a necessity in all sections where the free schools had been continuously sustained.

A brief experience showed us that the negro people were capable of education, with no limit that men could set to their capacity. What white men could learn or had learned, they, or some of them, could learn. There was one school diagonally across the street from my headquarters, named the Wayland Seminary. The pupils were from fourteen to twenty years of age. It was taught in 1866 by a lady, who, herself, was not only a fine scholar, but a thoroughly trained teacher. One day the Hon. Kenneth Raynor, of North Carolina, whom I had long known and valued as a personal friend, came to my room to labor with me and show me how unwise were some of my ideas.

He said in substance about this educating the freedmen:

"General Howard, do you not know that you are educating the colored youth above their business? You will only destroy them. Those young girls, for example; they will be too proud or vain to work, and the consequence will be that they will go to dance houses and other places of improper resort."

"Why, my friend," I replied, "do you really think that? I am astonished! That is not the way education affects the Yankee girls. Come with me to the Wayland school, across the street."

We went together to the large school building and entered the commodious room where the school was just commencing its morning exercises. After extending a pleasant welcome, the teacher gave us seats well back, where we could see the blackboards, which were near her desk, and the open school organ at her left, ready for use. She first sent up two nice-looking girls, of about fifteen years, to the instrument. One played, and the other, like a precentor, led the school in singing. There was evident culture in the singing and playing, and none of the melody was wanting. My friend's eyes moistened; but he whispered: "They always could sing!"

Next, we had a class of reading. It was grateful to cultured ears to have sentences well read and words correctly pronounced. Spelling and defining followed, with very few mistakes. The recitations at the blackboard in arithmetic that next came on were remarkable. To test the pupils beyond their text, I went forward and placed some hard problems there. With readiness and intelligence they were solved. The politeness and bearing of these young people to one another, to the teacher, and to us, struck my good friend with astonishment. Such a school, even of whites, so orderly, so well trained, and so accomplished, Mr. Raynor had seldom seen. As we returned across the street, arm in arm, he said to me: "General, you have converted me!" This fine seminary was tantamount to a normal school. It was preparing many excellent teachers for their subsequent work.

Miss M. R. Mann, a niece of the Hon. Horace Mann, through the aid of Massachusetts friends, had a handsome school building constructed in Washington, D. C., and it had the best possible appliances furnished—all for her own use. She charged tuition, except for those whose purpose was avowed to become teachers. She commenced at the foundation of instruction, and led her pupils step by step on and up, class by class, as high as she could conveniently take them. She began the enterprise in December, 1865. Pupils of different ages were admitted, so that teachers, still in embryo, might learn by experiment. It became before long the model school of the District of Columbia. The neatness and order, the elegant rooms for reciting, and the high grade of Miss Mann's classes in recitations always attracted and surprised visitors. From this school, also, several teachers graduated and proved themselves able and worthy in their subsequent successful career.

There were various other schools, as we know, in the United States which had been long in existence, preparing colored teachers, physicians, ministers, lawyers, and others for the coming needs of the new citizens—notably Oberlin College; Wilberforce University, of Xenia, O.; Berea Academy, Ky.; The Theological Institute (Baptist) at Washington, D. C., and Ashmun Institute at Oxford, Pa. The institute also for colored youth in Philadelphia, founded in 1837 by the bequest of a Friend, Richard Humphreys, was designed to teach agriculture and mechanical arts, and prepare teachers for their profession. By other gifts, and by the help of benevolent and friendly associations, this institute had come, in 1866, to have a capacity for three hundred (300) pupils; it was fairly endowed and doing well, giving excellent results. Its teachers were all colored persons. It had that year 48 graduates, 31 of whom became teachers. Still, notwithstanding these sources of supply, the need for more teachers was constant, and if any general system of free schools should be adopted, the demand would be a hundred times beyond the possibility of meeting it by competent instructors.

As the work of carrying forward the schools developed, the old negro clergymen of every name became inadequate for the religious instruction of the more enlightened people. Many ministers felt themselves to be unlearned, and so sought such knowledge of books as they could get. Negro pharmacists and other medical men were soon required, and contentions with white men in the courts demanded friendly advocates at law.

Under the evident and growing necessity for higher education, in 1866 and 1867, a beginning was made. Various good schools of a collegiate grade were started in the South, and normal classes were about this time added, as at Hampton, Charleston, Atlanta, Macon, Savannah, Memphis, Louisville, Mobile, Talladega, Nashville, New Orleans, and elsewhere.

In every way, as commissioner, I now encouraged the higher education, concerning which there was so much interest, endeavoring to adhere to my principle of Government aid in dealing with the benevolent associations. These, by 1867, had broken away from a common union, and were again pushing forward their denominational enterprises, but certainly, under the Bureau's supervision, nowhere did they hurtfully interfere with one another.

Each denomination desired to have, here and there, a college of its own. Such institutions the founders and patrons were eager to make different from the simple primary or grammar schools; these, it was hoped and believed, would be eventually absorbed in each

State in a great free school system. The educators naturally wished to put a moral and Christian stamp upon their students, especially upon those who would become instructors of colored youth. My own strong wish was ever to lay permanent substructures and build thereon as rapidly as possible, in order to give as many good teachers, professional men, and leaders to the rising generation of freedmen as we could, during the few years of Governmental control. . . .

Major John William De Forest of the Freedmen's Bureau Views His Southern Relief Clients and the Chivalrous Southrons

Among the alleged Carpetbaggers who came from New England with the Union Army was the talented novelist John W. De Forest (1826-1906), a man who discovered in the South a rich vein of literary ore in "the low-down people" later memorialized in *Tobacco Road*. He was the son of a successful merchant, but his father's early death led him to improvise his education. Fortunately his ability for sensitive writing gave him an early literary career which included several travel books and novels. During the Civil War, he recruited a New Haven company and served under Sheridan in the Shenandoah Valley. During 1865-1868 he was in command of a South Carolina district of the Freedmen's Bureau. As these selections show, he was ready to cut Bureau red tape to help the poverty-stricken mountaineers and Negroes who came to him for assistance, and he was ready to overlook their little lies about eligibility. He felt sympathy for the South's poverty, but noted the persistence of old social prejudices. His realistic descriptions and humor enrich his articles in *Harper's Magazine* and several novels, like *Miss Ravenel's Conversion from Secession to Loyalty* (1867) and especially *Kate Beaumont* (1872), although to a modern reader he may occasionally seem insensitive to the total tragic aspects of the situation. While he was never an abolitionist, he showed a strong nationalist viewpoint.

From John W. De Forest, "Drawing Bureau Rations," *Harper's New Monthly Magazine* XXXVII (June 1868), 75-76, and *idem* XXXVIII (Jan.-Feb. 1869), 339-41.

"Mornin. How ye git'n 'long? Got any thin for the lone wimmen?"

"Yes, ma'am. What do you need? How am I to know that you need any thing?"

"Oh Lord! I guess I'm poor enough. My ole man was killed in the war because he wouldn't jine the rebs. They shot him in the swamp, right whar they found him. We was always for your side. And I've got two small children, and nothin to go upon. Got any corn?"

Her old man was probably a "low down creetur" who was executed as a deserter, having refused to join the rebs just as he would have evaded joining any army or doing any thing that implied work. But looking at her haggard face and ragged clothing, how could I find it in my heart to doubt that she was a "Union woman?" My stores, it must be remembered, were properly distributable only to freedmen and refugees, the latter term meaning Southern loyalists who had been driven from their homes by the Confederacy.

I had intended to procrastinate and be mercilessly conscientious in my distribution, giving nothing except to persons whom I knew by personal inspection to be the very poorest in the district. But the pressure of an instantaneously aroused horde of dolorous applicants rendered it impossible to be either deliberate or fastidious. Amidst such an abundant supply of poverty there seemed to be no choice; and after a few days of heroic holding on to my goods, I let go with a run. Only in the over-coat business did I make a firm stand; the weather having turned mild, I boxed them up for another winter; indeed, I counterfeited innocence of over-coats. The remaining articles, one hundred and eighty in number, were distributed among ninety-four applicants, consisting of eleven white women, forty-nine colored women, and thirty-four colored men. All but one or two of the whites were widows with families of small children; and nearly all the blacks were deformed, rheumatic, blind, or crippled with extreme age.

In vain I resolved to issue but one article to an individual, in order to make the supply go further. A venerable, doubled-up contraband would say, "Boss, I got shoes now, but dey won't keep me warm o'nights. Can't I hev a blanket, Boss?" A woman furnished with a dress would show her bare or nearly bare feet, and put up a prayer for brogans. The wretched family from the brush house appeared, and in its grasping distress carried off three dresses, three pairs of shoes, and two blankets. Widows of Confederates though they were, how could I look on their muddy rags and tell them that they were not refugees, and had no claim upon Bureau charity? Had the Second Auditor and the Third Auditor discovered this pitiful rascality of mine, it would have been their duty to disallow my returns and stop my pay.

My little room, crammed with people of all colors elbowing each other in the equality of sordid poverty, looked as though it might be a Miscegenation Office. The two races got along admirably together; the whites put on no airs of superiority or aversion; the negroes were respectful, and showed no jealousy. There is little social distance at any time between the low-downer and the black. Two white women were pointed out to me as having children of mixed blood; and I heard that one rosy-cheeked girl of nineteen had taken a mulatto husband of fifty.

Now and then I was amused by a sparkle of female vanity. Two white widows of twenty-four or twenty-five, comely by nature, but now gaunt and haggard with the ailments which hardship surely brings upon women—charily exposed their muddy stockings of coarse home-spun wool, and, pipe in mouth, held the following dialogue:

"Miss Jackson, these shoes are a sight too big for me. I wear fours."

"That's so, Miss Jacocks. Fours is my number, too. And I hev worn threes."

Of my ninety-four recipients ninety-four signed with a mark; and in my subsequent issues I found that this was the usual proportion.

And now the public talk was of corn. The crop of 1866, both of cereals and other productions, had been a short one for various reasons. Capital, working stock, and even seed had been scarce; a new system of labor had operated, of course, bunglingly; finally, there had been a severe drought. During the autumn and early winter I was called upon to arrange a hundred or two of disputes between planters and their hands as to the division of the pittance which nature had returned them for their outlay and industry. The white, feeling that he ought to have a living out of his land, and fearing lest he should not get enough "to go upon" until the next harvest, held firmly to the terms of his contract, and demanded severe justice—in some cases more than justice. The negro could not understand how the advances which had been made to him during the summer should swallow up his half or third of the "crap."

Honesty bids me declare that, in my opinion, no more advantage was taken of the freedmen than a similarly ignorant class would be subjected to in any other region where poverty should be pinching and the danger of starvation imminent. So far as my observation goes, the Southerner is not hostile toward the negro as a negro, but only as a possible office-holder, as a juror, as a voter, as a political and social equal. He may cuff him, as he would his dog, into what he calls "his place;" but he is not vindictive toward him for being free, and he is willing to give him a chance in life.

On the other hand, the black is not the vicious and totally irrational creature described in reactionary journals. He is very ignorant, somewhat improvident, not yet aware of the necessity of persistent industry, and in short a grown-up child. I venture these statements after fifteen months of intercourse with the most unfair and discontented of both parties. The great majority of planters and laborers either did not dispute over their harvest of poverty, or came to an arrangement about it without appealing to me.

The ignorance of the freedmen was sometimes amusing and sometimes provoking. When Captain Britton, of the Sixth Infantry, acted as Bureau officer in a South Carolina district, a farmer and negro came before him to settle the terms of their contract, the former offering one-third of the crop, and the latter demanding one-sixth. It was only by the aid of six bits of paper, added and subtracted upon a table, that the Captain succeeded in shaking the faith of the darkey in his calculation.

"Well, Boss," he answered, doubtfully, "ef you say one-third is the most, I reckon it's so. But I allowed one-sixth was the most."

I passed nearly an entire forenoon in vainly endeavoring to convince an old freedman that his employer had not cheated him. I read to him, out of the planter's admirably kept books, every item of debit and credit: so much meal, bacon, and tobacco furnished, with the dates of each delivery of the same; so many bushels of corn and peas and bunches of "fodder" harvested. He admitted every item, admitted the prices affixed; and then, puzzled, incredulous, stubborn, denied the totals. His fat old wife, trembling with indignant suspicion, looked on grimly or broke out in fits of passion.

"Don you give down to it, Peter," she exhorted. "It ain't no how ris'ible that we should 'a worked all the year and git nothing to go upon."

The trouble with this man was that he had several small grandchildren to support, and that he had undertaken to do it upon a worn-out plantation. I could only assure him that he had "nothing coming," and advise him to throw himself upon the generosity of his employer. As the latter was himself woefully poor, and as it was my duty to set even-handed justice on its legs, any exaction in favor of the laborer beyond the terms of the contract was out of the question.

There were hundreds of cases like this; and there were the old, the widows, and the orphans. Although my district was a grain country, corn rose to two dollars a bushel, and bacon to forty cents a pound. In the lowlands of South Carolina the destitution was still more pinching and prices still higher. Governor Orr published a moving appeal for aid, composed mainly of letters showing a widespread want nearly approaching starvation. Evidently the hour was coming upon me when I should be obliged to make an issue of provisions. . . .

Proceeding with my sketches of our Southern and very nearly torrid brethren, I come to:

POLITICAL FEELING

Walking the streets of Greenville I met a child of six or seven—a blonde, blue-eyed girl with cheeks of faint rose—who, in return for my look of interest, greeted me with a smile. Surprised at the hospitable expression, and remembering my popularly abhorred blue uniform, I said, "Are you not afraid of me?"

"No," she answered; "I am not afraid. I met three Yankees the other day, and they didn't hurt me."

We of the North can but faintly imagine the alarm and hate which have trembled through millions of hearts at the South at the phrase, "The Yankees are coming!" The words meant war, the fall of loved ones, the burning of homes, the wasting of property, flight, poverty, subjugation, humiliation, a thousand evils, and a thousand sorrows. The Southern people had never before suffered any thing a tenth part so horrible as what befell them in consequence of this awful formula, this summons to the Afrites and Furies of desolation, this declaration of ruin. Where the conquering army sought to be gentlest it still devoured the land like locusts; where it came not at all it nevertheless brought social revolution, bankruptcy of investments, and consequently indigence. A population of bereaved parents, of widows, and of orphans, steeped in sudden poverty, can hardly love the cause of its woes. The great majority of the Southerners, denying that they provoked the war, looking upon us not as the saviours of a common country, but as the subjugators of their sovereign States, regard us with detestation.

I speak of the "chivalrous Southrons," the gentry, the educated, the socially influential, the class which before the war governed the South, the class which may soon govern it again. Even if
these people knew that they had been in the wrong they would still
be apt to feel that their punishment has exceeded their crime, because it has been truly tremendous and has reached many who
could not be guilty. I remember a widowed grandmother of eighty
and an orphan grand-daughter of seven from each of whom a large
estate on the Sea Islands had passed deyond redemption, and who
were in dire poverty. When the elder read aloud from a newspaper a
description of some hundreds of acres which had been divided
among negroes, and said, "Chattie, that is your plantation," the
child burst into tears. I believe that it is unnatural not to sympathize with this little plundered princess, weeping for her lost
domains in fairy-land.

Imagine the wrath of a fine gentleman, once the representative
of his country abroad, who finds himself driven to open a beer
saloon. Imagine the indignation of a fine lady who must keep
boarders; of another who must go out to service little less than
menial; of another who must beg rations with low-downers and negroes. During the war I saw women of good families at the South
who had no stockings; and here I beg leave to stop and ask the
reader to conceive fully, if he can, the sense of degradation which
must accompany such poverty; a degradation of dirt and nakedness, and slatternly uncomeliness, be it observed; a degradation
which seemed to place them beside the negro. Let us imagine the
prosperous ladies of our civilization prevented only from wearing the
latest fashions; what manliest man of us all would like to assume
the responsibility of such a piece of tyranny?

Moreover, "Our Lady of Tears," the terrible *Mater Lachryma-
rum* of De Quincey's visions, fills the whole South with her outcries
for the dead. It is not so much a wonder as a pity that the women
are bitter, and teach bitterness to their children.

Of course there are lower and more ridiculous motives for this
hate. Non-combatants, sure of at least bodily safety, are apt to be

war-like, and to blow cheap trumpets of mock heroism. Futher-more, it is aristocratic to keep aloof from Yankees; and what woman does not desire to have the tone of good society?

When will this sectional aversion end? I can only offer the obvious reflection that it is desirable for both North and South, but espe-cially for the weaker of the two, that it should end as quickly as possible. For the sake of the entire republic we should endeavor to make all our citizens feel that they are Americans, and nothing but Americans. If we do not accomplish this end, we shall not rival the greatness of the Romans. It was not patricianism which made Rome great so much as the vast community and bonded strength of Roman citizenship. Let us remember in our legislation the law of solidarity: the fact that no section of a community can be injured without injuring the other sections; that the perfect prosperity of the whole depends upon the prosperity of all the parts.

This idea should be kept in view despite of provocations; this policy will in the end produce broad and sound national unity. As the Southerners find that the republic brings them prosperity they will, little by little, and one by one, become as loyal as the people of other sections.

FINANCIAL CONDITION

In Naples and Syria I have seen more beggarly communities than the South, but never one more bankrupt. Judging from what I learned in my own district I should say that the great majority of planters owed to the full extent of their property, and that, but for stay-laws and stay-orders, all Dixie would have been brought to the hammer without meeting its liabilities. When I left Greenville there were something like a thousand executions awaiting action; and, had the Commanding General allowed their collection, another thousand would have been added to the docket. I have known land to go at auction for a dollar and twelve cents an acre, which before the war was valued, I was told, at seven or eight dollars the acre. Labor was equally depreciated, able-bodied men hiring out at seventy-five cents a day if they found themselves; at twenty-five cents if found by their employers. The great mass of the farmers could not pay even these wretched wages, and were forced to plant upon shares, a system unsuited to a laboring class so ignorant and thoughtless as the negroes.

It seemed unjust that debts should retain their full valuation when all other property was thus depreciated. Yet I doubt the practical wisdom of the stay-orders. I think it would have been better to let the whole row of staggering bricks go over; then every one would have known where he was, and industry would have resumed its life. As it was, there was a prolonged crisis of bankruptcy, in which neither debtor nor creditor dared or could take a step. It was a carnival of Micawberism; hundreds of thousands of people were waiting to see what would turn up; they were living on what remained of their property without working to increase it; why should they accumulate when the creditor might seize the accumulation?

This financial and moral paralysis was fostering dishonesty. People who had in other days been honorable descended to all sorts of trickeries, in the hope of saving property which did not seem to be covered by the stay-orders. I was teased with applications to use my authority in preventing the collection of debts, the administration of estates, and the levying of taxes. In short, the stay-system was transforming the chivalrous Southrons into a race of —Micawbers.

There would have been more hope in the future of my district but for the exhausted soil and the wretched agriculture which had been bequeathed to it by slavery. Land which, under proper cultivation, will produce two generous crops a year, had been reduced, by lack of manure and of management, to one crop, varying from ten to two bushels the acre. The common plow-share of the country is about six inches wide by ten long, and this is used until it is worn into what is called a "bull-tongue," a phrase which aptly describes its shape and size. This triviality does not turn a furrow; it scratches the earth like a harrow.

Here and there, at monstrous intervals, a planter uses Northern plows and manure, gathering his forty and eighty bushels of corn to the acre. His neighbors look on with astonishment, but without imitating him, as if his results were magic, and beyond merely human accomplishment. A German colony, planted at Walhalla, in the northwestern corner of South Carolina, has converted a tract of some thousands of acres into a garden of fertility. Among their Anglo-Saxon neighbors you can not discover a sign of their influence. What is to become of this bull-tongued and bull-headed race? I sometimes thought that there was no hope of the physical regeneration of the South until immigration should have rooted out and replaced its present population.

In this same land numberless water-privileges send their ungathered riches to the sea, and the earth is crowded with underground palaces of mineral wealth. The climate, too, is unrivaled: the summer heat in Greenville was rarely too great for walking, its highest point being usually eighty-four; while the winter brought at the worst two or three falls of snow, which melted in two or three days. Neither in Europe, nor along the shores of the Mediterranean, have I found a temperature which, during the year round, was so agreeable and healthful. You can see what it is in the remarkable stature of the men, and in the height, fullness of form, and beauty of the women. My impression is that the entire Alleghany region, from Maryland down into the north of Georgia, is a paradise for the growth of the human plant. If bodily comforts and intellectual pleasures existed there, I should advise all New England to emigrate to it.

Yet it is poorer than Naples, and before the war it was not richer. So much for the political economy of the chivalrous Southron, and so much for his rule-or-ruin statesmanship, and, in one word, so much for slavery!

SOUTHERN LOYALISTS

I class the loyalists of my district under the head of "semi-chivalrous Southrons," because, being seldom large planters or even slaveholders, they do not exhibit all the characteristics of the "high-toned" population. They are mostly small farmers, inhabiting the mountains of Pickens and of a certain portion of Greenville known as the Dark Corner. I did not always find it easy to distinguish them from rebels. One gaunt old female laid claim to Bureau rations on the double ground that she was a good Union woman, and that she had lost two sons in the Confederate army. This story was so contradictory that I believed it, remembering first that truth is often much more improbable than falsehood; and, second, that many loyal families saw their children carried off by rebel press-gangs.

These poor, uncultured, and, in some cases, half-wild people have always been true to the United States Government. In the days of Nullification, and in other subsequent disunion excitements, when Governor Perry (or, as they called him, Ben Perry) fought a good fight against Calhounism, they were his firmest supporters, and regarded him with something like adoration. As a Greenvilleite said to me, "They believed they would go to him when they died."

"But now," in the words of one of their patriarchs, "Ben Perry has fallen from the faith"; and consequently the mountaineers have deserted him in a body, and stigmatize him as "the biggest reb agoing." One of the prime staples of the Republican speeches which I heard in that region was the showing up of the apostasy of this distinguished "central monkey."

THE MOUNTAINEERS DURING THE WAR

It is a striking instance of the reliability of history that I never learned to my satisfaction the date or manner of the famous advance of the mountaineers upon Greenville during the war. One informant assured me that it took place before Bull Run; that the loyal men of the Dark Corner and vicinity mustered six hundred strong; that they marched toward the low-country with the intention of forcing South Carolina back into the Union; that Greenville, unable to meet such a host in the field, sent forth Governor Perry to dissipate it by the breath of his eloquence. This dramatic informant, rising from his chair and extending his arm, proceeded to deliver with flashing eye and thunderous tongue a fragment of the Governor's oration:

"Men of Greenville," he represented him as saying, "the government under which you were born no longer exists; and that loyalty which you formerly owed it, and which you rendered so nobly, is now due to the Confederate States." Whereupon the invaders separated into two bodies, one of which went back to its mountains in wrath and discouragement, while the other formed two companies for the rebel army and fought heroically at Bull Run.

The other version of this affair is, that it took place late in the struggle; that there was no advance upon the low-country, but only a general marauding of deserters and other desperadoes; that the Confederate authorities offered them pardon in case they would surrender and agree to lead peaceful lives; that sixty or seventy of them were got together, and that Governor Perry was induced to make them a pacificatory speech; the result being that the majority of them laid down their bushwhacking rifles and resumed the ways of peace. As I had both these tales from good local authority the reader will be justified in believing them both. My own opinion inclines to accept the latter of the two as the most probable.

It is certain that the majority of the able-bodied men of the mountains were eventually bullied or dragged by main force into the rebel army. They sought to remain loyal; there is no reasonable doubt of that; but the conscription details were too much for them. Long lines of videttes were run clear through the mountains, and the distances between the lines were traversed by relentless patrols. Men who fled on being summoned to surrender were shot at once; they were massacred in their own door-yards in the presence of their families. It must be understood that by the Conscription Act every male Southerner was placed on the rolls of the Confederate army, and thus was constituted a deserter in case he failed to repair to the dépôt of the regiment to which he had been assigned. It was nominally as deserters, and not as Unionists, that these victims were murdered.

The rebel authorities even used blood-hounds to aid their troops in scouring the refractory mountains. "But that didn't amount to much," said a stalwart old mountaineer to me, with a chuckle. "The dawgs would run ahead yelping, and the boys would take a crack or two at 'em with a rifle, and that would be the end of the dawgs."

It took at least two lowlanders to catch one highlander, and when caught he was very nearly worthless as a soldier. He seldom fired a gun at the Yankees; if there was a chance to desert he improved it; if he got back to his native rocks he was a bigger pest than ever. Nearly all the youth of the Dark Corner were at one time or another chased into the rebel army, without doing it a particle of benefit.

Meantime, the elders of the mountains harbored such of our men as escaped to them from Columbia or Andersonville, and acted as guides in running them through the rebel lines to Eastern Tennessee. Several of them have shown me certificates to this effect from Union officers whom they had thus befriended. . . .

PART THREE

THE DEBATE OVER RADICAL RECONSTRUCTION

Frederick Douglass, Freedman and Abolitionist
Editor, Calls for Radical Reconstruction

The tradition of Negro militancy is usually symbolized by the ex-slave Frederick Douglass (1817?-1895), born on a Talbot County, Maryland, plantation, of a white father and slave mother. When he escaped to New York City, where he became a laborer, and then to Massachusetts, his talents as a speaker, writer, and idealist were soon recognized by the Garrison abolitionists. Douglass campaigned against disfranchisement and social discrimination and acted as an agent of the Massachusetts Antislavery Society. He published an autobiography that has become a classic of freedom. As an editor of the *North Star* for seventeen years, he fought for a broadly liberal program for both races, including female suffrage and Negro education. As this selection suggests, he was particularly proud of his role in convincing moderates that slavery was the real cause of the war and that the Union Army must welcome the Negro as a soldier. Lincoln conferred on key racial issues with Douglass, who pressed for immediate Negro suffrage as an indispensable protection for the Southern freedman and also urged the enforcement of civil rights for Negroes. In this cause he published the *National New Era*. He was duped into accepting the presidency of the failing Freedmen's Savings and Trust Company. This institution, with branches in all the Southern states, was intended to encourage freedmen to save their earnings and to rise in ambition, but its collapse meant tragedy for thousands of Negroes and only the well-known integrity of Douglass enabled him to escape suspicion. In later years he served as the first United States minister to Haiti and continued to fight for his race, especially in the years before his death, against the rising tide of lynching.

Selection: Frederick Douglass, "Reconstruction," *Atlantic Monthly* XVIII (1866), 761-65.

The assembling of the Second Session of the Thirty-ninth Congress may very properly be made the occasion of a few earnest words on the already much-worn topic of reconstruction.

Seldom has any legislative body been the subject of a solicitude more intense, or of aspirations more sincere and ardent. There are the best of reasons for this profound interest. Questions of vast moment, left undecided by the last session of Congress, must be manfully grappled with by this. No political skirmishing will avail. The occasion demands statesmanship.

Whether the tremendous war so heroically fought and so victoriously ended shall pass into history a miserable failure, barren of permanent results,—a scandalous and shocking waste of blood and treasure,—a strife for empire, as Earl Russell characterized it, of no value to liberty or civilization,—an attempt to re-establish a Union by force, which must be the merest mockery of a Union,—an effort to bring under Federal authority States into which no loyal man from the North may safely enter, and to bring men into the national councils who deliberate with daggers and vote with revolvers, and who do not even conceal their deadly hate of the country that conquered them; or whether, on the other hand, we shall, as the rightful reward of victory over treason, have a solid nation, entirely delivered from all contradictions and social antagonisms, based upon loyalty, liberty, and equality, must be determined one way or the other by the present session of Congress. The last session really did nothing which can be considered final as to these questions. The Civil Rights Bill and the Freedmen's Bureau Bill and the proposed constitutional amendments, with the amendment already adopted and recognized as the law of the land, do not reach the difficulty, and cannot, unless the whole structure of the government is changed from a government by States to something like a despotic central government, with power to control even the municipal regulations of States, and to make them conform to its own despotic will. While there remains such an idea as the right of each State to control its own local affairs,—an idea, by the way, more deeply rooted in the minds of men of all sections of the country than perhaps any one other political idea,—no general assertion of human rights can be of any practical value. To change the character of the government at this point is neither possible nor desirable. All that is necessary to be done is to make the government consistent with itself and render the rights of the States compatible with the sacred rights of human nature.

The arm of the Federal government is long, but it is far too short to protect the rights of individuals in the interior of distant States. They must have the power to protect themselves, or they will go unprotected, in spite of all the laws the Federal government can put upon the national statute-book.

Slavery, like all other great systems of wrong, founded in the depths of human selfishness, and existing for ages, has not neglected its own conservation. It has steadily exerted an influence upon all around it favorable to its own continuance. And to-day it is so strong that it could exist, not only without law, but even against law. Custom, manners, morals, religion, are all on its side everywhere in the South; and when you add the ignorance and servility of the ex-slave to the intelligence and accustomed authority of the master, you have the conditions, not out of which slavery will again grow, but under which it is impossible for the Federal government to wholly destroy it, unless the Federal government be armed with despotic power, to blot out State authority, and to station a Federal officer at every cross-road. This, of course, cannot be done, and ought not even if it could. The true way and the easiest way is to make our government entirely consistent with itself, and give to every loyal citizen the elective franchise,—a right and power which will be ever present, and will form a wall of fire for his protection.

One of the invaluable compensations of the late Rebellion is the highly instructive disclosure it made of the true source of danger to republican government. Whatever may be tolerated in monarchical and despotic governments, no republic is safe that tolerates a privileged class, or denies to any of its citizens equal rights and equal means to maintain them. What was theory before the war has been made fact by the war.

There is cause to be thankful even for rebellion. It is an impressive teacher, though a stern and terrible one. In both characters it has come to us, and it was perhaps needed in both. It is an instructor never a day before its time, for it comes only when all other means of progress and enlightenment have failed. Whether the oppressed and despairing bondman, no longer able to repress his deep yearnings for manhood, or the tyrant, in his pride and impatience, takes the initiative, and strikes the blow for a firmer hold and a longer lease of oppression, the result is the same,—society is instructed, or may be.

Such are the limitations of the common mind, and so thoroughly engrossing are the cares of common life, that only the few among men can discern through the glitter and dazzle of present prosperity the dark outlines of approaching disasters, even though they may have come up to our very gates, and are already within striking distance. The yawning seam and corroded bolt conceal their defects from the mariner until the storm calls all hands to the pumps. Prophets, indeed, were abundant before the war; but who cares for prophets while their predictions remain unfulfilled, and the calamities of which they tell are masked behind a blinding blaze of national prosperity?

It is asked, said Henry Clay, on a memorable occasion, Will slavery never come to an end? That question, said he, was asked fifty years ago, and it has been answered by fifty years of unprecedented prosperity. In spite of the eloquence of the earnest Abolitionists,—poured out against slavery during thirty years,— even they must confess, that, in all the probabilities of the case, that system of barbarism would have continued its horrors far beyond the limits of the nineteenth century but for the Rebellion, and perhaps only have disappeared at last in a fiery conflict, even more fierce and bloody than that which has now been suppressed.

It is no disparagement to truth, that it can only prevail where reason prevails. War begins where reason ends. The thing worse than rebellion is the thing that causes rebellion. What that thing is, we have been taught to our cost. It remains now to be seen whether we have the needed courage to have that cause entirely removed from the Republic. At any rate, to this grand work of national regeneration and entire purification Congress must now address itself, with full purpose that the work shall this time be thoroughly done. The deadly upas, root and branch, leaf and fibre, body and sap, must be utterly destroyed. The country is evidently not in a condition to listen patiently to pleas for postponement, however plausible, nor will it permit the responsibility to be shifted to other shoulders. Authority and power are here commensurate with the duty imposed. There are no cloud-flung shadows to obscure the way. Truth shines with brighter light and intenser heat at every moment, and a country torn and rent and bleeding implores relief from its distress and agony.

If time was at first needed, Congress has now had time. All the requisite materials from which to form an intelligent judgment are now before it. Whether its members look at the origin, the progress, the termination of the war, or at the mockery of a peace now existing, they will find only one unbroken chain of argument in favor of a radical policy of reconstruction. For the omissions of the last session, some excuses may be allowed. A treacherous President stood in the way; and it can be easily seen how reluctant good men might be to admit an apostasy which involved so much of baseness and ingratitude. It was natural that they should seek to save him by bending to him even when he leaned to the side of error. But all is changed now. Congress knows now that it must go on without his aid, and even against his machinations. The advantage of the present session over the last is immense. Where that investigated, this has the facts. Where that walked by faith, this may walk by sight. Where that halted, this must go forward, and where that failed, this must succeed, giving the country whole measures where that gave us half-measures, merely as a means of saving the elections in a few doubtful districts. That Congress saw what was right, but distrusted the enlightenment of the loyal masses; but what was forborne in distrust of the people must now be done with a full knowledge that the people expect and require it. The members go to Washington fresh from the inspiring presence of the people. In every considerable public meeting, and in almost every conceivable way, whether at court-house, school-house, or cross-roads, indoors and out, the subject has been discussed, and the people have emphatically pronounced in favor of a radical policy. Listening to the doctrines of expediency and compromise with pity, impatience, and disgust, they have everywhere broken into demonstrations of the wildest enthusiasm when a brave word has been spoken in favor of equal rights and impartial suffrage. Radicalism, so far from being odious, is now the popular passport to power. The men most bitterly charged with it go to Congress with the largest majorities, while the timid and doubtful are sent by lean majorities, or else left at home. The strange controversy between the President and Congress, at one time so threatening, is disposed of by the people. The high reconstructive powers which he so confidently, ostentatiously, and haughtily claimed, have been disallowed, denounced, and utterly repudiated; while those claimed by Congress have been confirmed.

Of the spirit and magnitude of the canvass nothing need be said. The appeal was to the people, and the verdict was worthy of the tribunal. Upon an occasion of his own selection, with the advice and approval of his astute Secretary, soon after the members of Congress had returned to their constituents, the President quitted the executive mansion, sandwiched himself between two recognized heroes,—men whom the whole country delighted to honor,—and, with all the advantage which such company could give him, stumped the country from the Atlantic to the Mississippi, advocating everywhere his policy as against that of Congress. It was a strange sight, and perhaps the most disgraceful exhibition ever made by any President; but, as no evil is entirely unmixed, good has come of this, as from many others. Ambitious, unscrupulous, energetic, indefatigable, voluble, and plausible,—a political gladiator, ready for a "set-to" in any crowd,—he is beaten in his own chosen field, and stands to-day before the country as a convicted usurper, a political criminal, guilty of a bold and persistent attempt to possess himself of the legislative powers solemnly secured to Congress by the Constitution. No vindication could be more complete, no condemnation could be more absolute and humiliating. Unless reopened by the sword, as recklessly threatened in some circles, this question is now closed for all time.

Without attempting to settle here the metaphysical and somewhat theological question (about which so much has already been said and written), whether once in the Union means always in the Union,—agreeably to the formula, Once in grace always in grace,—it is obvious to common sense that the rebellious States stand to-day, in point of law, precisely where they stood when, exhausted, beaten, conquered, they fell powerless at the feet of Federal authority. Their State governments were overthrown, and the lives and property of the leaders of the Rebellion were forfeited. In reconstructing the institutions of these shattered and overthrown States, Congress should begin with a clean slate, and make clean work of it. Let there be no hesitation. It would be a cowardly deference to a defeated and treacherous President, if any account were made of the illegitimate, one-sided, sham governments hurried into existence for a malign purpose in the absence of Congress. These pretended governments, which were never submitted to the people, and from participation in which four millions of the loyal people were excluded by Presidential order, should now be treated according to their true character, as shams and impositions, and supplanted by true and legitimate governments, in the formation of which loyal men, black and white, shall participate.

It is not, however, within the scope of this paper to point out the precise steps to be taken, and the means to be employed. The people are less concerned about these than the grand end to be attained. They demand such a reconstruction as shall put an end to the present anarchical state of things in the late rebellious States, —where frightful murders and wholesale massacres are perpetrated in the very presence of Federal soldiers. This horrible business they require shall cease. They want a reconstruction such as will protect loyal men, black and white, in their persons and property;

such a one as will cause Northern industry, Northern capital, and Northern civilization to flow into the South, and make a man from New England as much at home in Carolina as elsewhere in the Republic. No Chinese wall can now be tolerated. The South must be opened to the light of law and liberty, and this session of Congress is relied upon to accomplish this important work.

The plain, common-sense way of doing this work, as intimated at the beginning, is simply to establish in the South one law, one government, one administration of justice, one condition to exercise of the elective franchise, for men of all races and colors alike. This great measure is sought as earnestly by loyal white men as by loyal blacks, and is needed alike by both. Let sound political prescience but take the place of an unreasoning prejudice, and this will be done.

Men denounce the negro for his prominence in this discussion; but it is no fault of his that in peace as in war, that in conquering Rebel armies as in reconstructing the rebellious States, the right of the negro is the true solution of our national troubles. The stern logic of events which goes directly to the point, disdaining all concern for the color or features of men, has determined the interests of the country as identical with and inseparable from those of the negro.

The policy that emancipated and armed the negro—now seen to have been wise and proper by the dullest—was not certainly more sternly demanded than is now the policy of enfranchisement. If with the negro was success in war, and without him failure, so in peace it will be found that the nation must fall or flourish with the negro.

Fortunately, the Constitution of the United States knows no distinction between citizens on account of color. Neither does it know any difference between a citizen of a State and a citizen of the United States. Citizenship evidently includes all the rights of citizens, whether State or national. If the Constitution knows none, it is clearly no part of the duty of a Republican Congress now to institute one. The mistake of the last session was the attempt to do this very thing by a renunciation of its power to secure political rights to any class of citizens, with the obvious purpose to allow the rebellious States to disfranchise, if they should see fit, their colored citizens. This unfortunate blunder must now be retrieved, and the emasculated citizenship given to the negro supplanted by that contemplated in the Constitution of the United States, which declares that the citizens of each State shall enjoy all the rights and immunities of citizens of the several States,—so that a legal voter in any State shall be a legal voter in all the States.

Thaddeus Stevens Demands Territorial Status and Prolonged Military Government for the South

The lifelong record of Thaddeus Stevens (1792-1868) for progressive causes, especially that of the Negro, suggests that his critics have over-emphasized his personality quirks, his inflexibility, his pathological hatred of the South, his handicaps such as lameness and a loose wig that aroused much mirth. Born in Vermont and educated at Dartmouth, pursuing a career as lawyer and politician, he shared the strong antislavery views of many New Englanders. While a member of the Pennsylvania legislature (he was then an iron manufacturer near Chambersburg), he fought secret societies as a leader of the antimasonic movement, strongly championed the free-school movement and the right of petition, defended numerous fugitive slaves without fee, and angered a mob by his obstinacy upon issues of principle. He was elected to Congress in 1848 as a Whig and Free-Soiler; there he refused to make concessions to slavery in the territories, bitterly fought the Fugitive Slave Act, and taunted Southerners as being slave-drivers.

During the Civil War, he supported Lincoln's policies, except for his seemingly too-generous Reconstruction policies and his "soft" solution of compensated emancipation. When Johnson revealed that he intended to continue the Lincoln policy of early readmission for seceded states, he took issue with him, as the speech reproduced here indicates. The real quarrel began after Johnson vetoed a series of such Radical bills as the Freedman's Bureau Bill and the Radical Reconstruction bills. In Congress Stevens led the Radicals as chairman of the powerful Ways and Means Committee. After the great Congressional victories of the Radicals in 1866, he was ready for a more extreme program in the direction of Negro suffrage, pro-longed military control of the South, and "the perpetual ascendancy of the party of the Union." As the powerful chairman of the Joint Committee on Reconstruction, Stevens pushed through the omnibus Fourteenth Amendment and then pressed for Johnson's impeachment.

From Speech on Reconstruction, December 18, 1865, *Cong. Globe,* 39 Cong., 1st Sess., Vol. 36, pp. 74-75.

. . . It is obvious from all this that the first duty of Congress is to pass a law declaring the condition of these outside or defunct States, and providing proper civil governments for them. Since the conquest they have been governed by martial law. Military rule is necessarily despotic, and ought not to exist longer than is absolutely necessary. As there are no symptoms that the people of these provinces will be prepared to participate in constitutional government for some years, I know of no arrangement so proper for them as territorial governments. There they can learn the principles of freedom and eat the fruit of foul rebellion. Under such governments, while electing members to the Territorial Legislatures, they will necessarily mingle with those to whom Congress shall extend the right of suffrage. In Territories Congress fixes the qualifications of electors; and I know of no better place nor better occasion for the conquered rebels and the conqueror to practice justice to all men, and accustom themselves to make and to obey equal laws.

As these fallen rebels cannot at their option reënter the heaven which they have disturbed, the garden of Eden which they have deserted, and flaming swords are set at the gates to secure their exclusion, it becomes important to the welfare of the nation to inquire when the doors shall be reopened for their admission.

According to my judgment they ought never to be recognized as capable of acting in the Union, or of being counted as valid States, until the Constitution shall have been so amended as to make it what its framers intended; and so as to secure perpetual ascendency to the party of the Union; and so as to render our republican Government firm and stable forever. The first of those amendments is to change the basis of representation among the States from Federal numbers to actual voters. Now all the colored freemen in the slave States, and three-fifths of the slaves, are represented, though none of them have votes. The States have nineteen representatives of colored slaves. If the slaves are now free then they can add, for the other two-fifths, thirteen more, making the slave representation thirty-two. I suppose the free blacks in those States will give at least five more, making the representation of non-voting people of color about thirty-seven. The whole number of representatives now from the slave States is seventy. Add the other two-fifths and it will be eighty-three.

If the amendment prevails, and those States withhold the right of suffrage from persons of color, it will deduct about thirty-seven, leaving them but forty-six. With the basis unchanged, the eighty-three southern members, with the Democrats that will in the best times be elected from the North, will always give them a majority in Congress and in the Electoral College. They will at the very first election take possession of the White House and the halls of Congress. I need not depict the ruin that would follow. Assumption of the rebel debt or repudiation of the Federal debt would be sure to follow. The oppression of the freedmen; the reamendment of their State constitutions, and the reëstablishment of slavery would be the inevitable result. That they would scorn and disregard their present constitutions, forced upon them in the midst of martial law, would be both natural and just. No one who has any regard for freedom of elections can look upon those governments, forced upon them in duress, with any favor. If they should grant the right of suffrage to persons of color, I think there would always be Union white men enough in the South, aided by the blacks, to divide the representation, and thus continue the Republican ascendancy. If they should refuse to thus alter their election laws it would reduce the representatives of the late slave States to about forty-five and render them powerless for evil.

It is plain that this amendment must be consummated before the defunct States are admitted to be capable of State action, or it never can be.

The proposed amendment to allow Congress to lay a duty on exports is precisely in the same situation. Its importance cannot well be overstated. It is very obvious that for many years the South will not pay much under our internal revenue laws. The only article on which we can raise any considerable amount is cotton. It will be grown largely at once. With ten cents a pound export duty it would be furnished cheaper to foreign markets than they could obtain it from any other part of the world. The late war has shown that. Two million bales exported, at five hundred pounds to the bale, would yield $100,-000,000. This seems to be the chief revenue we shall ever derive from the South. Besides, it would be a protection to that amount to our domestic manufactures. Other proposed amendments—to make all laws uniform; to prohibit the assumption of the rebel debt—are of vital importance, and the only thing that can prevent the combined forces of copperheads and secessionists from legislating against the interests of the Union whenever they may obtain an accidental majority.

But this is not all that we ought to do before these inveterate rebels are invited to participate in our legislation. We have turned, or are about to turn, loose four million slaves without a hut to shelter them or a cent in their pockets. The infernal laws of slavery have prevented them from acquiring an education, understanding the commonest laws of contract, or of managing the ordinary business of life. This Congress is bound to provide for them until they can take care of themselves. If we do not furnish them with homesteads, and hedge them around with protective laws; if we leave them to the legislation of their late masters, we had better have left them in bondage. Their condition would be worse than that of our prisoners at Andersonville. If we fail in this great duty now, when we have the power, we shall deserve and receive the execration of history and of all future ages.

Two things are of vital importance.

1. So to establish a principle that none of the rebel States shall be counted in any of the amendments of the Constitution until they are duly admitted into the family of States by the law-making power of their conqueror. For more than six months the amendment of the Constitution abolishing slavery has been ratified by the Legislatures of three-fourths of the States that acted on its passage by Congress, and which had Legislatures, or which were States capable of acting, or required to act, on the question.

I take no account of the aggregation of whitewashed rebels, who without any legal authority have assembled in the capitals of the late rebel States and simulated legislative bodies. Nor do I regard with any respect the cunning byplay into which they deluded the Secretary of State by frequent telegraphic announcements that "South Carolina had adopted the amendment;" "Alabama has adopted the amendment, being the twenty-seventh State," &c. This was intended to delude the people, and accustom Congress to hear repeated the names of these extinct States as if they were alive; when, in truth, they have now no more existence than the revolted cities of Latium, two-thirds of whose people were colonized and their property confiscated, and their right of citizenship withdrawn by conquering and avenging Rome.

2. It is equally important to the stability of this Republic that it should now be solemnly decided what power can revive, recreate, and reinstate these provinces into the family of States, and invest them with the rights of American citizens. It is time that Congress should assert its sovereignty, and assume something of the dignity of a Roman senate. It is fortunate that the President invites Congress to take this manly attitude. After stating with great frankness in his able message his theory, which, however, is found to be impracticable, and which I believe very few now consider tenable, he refers the whole matter to the judgment of Congress. If Congress should fail firmly and wisely to discharge that high duty it is not the fault of the President.

This Congress owes it to its own character to set the seal of reprobation upon a doctrine which is becoming too fashionable, and unless rebuked will be the recognized principle of our Government. Governor Perry and other provisional governors and orators proclaim that "this is the white man's Government." The whole copperhead party, pandering to the lowest prejudices of the ignorant, repeat the cuckoo cry, "This is the white man's Government." Demagogues of all parties, even some high in authority, gravely shout, "This is the white man's Government." What is implied by this? That one race of men are to have the exclusive right forever to rule this nation, and to exercise all acts of sovereignty, while all other races and nations and colors are to be their subjects, and have no voice in making the laws and choosing the rulers by whom they are to be governed. Wherein does this differ from slavery except in degree? Does not this contradict all the distinctive principles of the Declaration of Independence? When the great and good men promulgated that instrument, and pledged their lives and sacred honors to defend it, it was supposed to form an epoch in civil government. Before that time it was held that the right to rule was vested in families, dynasties, or races, not because of superior intelligence or virtue, but because of a divine right to enjoy exclusive privileges.

Our fathers repudiated the whole doctrine of the legal superiority of families or races, and proclaimed the equality of men before the law. Upon that they created a revolution and built the Republic. They were prevented by slavery from perfecting the superstructure whose foundation they had thus broadly laid. For the sake of the Union they consented to wait, but never relinquished the idea of its final completion. The time to which they looked forward with anxiety has come. It is our duty to complete their work. If this Republic is not now made to stand on their great principles, it has no honest foundation, and the Father of all men will still shake it to its center. If we have not yet been sufficiently scourged for our national sin to teach us to do justice to all God's creatures, without distinction of race or color, we must expect the still more heavy vengeance of an offended Father, still increasing his inflictions as he increased the severity of the plagues of Egypt until the tyrant consented to do justice. And when that tyrant repented of his reluctant consent, and attempted to reenslave the people, as our southern tyrants are attempting to do now, he filled the Red sea with broken chariots and drowned horses, and strewed the shores with dead carcasses.

Mr. Chairman, I trust the Republican party will not be alarmed at what I am saying. I do not profess to speak their sentiments, nor must they be held responsible for them. I speak for myself, and take the responsibility, and will settle with my intelligent constituents.

This is not a "white man's Government," in the exclusive sense in which it is used. To say so is political blasphemy, for it violates the fundamental principles of our gospel of liberty. This is man's Government; the Government of all men alike; not that all men will have equal power and sway within it. Accidental circumstances, natural and acquired endowment and ability, will vary their fortunes. But equal rights to all the privileges of the Government is innate in every immortal being, no matter what the shape or color of the tabernacle which it inhabits.

If equal privileges were granted to all, I should not expect any but white men to be elected to office for long ages to come. The prejudice engendered by slavery would not soon permit merit to be preferred to color. But it would still be beneficial to the weaker races. In a country where political divisions will always exist, their power, joined with just white men, would greatly modify, if it did not entirely prevent, the injustice of majorities. Without the right of suffrage in the late slave States. (I do not speak of the free States), I believe the slaves had far better been left in bondage. I see it stated that very distinguished advocates of the right of suffrage lately declared in this city that they do not expect to obtain it by congressional legislation, but only by administrative action, because as one gallant gentleman said, the States had not been out of the Union. Then they will never get it. The President is far sounder than they. He sees that administrative action has nothing to do with it. If it ever is to come, it must be constitution amendments or congressional action in the Territories, and in enabling acts.

How shameful that men of influence should mislead and miseducate the public mind! They proclaim, "This is the white man's Government," and the whole coil of copperheads echo the same sentiment, and upstart, jealous Republicans join the cry. Is it any wonder ignorant foreigners and illiterate natives should learn this doctrine, and be led to despise and maltreat a whole race of their fellow-men?

Sir, this doctrine of a white man's Government is as atrocious as the infamous sentiment that damned the late Chief Justice to everlasting fame; and, I fear, to everlasting fire.

President Johnson Vetoes Radical Reconstruction as an Invasion of States' Rights: Fears Amalgamation of Races and Africanization

The controversial President (1808-1875) was born in Raleigh, North Carolina, of humble parentage. He had no formal schooling and early knew poverty. When he moved to eastern Tennessee, he advanced himself by self-education, aided by his wife, and by considerable reading and debating. His tailor shop proved successful and enabled him to turn to politics—first as alderman, then as mayor, state legislator, Congressman (1843-53), Governor (elected twice), and then United States Senator from Tennessee. He appeared to be a radical Jacksonian, judging from his praises of the common man, his hatred of planters and the upper classes, his sponsorship of the Homestead Bill (which did not affect Tennessee because it had little federal land, but which appealed to Eastern labor and the frontier), and his concern for federal economy. But his racial attitudes were orthodox-Southern. He attacked abolitionism and, while accepting the Kansas–Nebraska Act, went along with the more conservative resolution of Senator Jefferson Davis, who wished the federal government not only to abstain from interfering with slavery but also to protect it. In the 1860 election, when his Democratic Party split between Douglas and Breckinridge, Johnson supported the latter and urged compromises to freeze the *status quo* of slavery. However, he not only shocked the secessionists by declaring himself for the Union, but also remained in the Senate after all of the other Southern representatives withdrew.

Lincoln appointed Johnson military governor of Tennessee, and although his eastern Tennessee homeland was overrun, the governor managed to introduce the first Reconstruction policy by state action alone based on the abolition of slavery and loyalty to the Union. The National Union Convention of 1864 that nominated Lincoln also chose Johnson as the Vice-presidential candidate, a strategic move that freed the Republicans from the stigma of sectionalism. The subsequent story has already been told (see pp. xviii-xxiv).

The veto message of March 23, 1867, is reprinted from James D. Richardson (ed.), *A Compilation of the Messages and Papers of the Presidents* (New York, 1897), VIII, 3731-33; the Annual Message of December 3, 1867, is also from Richardson, VIII, 3760-64.

. . . I do not deem it necessary further to investigate the details of this bill. No consideration could induce me to give my approval to such an election law for any purpose, and especially for the great purpose of framing the constitution of a State. If ever the American citizen should be left to the free exercise of his own judgment it is when he is engaged in the work of forming the fundamental law under which he is to live. That work is his work, and it can not properly be taken out of his hands. All this legislation proceeds upon the contrary assumption that the people of each of these States shall have no constitution except such as may be arbitrarily dictated by Congress and formed under the restraint of military rule. A plain statement of facts makes this evident.

In all these States there are existing constitutions, framed in the accustomed way by the people. Congress, however, declares that these constitutions are not "loyal and republican," and requires the people to form them anew. What, then, in the opinion of Congress, is necessary to make the constitution of a State "loyal and republican"? The original act answers the question: It is universal negro suffrage—a question which the Federal Constitution leaves exclusively to the States themselves. All this legislative machinery of martial law, military coercion, and political disfranchisement is avowedly for that purpose and none other. The existing constitutions of the ten States conform to the acknowledged standards of loyalty and republicanism. Indeed, if there are degrees in republican forms of government, their constitutions are more republican now than when these States, four of which were members of the original thirteen, first became members of the Union.

Congress does not now demand that a single provision of their constitutions be changed except such as confine suffrage to the white population. It is apparent, therefore, that these provisions do not conform to the standard of republicanism which Congress seeks to establish.

That there may be no mistake, it is only necessary that reference should be made to the original act, which declares "such constitution shall provide that the elective franchise shall be enjoyed by all such persons as have the qualifications herein stated for electors of delegates." What class of persons is here meant clearly appears in the same section; that is to say, "the male citizens of said State 21 years old and upward of whatever race, color, or previous condition, who have been resident in said State for one year previous to the day of such election."

Without these provisions no constitution which can be framed in any one of the ten States will be of any avail with Congress. This, then, is the test of what the constitution of a State of this Union must contain to make it republican. Measured by such a standard, how few of the States now composing the Union have republican constitutions! If in the exercise of the constitutional guaranty that Congress shall secure to every State a republican form of government universal suffrage for blacks as well as whites is a *sine qua non,* the work of reconstruction may as well begin in Ohio as in Virginia, in Pennsylvania as in North Carolina.

When I contemplate the millions of our fellow-citizens of the South with no alternative left but to impose upon themselves this fearful and untried experiment of complete negro enfranchisement—and white disfranchisement, it may be, almost as complete—or submit indefinitely to the rigor of martial law, without a single attribute of freemen, deprived of all the sacred guaranties of our Federal Constitution, and threatened with even worse wrongs, if any worse are possible, it seems to me their condition is the most deplorable to which any people can be reduced. It is true that they have been engaged in rebellion and that their object being a separation of the States and a dissolution of the Union there was an obligation resting upon every loyal citizen to treat them as enemies and to wage war against their cause.

Inflexibly opposed to any movement imperiling the integrity of the Government, I did not hesitate to urge the adoption of all measures necessary for the suppression of the insurrection. After a long and terrible struggle the efforts of the Government were triumphantly successful, and the people of the South, submitting to the stern arbitrament, yielded forever the issues of the contest. Hostilities terminated soon after it became my duty to assume the responsibilities of the chief executive officer of the Republic, and I at once endeavored to repress and control the passions which our civil strife had engendered, and, no longer regarding those erring millions as enemies, again acknowledged them as our friends and our countrymen. The war had accomplished its objects. The nation was saved and that seminal principle of mischief which from the birth of the Government had gradually but inevitably brought on the rebellion was totally eradicated. Then, it seemed to me, was the auspicious time to commence the work of reconciliation; then, when these people sought once more our friendship and protection, I considered it our duty generously to meet them in the spirit of charity and forgiveness and to conquer them even more effectually by the magnanimity of the nation than by the force of its arms. I yet believe that if the policy of reconciliation then inaugurated, and which contemplated an early restoration of these people to all their political rights, had received the support of Congress, every one of these ten States and all their people would at this moment be fast anchored in the Union and the great work which gave the war all its sanction and made it just and holy would have been accomplished. Then all over the vast and fruitful regions of the South peace and its blessings would have prevailed, while now millions are deprived of rights guaranteed by the Constitution to every citizen and after nearly two years of legislation find themselves placed under an absolute military despotism. . . .

. . . I repeat the expression of my willingness to join in any plan within the scope of our constitutional authority which promises to better the condition of the negroes in the South, by encouraging them in industry, enlightening their minds, improving their morals, and giving protection to all their just rights as freedmen. But the transfer of our political inheritance to them would, in my opinion, be an abandonment of a duty which we owe alike to the memory of our fathers and the rights of our children.

The plan of putting the Southern States wholly and the General Government partially into the hands of negroes is proposed at a time peculiarly unpropitious. The foundations of society have been broken up by civil war. Industry must be reorganized, justice reestablished, public credit maintained, and order brought out of confusion. To accomplish these ends would require all the wisdom and virture of the great men who formed our institutions originally. I confidently believe that their descendants will be equal to the arduous task before them, but it is worse than madness to expect that negroes will perform it for us. Certainly we ought not to ask their assistance till we despair of our own competency.

The great difference between the two races in physical, mental, and moral characteristics will prevent an amalgamation or fusion of them together in one homogeneous mass. If the inferior obtains the ascendancy over the other, it will govern with reference only to its own interests—for it will recognize no common interest—and create such a tyranny as this continent has never yet witnessed. Already the negroes are influenced by promises of confiscation and plunder. They are taught to regard as an enemy every white man who has any respect for the rights of his own race. If this continues it must become worse and worse, until all order will be subverted, all industry cease, and the fertile fields of the South grow up into a wilderness. Of all the dangers which our nation has yet encountered, none are equal to those which must result from the success of the effort now making to Africanize the half of our country.

I would not put considerations of money in competition with justice and right; but the expenses incident to "reconstruction" under the system adopted by Congress aggravate what I regard as the intrinsic wrong of the measure itself. It has cost uncounted millions already, and if persisted in will add largely to the weight of taxation, already too oppressive to be borne without just complaint, and may finally reduce the Treasury of the nation to a condition of bankruptcy. We must not delude ourselves. It will require a strong standing army and probably more than $200,000,000 per annum to maintain the supremacy of negro governments after they are established. The sum thus thrown away would, if properly used, form a sinking fund large enough to pay the whole national debt in less than fifteen years. It is vain to hope that negroes will maintain their ascendancy themselves. Without military power they are wholly incapable of holding in subjection the white people of the South.

I submit to the judgment of Congress whether the public credit may not be injuriously affected by a system of measures like this. With our debt and the vast private interests which are complicated with it, we can not be too cautious of a policy which might by possibility impair the confidence of the world in our Government. That confidence can only be retained by carefully inculcating the principles of justice and honor on the popular mind and by the most scrupulous fidelity to all our engagements of every sort. Any serious breach of the organic law, persisted in for a considerable time, can not but create fears for the stability of our institutions. Habitual violation of prescribed rules, which we bind ourselves to observe, must demoralize the people. Our only standard of civil duty being set at naught, the sheet anchor of our political morality is lost, the public conscience swings from its moorings and yields to every impulse of passion and interest. If we repudiate the Constitution, we will not be expected to care much for mere pecuniary obligations. The violation of such a pledge as we made on the 22d day of July, 1861, will assuredly diminish the market value of our other promises. Besides, if we acknowledge that the national debt was created, not to hold the States in the Union, as the taxpayers were led to suppose, but to expel them from it and hand them over to be governed by negroes, the moral duty to pay it may seem much less clear. I say it may *seem* so, for I do not admit that this or any other argument in favor of repudiation can be entertained as sound; but its influence on some classes of minds may well be apprehended. The financial honor of a great commercial nation, largely indebted and with a republican form of government administered by agents of the popular choice, is a thing of such delicate texture and the destruction of it would be followed by such unspeakable calamity that every true patriot must desire to avoid whatever might expose it to the slightest danger. . . .

Senator Charles Sumner Says that the Confederacy Committed Suicide and that Congress Alone Can Provide "Equal Rights For All" to Insure Safety and Justice

Charles Sumner (1811-1874) spent his life bitterly attacking injustice with the violence of an Old Testament prophet. He apparently learned much from his father, a Boston lawyer who combined love of learning with opposition to slavery, to segregation in the schools, and to the Massachusetts law forbidding racial intermarriage. Charles was a brilliant student at Harvard and the Harvard Law School, where he became a lecturer and a contributor to law publications. As a radical Free-Soiler, he attacked the War with Mexico and assailed the conspiracy between "the lords of the lash and the lords of the loom." In 1849, he became a counsel for a Negro group in the famous Roberts case, in which he defended the right of Negro children to attend white public schools in Boston under the principle of "equality before the law." Although he lost the case, school desegregation won out a few years later and the idea became the heart of the Fourteenth Amendment in 1868.

As a militant United States Senator from Massachusetts after 1851, Sumner fought the Fugitive Slave Act and the Kansas–Nebraska Act. His severest philippic, "The Crime Against Kansas," spared no reputations among proslavery and compromising politicians and inspired Congressman Preston Brooks of South Carolina to beat him mercilessly with a cane, forcing him out of public life for more than three years. Lincoln in 1861 made him chairman of the Committee on Foreign Relations in the Senate, a powerful post in which he prevented the seizure of Confederate envoys Mason and Slidell on a British ship from erupting into war. He also worked to promote the principle of international arbitration in the *Alabama* claims dispute. During Reconstruction, he cooperated with Thaddeus Stevens in combating the Johnson program and in securing the passage of the Fourteenth Amendment.

Sumner's motives in fighting for Johnson's impeachment are given in the second selection, "Opinion of Hon. Charles Sumner," *Proceedings in the Trial of Andrew Johnson* (Washington, D. C., 1868), 958-67. The first selection, expressing a lifelong theme of equality and an argument for thorough Radical Reconstruction, is "The Equal Rights of All," in *Charles Sumner: His Complete Works* (Boston, 1890), Senate Speech of February 5 and 6, 1866, pp. 124-35.

MR. PRESIDENT,—In opening this great question, I begin by expressing a heartfelt aspiration that the day may soon come, when the States lately in rebellion may be received again into the copartnership of political power and the full fellowship of the Union. But I see too well that it is vain to expect this day, so much longed for, until we have obtained that security for the future which is found only in the Equal Rights of All, at the ballot-box as in the court-room. This is the Great Guaranty without which all other guaranties will fail. This is the sole solution of present troubles and anxieties. This is the only sufficient assurance of peace and reconciliation. To the establishment of this Great Guaranty, as a measure of safety and of justice, I now ask your best attention.

The powers of Congress over this subject are ample as they are beneficent. From four specific fountains they flow, each sufficient, all four swelling into an irresistible current, and tending to one conclusion: first, the necessity of the case, by which, according to analogy of the Territories, disloyal States, having no local government, lapse under the authority of Congress; secondly, the Rights of War, which do not expire or lose their grasp, except with the establishment of all needful guaranties; thirdly, the constitutional injunction to guaranty a republican form of government; and, fourthly, the Constitutional Amendment, by which Congress, in words of peculiar energy, is empowered to "enforce" the abolition of Slavery by "appropriate legislation." According to the proverb of catholic Europe, all roads lead to Rome; and so do all these powers lead to the jurisdiction of Congress over this whole subject. No matter which road you take, you arrive at the same point. The first two have already been discussed exhaustively.[1] The two latter have been considered less, and it is on these that I shall speak especially to-day. I propose, with the permission of the Senate, to show the necessity and duty of exercising the jurisdiction of Congress so as to secure that essential condition of a republican government, the Equal Rights of All. And I put aside, at the outset, the metaphysical question, worthy of schoolmen in the Dark Ages, whether certain States are *in* the Union or *out of* the Union. That is a question of form, and not of substance,—of words only, and not of facts; for the substance is clear, and the facts are unanswerable. All are agreed, according to the authority of President Lincoln, in his latest utterance before his lamented death, that these States have ceased to be in "practical relation with the Union";[1] and this is enough to sustain the jurisdiction of Congress, even without the plain words of the Constitution in two separate texts.

The time has passed for phrases, which have been the chief resource in opposition to a just reconstruction. It is not enough to say "a State cannot secede," "a State cannot get out of the Union," "Louisiana is a State in the Union." These are mere words, having no positive meaning, and improper for this debate. So far as they have meaning, they confound law and fact. It is very obvious that a State may, in point of *law*, be still in the list of States, and yet, in point of *fact*, its relations to the Union may have ceased through violence, foreign or domestic. In point of law, no man can commit suicide; but in point of fact, men do. The absurdity of denying that a man has committed suicide, because it is unlawful, is equalled by the kindred absurdity of saying that a State cannot do a certain thing, because it is unlawful. Unhappily, in this world, the fact is not always in conformity with the law.

Therefore I put aside all fine-spun theories running into the metaphysics of Constitutional Law. All such subtleties are absolutely futile. They must end in nothing. I found myself on existing facts, which are undeniable. Of these I select two.

Whatever may have been the effect of the acts of Secession in point of law, it is plain that *de facto* the Rebel States have ceased to take any part in the National Government. All loyal government in those States has been *de facto* subverted. They are all without magistrates or officers bound by oath to support the National Constitution according to its requirement, so that *de facto* there are no magistrates or

[1] Speech in Washington, April 11, 1865: McPherson's *Political History of the United States during the Rebellion*, p. 609.

officers of the Union in these States; nor are there any *de facto* Senators or Representatives in Congress from those States. Such are unquestionable facts, all of which concentre in the great unquestionable *fact*, that for the time being there are no State Governments in these States which the National Government can recognize as such.

There is another fact equally unquestionable. It is that the Rebel States have been *de facto* in war against the National Government. Armies have been mustered, battles have been fought, and the whole country has been convulsed by this war. An immense national debt, mourning families, widows and orphans, attest this terrible fact.

Everything has a natural consequence, and the consequence of this condition of things is that necessity which I have announced. These States cannot subsist without legal governments in just correlation with the other States and with the Nation.

Necessity and duty commingle. If what is necessary is not always according to duty, surely duty is always a necessity. On the present occasion they unite in one voice for the Great Guaranty. It is at once necessity and duty. Glancing at the promises of the Fathers, I shall exhibit,—

First, the overruling necessity of the times;

And, *secondly,* the positive mandate of the Constitution, compelling us to guaranty "a republican form of government," and thus to determine what is meant by this requirement; all of which has been fortified by continuing Rights of War, and by the Constitutional Amendment authorizing Congress to enforce the abolition of Slavery.

In the life of a nation, as in that of an individual, there are moments when outstanding promises must be performed under peril of ruin and dishonor. Such is the present moment in the life of the Republic. Sacred promises, beginning with our history, are yet unperformed, although the hour has sounded when continued failure on our part will open the door to a long train of woes. And there are yet other promises, recently made, for the national defence against a wicked rebellion, which, like those of earlier date, are also unperformed. . . .

As an act of justice, Enfranchisement has a necessity of its own. No individual and no people can afford to be unjust. Such an offence carries a curse, which, sooner or later, must drag its perpetrator to ruin. But here necessity from considerations of justice is completed and intensified by positive requirements of the national safety, plainly involved in the performance of these promises.

Look at the unhappy freedman blasted by the ban of exclusion. He has always been loyal, and now it is he, and not the Rebel master, who pays the penalty. From the nature of the case, he must be discontented, restless, anxious, smarting with sense of wrong and consciousness of rights denied. He does not work as if taken by the hand and made to feel the grasp of friendship. He is idle, thriftless, unproductive. Industry suffers. Cotton does not grow. Commerce does not thrive. Credit fails; nay, it dies before it is born. On the other hand, his Rebel master, with hands still red with the blood of fellow-countrymen, is encouraged in that assumption of superiority which is part of the Barbarism of Slavery; he dominates as in times past; he is exacting as of old; he is harsh, cruel, and vindictive; he makes the unprotected and trembling freedman suffer for the losses and disappointments of the Rebellion; he continues to insult and prostitute the wife and children, who, ceasing to be chattels, have not ceased to be dependants; he follows the freedman to by-ways and obscure places, where once again he plays master and asserts his ancient title as lord of the lash. Scenes of savage brutality and blood ensue. All this, which reason foretells, the short experience of a few months already confirms. And all this you sanction, when you leave the freedman despoiled of his rights.

But the freedman, though forbearing and slow to anger, will not always submit to outrage. He will resist. Resistance will be organized. And here begins the terrible war of races foreseen by Jefferson, where God, in all His attributes, has none which can take part with the oppressor. The tragedy of San Domingo will be renewed on a wider theatre, with bloodier incidents. Be warned, I entreat you, by this historic example. It was the denial of rights to colored people, upon successive promises, which caused that fearful insurrection. After various vicissitudes, during which the rights of citizenship were conferred on free people of color and then resumed, the slaves at last rose; and here the soul sickens at the recital. Then came Toussaint l'Ouverture, a black of unmixed blood, who placed himself at the head of his race, showing the genius of war, and the genius of statesmanship also. Under his magnanimous rule the beautiful island began to smile once more: agriculture revived; commerce took a new start; the whites were protected in person and property; and a Constitution was adopted acknowledging the authority of France, but making no distinction of race or color. In an evil hour this policy was reversed by a decree of Napoleon Bonaparte. War revived, and the French army was compelled to succumb. The connection of San Domingo with France was broken, and this island became a black republic. All this dreary catalogue of murder, battle, sorrow, and woe began in denial of justice to the colored race. And only recently we have listened to a similar tragedy from Jamaica, thus swelling the terrible testimony. Like causes produce like effects; therefore all this will be ours, if we madly persist in the same denial. The freedmen among us are not unlike the freedmen of San Domingo or Jamaica; they have the same "organs, dimensions, senses, affections, passions," and, above all, the same sense of wrong, and the same revenge.

To avoid insurrection and servile war, big with measureless calamity, and even to obtain the security essential to industry, agriculture, commerce, and the national credit, you must perform the promises of the Republic, originally made by our fathers, and recently renewed by ourselves. But duty done will not only save you from calamity and give you security; it will also prepare the way for the great triumphs of the future, when through assured peace there shall be tranquillity, prosperity, and reconciliation, all of which it is vain to expect without justice.

The freedman must be protected. To this you are solemnly pledged by the Proclamation of President Lincoln, which, after declaring him "free," promises to *maintain* this freedom, not for any limited period, but for all time. But this cannot be, so long as you deny him the shield of *impartial laws*. Let him be heard in court, and let him vote. Let these rights be guarded sacredly. Beyond even the shield of *impartial laws*, he will then have the protection which comes from the consciousness of manhood. Clad in the full panoply of citizenship, he will feel at last that he is a man. . . .

Sometimes it is said that we must not require justice to the freedman, because justice is still denied to the colored citizen in Connecticut and New York. Idle words, of inconceivable utterance! as if the two cases bore any imaginable resemblance! There are rivers in the North and rivers in the South, but who says that on this account the two regions are alike? The denial of justice to the colored citizens in Connecticut and New York is wrong and mean; but it is on so small a scale that it is not perilous to the Republic, nor is it vital to the protection of the colored citizen and the protection of the national creditor. You are moved to Enfranchisement in Connecticut and New York for justice to a few individuals only; but you are moved to it in the Rebel States for justice to multitudes, also to save the Republic, imperilled by injustice on a gigantic scale, and to supply needful protection to the national freedman and the national creditor. From failure on our part, there is in one case little more than shame, while in the other there is positive danger, involving the fate of the national freedman and the national creditor, to whom we are bound by the most solemn ties. To a good man, injustice, even on a small scale, is not tolerable; he feels the necessity of resisting it; but where the victims are counted by millions, this necessity becomes a transcendent duty, quickened and invigorated by all the instincts of self-preservation. Therefore, I say again, for the national safety, redeem these promises of the Fathers, and your own. . . .

I voted against the rule of the Senate allowing opinions to be filed in this proceeding, and regretted its adoption. With some hesitation I now take advantage of the opportunity, if not the invitation, which it affords. Voting "guilty" on all the articles, I feel that there is no need of explanation or apology. Such a vote is its own best defender. But I follow the example of others.

BATTLE WITH SLAVERY

This is one of the last great battles with slavery. Driven from these legislative Chambers; driven from the field of war, this monstrous power has found a refuge in the Executive Mansion, where, in utter disregard of the Constitution and laws, it seeks to exercise its ancient far-reaching sway. All this is very plain. Nobody can question it. Andrew Johnson is the impersonation of the tyrannical Slave Power. In him it lives again. He is the lineal successor of John C. Calhoun and Jefferson Davis. And he gathers about him the same supporters. Original partisans of slavery North and South; habitual compromisers of great principles; maligners of the Declaration of Independence; politicians without heart; lawyers, for whom a technicality is everything, and a promiscuous company who at every stage of the battle have set their faces against Equal Rights;—these are his allies. It is the old troop of slavery, with a few recruits, ready as of old for violence—cunning in device and heartless in quibble. With the President at their head, they are now entrenched in the Executive Mansion.

Not to dislodge them is to leave this country a prey to one of the most hateful tyrannies of history. Especially is it to surrender the Unionists of the rebel States to violence and bloodshed. Not a month, not a week, not a day should be lost. *The safety of the Republic requires action at once.* The lives of innocent men must be rescued from sacrifice.

I would not in this judgment depart from that moderation which belongs to the occasion; but God forbid that, when called to deal with so great an offender, I should affect a coldness which I cannot feel. Slavery has been our worst enemy, murdering our children, filling our homes with mourning, and darkening the land with tragedy; and now it rears its crest anew with Andrew Johnson as its representative. Through him it assumes once more to rule the Republic and to impose its cruel law. The enormity of his conduct is aggravated by his bare-faced treachery. He once declared himself the Moses of the colored race. Behold him now the Pharaoh. With such treachery in such a cause there can be no parley. Every sentiment, every conviction, every vow against slavery must now be directed against him. Pharaoh is at the bar of the Senate for judgment.

The formal accusation is founded on certain recent transgressions, enumerated in articles of impeachment, but it is wrong to suppose that this is the whole case. It is very wrong to try this impeachment merely on these articles. It is unpardonable to higgle over words and phrases when for more than two years the tyrannical pretensions of this offender, now in evidence before the Senate, as I shall show, have been manifest in their terrible, heart-rending consequences. . . .

Meanwhile the President proceeded in his transgressions. There is nothing of usurpation which he has not attempted. Beginning with an assumption of all power in the rebel States, he has shrunk from nothing in the maintenance of this unparalleled assumption. This is a plain statement of fact. Timid at first he grew bolder and bolder. He saw too well that his attempt to substitute himself for Congress in the work of reconstruction was sheer usurpation, and, therefore, by his Secretary of State, did not hesitate to announce that "it must be distinctly understood that the restoration will be *subject to the decision of Congress.*" On two separate occasions, in July and September, 1865, he confessed the power of Congress over the subject; but when Congress came together in December, this confesser of congressional power found that he alone had this great prerogative. According to his new-fangled theory, Congress had nothing to do but admit the States with the governments which had been instituted through his will alone. It is difficult to measure the vastness of this usurpation, involving as it did a general nullification. Strafford was not bolder, when, speaking for Charles I, he boasted that "the little finger of prerogative was heavier than the loins of the law;" but these words helped the proud minister to the scaffold. No monarch, no despot, no Sultan, could claim more than an American President; for he claimed all. By his edict alone governments were organized, taxes were levied, and even the franchises of the citizen were determined.

Had this assumption of power been incidental, for the exigency of the moment, as under the pressure of war, and especially to serve the cause of Human Rights to which before his elevation the President had professed such loud-mouthed devotion, it might have been pardoned. It would have passed into the chapter of unauthorized acts which a patriot people had condoned. But it was the opposite in every particular. Beginning and continuing in usurpation, it was hateful beyond pardon, because it sacrificed the rights of Unionists, white and black, and was in the interest of the rebellion and of those very rebels who had been in arms against their country.

More than one person was appointed Provisional Governor, who could not take the oath of office required by act of Congress. Other persons in the same predicament were appointed in the revenue service. The effect of these appointments was disastrous. They were in the nature of notice to rebels everywhere, that participation in the rebellion was no bar to office. If one of their number could be appointed Governor, if another could be appointed to a confidential position in the Treasury Department, then there was nobody on the long list of blood who might not look for preferment. And thus all offices, from Governor to constable, were handed over to a disloyal scramble. Rebels crawled forth from their retreats. Men who had hardly ventured to expect their lives were now candidates for office, and the Rebellion became strong again. The change was felt in all the gradations of government, whether in States, counties, towns, or villages. Rebels found themselves in places of trust, while the true-hearted Unionists, who had watched for the coming of our flag and ought to have enjoyed its protecting power, were driven into hiding-places. All this was under the auspices of Andrew Johnson. It was he who animated the wicked crew. He was at the head of the work. Loyalty everywhere was persecuted. White and black, whose only offense was that they had been true to their country, were insulted, abused, murdered. There was no safety for the loyal man except within the flash of our bayonets. The story is as authentic as hideous. More than two thousand murders have been reported in Texas alone since the surrender of Kirby Smith. In other States there was a similar carnival. Property, person, life, were all in jeopardy. Acts were done "to make a holiday in Hell." At New Orleans there was a fearful massacre, which, considering the age and the place, was worse than that of St. Bartholomew, which darkens a century of France, or that of Glencoe, which has printed an ineffaceable stain upon one of the greatest reigns of English history. All this is directly traced to Andrew Johnson. The words of bitterness uttered at another time are justified, while Fire, Famine, and Slaughter shriek forth—

> "He let me loose, and cried Halloo!
> To him alone the praise is due."

ACCUMULATION OF IMPEACHABLE OFFENSES

This is nothing but the outline, derived from historic sources *which the Senate on this occasion is bound to recognize*. Other acts fall within the picture. The officers he had appointed in defiance of law were paid also in the same defiance. Millions of property were turned over without consideration to railroad companies, whose special recommendation was their participation in the rebellion. The Freedman's Bureau, that sacred charity of the Republic, was despoiled of its possessions for the sake of rebels, to whom their forfeited estates were given back after they had been vested by law in the United States. The proceeds of captured and abandoned property, lodged under the law in the national Treasury, were ravished from their place of deposit and sacrificed. Rebels were allowed to fill the ante-chambers of the

Executive Mansion and to enter into his counsels. The pardoning power was prostituted, and pardons were issued in lots to suit rebels, thus grossly abusing that trust whose discreet exercise is so essential to the administration of justice. The powers of the Senate over appointments were trifled with and disregarded, by reappointing persons who had been already rejected, and by refusing to communicate the names of others appointed by him during the recess. The veto power, conferred by the Constitution as a remedy for ill-considered legislation, was turned by him into a weapon of offense against Congress and into an instrument to beat down the just opposition which his usurpation had aroused. The power of removal, which patriot Presidents had exercised so sparingly, was seized as an engine of tryanny and openly employed to maintain his wicked purposes by the sacrifice of good citizens, who would not consent to be his tools. Incompetent and dishonest creatures, whose only recommendation was that they echoed his voice, were appointed to office, especially in the collection of the Internal Revenue, through whom a new organization, known as the "Whisky Ring," has been able to prevail over the Government, and to rob the Treasury of millions, at the cost of tax-paying citizens, whose burdens are thus increased. Laws enacted by Congress for the benefit of the colored race, including that great statute for the establishment of the Freedman's Bureau, and that other great statute for the establishment of civil rights, were first attacked by his veto, and when finally passed by the requisite majority over his veto were treated by him as little better than dead letters, which he boldly attempted to prevent the adoption of a constitutional amendment by which the right of citizens and the national debt were placed under the guarantee of irrepealable law. During these successive assumptions, usurpations, and tyrannies, utterly without precedent in our history, this deeply guilty man ventured upon public speeches, each an offense to good morals, where, lost to all shame, he appealed in coarse words to the coarse passions of the coarsest people—scattering firebrands of sedition—inflaming anew the rebel spirit—insulting good citizens, and, with regard to office-holders, announcing in his own characteristic phrase that he would "kick them out"—the whole succession of speeches being from their brutalities and indecencies in the nature of a "criminal exposure of his person," indictable at common law, for which no judgment can be too severe; but even this revolting transgression is aggravated when it is considered that through these utterances the cause of justice was imperiled and the accursed demon of civil feud was lashed again into vengeful fury. All these things from beginning to end are plain facts, already recorded in history and known to all. And it is further recorded in history, and known to all, that, through these enormities, any one of which is enough for condemnation, while all together present an aggregation of crime, untold calamities have been brought upon our country; disturbing business and finance; diminishing the national revenues; postponing specie payments; dishonoring the Declaration of Independence in its grandest truths; arresting the restoration of the rebel States; reviving the dying rebellion; and instead of that peace and reconciliation so much longed for, sowing strife and wrong, whose natural fruit is violence and blood.

OPEN DEFIANCE OF CONGRESS

For all of these or any one of them Andrew Johnson should have been impeached and expelled from office. The case required a statement only; not an argument. Unhappily this was not down. As a petty substitute for the judgment which should have been pronounced and as a bridle on presidential tyranny in "kicking out of office," Congress enacted a law known as the Tenure-of-Office Act, passed March 2, 1867, over his veto by the vote of two thirds of both Houses. And, in order to prepare the way for impeachment, by removing certain scruples of technicality, its violation was expressly declared to be a high misdemeanor. The President began at once to chafe under its restraint.

Recognizing the act and following its terms he first suspended Mr. Stanton from office, and then, on his restoration by the Senate, made an attempt to win General Grant into a surrender of the Department, as so to oust Mr. Stanton and to render the restoration by the Senate ineffectual. Meanwhile Sheridan in Louisiana, Pope in Alabama, and Sickles in South Carolina, who, as military commanders, were carrying into the pacification of these States all the energies which had been so brilliantly displayed in the war, were pursued by the same vindictive spirit. They were removed by the President, and rebellion throughout that whole region clapped its hands. This was done in the exercise of his powers as Commander-in-Chief. At last, in his unappeased rage, he openly violated the Civil-Tenure Act, so as to bring himself under its judgment, by the defiant attempt to remove Mr. Stanton from the War Department without the consent of the Senate and the appointment of Lorenzo Thomas, Adjutant General of the United States, as Secretary of War *ad interim*.

IMPEACHMENT AT LAST

The Grand Inquest of the nation, which had slept on so many enormities, was awakened by this open defiance. The gauntlet was flung into its very Chamber, and there it lay on the floor. The President, who had already claimed everything for the Executive with impunity, now rushed into conflict with Congress on the very ground selected in advance by the latter. The field was narrow, but sufficient. There was but one thing for the House of Representatives to do. Andrew Johnson must be impeached, or the Tenure-of-Office Act would become a dead letter, while his tyranny would receive a letter of license, and impeachment as a remedy for wrong-doing would be blotted from the Constitution.

Accordingly it was resolved that the offender, whose crimes had so long escaped judgment, should be impeached. Once entered upon this work, the House of Representatives, after setting forth the removal of Mr. Stanton and the appointment of General Thomas in violation of the law and Constitution, proceeded further to charge him in different forms with conspiracy wrongfully to get possession of the War Department; also with an attempt to corrupt General Emory and induce him to violate an act of Congress; also with scandalous speeches, such as no President could be justified in making; concluding with a general article setting forth attempts on his part to prevent the execution of certain acts of Congress.

Such is a simple narrative, which brings us to the Articles of Impeachment. Nothing that I have said thus far is superfluous; for it shows the origin of this proceeding, and illustrates its moving cause. The articles themselves are narrow if not technical. But they are filled and broadened by the transgressions of the past, all of which enter into the present offenses. The whole is an unbroken series with a common life. As well separate the Siamese twins as separate the offenses now charged from that succession of antecedent crimes with which they are linked, any one of which is enough for judgment. The present springs from the past and can be truly seen only in its light, which in this case is nothing less than "darkness visible."

PART FOUR

GRANT'S MILITARY INTERVENTIONS IN THE SOUTH

President Ulysses S. Grant Assails Southern Terrorism but Regrets Necessity of Federal Military Intervention

Grant's father, a descendant of Puritans, came from an undistinguished but hard-working family. Hiram Ulysses Grant (1822-1885) toiled as a child in his father's tannery in a small Ohio town (he was born in Point Pleasant). He entered the United States Military Academy, and earned above-average grades. He was especially interested in the cavalry. Although unsympathetic to the War with Mexico, he distinguished himself in most of Taylor's battles. He served eleven years in the Army, married and raised a family, moved to St. Louis and then worked briefly as a clerk in a Galena, Illinois, leather shop owned by two of his brothers. He was never active in politics, usually voted Democrat when he voted at all, and never identified himself with the antislavery movement. However, his tremendous record in the Civil War made him a national hero; he was put in charge of the Army during the crucial years of Reconstruction.

As one of President Johnson's chief emissaries to the South following the war, Grant returned with a most reassuring report that the "mass of thinking people in the South" accepted the results of the war. However, he later moved closer to the Radicals and refused to aid the President politically in the quarrel with Congress. When Johnson tried to eliminate Secretary of War Stanton, a supporter of the Radicals, and turned over his duties to Grant, the general decided to return the office to Stanton. Angry, Johnson implied publicly that Grant had violated their understanding, a charge the general never forgave.

In 1868 Grant was elected President only with the aid of the Negro vote, a situation which led the Radicals to insist on the Fifteenth Amendment. While he pleased the country by urging "Let Us Have Peace," Grant faced the terrorist upsurge of the Klan and the growing disillusionment of Northern antislavery men concerning the results of Reconstruction. Even Horace Greeley, always in the vanguard of the old antislavery forces, agreed to face Grant in the election of 1872 as a compromise candidate of the Liberal Republicans and the Democrats who opposed further federal military

The first selection, "Annual Message of Ulysses S. Grant, December 7, 1874," is from James Richardson (ed.), *Compilation of the Messages and Papers of the Presidents*, pp. 4250-53. The President states his role in the Louisiana and Arkansas interventions, but points out that the total of all federal troops stationed in the garrisons of all the forts from the Delaware to the Gulf amounted to only 4082. While he deplores the need for intervention, he urges the continued support of the Negro as a citizen and as a voter. In the second selection, Andrew Johnson's last and major speech as a newly elected Senator from Tennessee, there is a direct attack on Grant's policy of military intervention. As in the past, Johnson argues from the standpoint of States' Rights and the fears of a military despotism. From the *Congressional Record*, March 22, 1875.

intervention in the South. Grant faithfully but unenthusiastically used federal power to destroy the Klan and to enforce the Fourteenth Amendment, and he called out troops against dissident groups in Louisiana and Arkansas. Meanwhile, the conservative counter-revolution, encouraged by Northern acquiescence, moved rapidly against the Radical state governments and "redeemed" a crystallizing Solid South by 1876. At the same time the federal government was suffering in prestige from the notorious scandals of the Grant regime.

. . . On the 14th of September last the governor of Louisiana called upon me, as provided by the Constitution and laws of the United States, to aid in suppressing domestic violence in that State. This call was made in view of a proclamation issued on that day by D. B. Penn, claiming that he was elected lieutenant-governor in 1872, and calling upon the militia of the State to arm, assemble, and drive from power the usurpers, as he designated the officers of the State government. On the next day I issued my proclamation commanding the insurgents to disperse within five days from the date thereof, and subsequently learned that on that day they had taken forcible possession of the statehouse. Steps were taken by me to support the existing and recognized State government, but before the expiration of the five days the insurrectionary movement was practically abandoned, and the officers of the State government, with some minor exceptions, resumed their powers and duties. Considering that the present State administration of Louisiana has been the only government in that State for nearly two years; that it has been tacitly acknowledged and acquiesced in as such by Congress, and more than once expressly recognized by me, I regarded it as my clear duty, when legally called upon for that purpose, to prevent its overthrow by an armed mob under pretense of fraud and irregularity in the election of 1872. I have heretofore called the attention of Congress to this subject, stating that on account of the frauds and forgeries committed at said election, and because it appears that the returns thereof were never legally canvassed, it was impossible to tell thereby who were chosen; but from the best sources of information at my command I have always believed that the present State officers received a majority of the legal votes actually cast at that election. I repeat what I said in my special message of February 23, 1873, that in the event of no action by Congress I must continue to recognize the government heretofore recognized by me.

I regret to say that with preparations for the late election decided indications appeared in some localities in the Southern States of a determination, by acts of violence and intimidation, to deprive citizens of the freedom of the ballot because of their political opinions. Bands of men, masked and armed, made their appearance; White Leagues and other societies were formed; large quantities of arms and ammunition were imported and distributed to these organizations; military drills, with menacing demonstrations, were held, and with all these murders enough were committed to spread terror among those whose political action was to be suppressed, if possible, by these intolerant and criminal proceedings. In some places colored laborers were compelled to vote according to the wishes of their employers, under threats of discharge if they acted otherwise; and there are too many instances in which, when these threats were disregarded, they were remorselessly executed by those who made them. I understand that the fifteenth amendment to the Constitution was made to prevent this and a like state of things, and the act of May 31, 1870, with amendments, was passed to enforce its provisions, the object of both being to guarantee to all citizens the right to vote and to protect them in the free enjoyment of that right. Enjoined by the Constitution "to take care that the laws be faithfully executed," and convinced by undoubted evidence that violations of said act had been committed and that a widespread and flagrant disregard of it was contemplated, the proper officers were instructed to prosecute the offenders, and troops were stationed at convenient points to aid these officers, if necessary, in the performance of their official duties. Complaints are made of this interference by Federal authority; but if said amendment and act do not provide for such interference under the circumstances as above stated, then they are without meaning, force, or effect, and the whole scheme of colored enfranchisement is worse than mockery and little better than a crime. Possibly Congress may find it due to truth and justice to ascertain, by means of a committee, whether the alleged wrongs to colored citizens for political purposes are real or the reports thereof were manufactured for the occasion.

The whole number of troops in the States of Louisiana, Alabama, Georgia, Florida, South Carolina, North Carolina, Kentucky, Tennessee, Arkansas, Mississippi, Maryland, and Virginia at the time of the election was 4,082. This embraces the garrisons of all the forts from the Delaware to the Gulf of Mexico.

Another trouble has arisen in Arkansas. Article 13 of the constitution of that State (which was adopted in 1868, and upon the approval of which by Congress the State was restored to representation as one of the States of the Union) provides in effect that before any amendments proposed to this constitution shall become a part thereof they shall be passed by two successive assemblies and then submitted to and ratified by a majority of the electors of the State voting thereon. On the 11th of May, 1874, the governor convened an extra session of the general assembly of the State, which on the 18th of the same month passed an act providing for a convention to frame a new constitution. Pursuant to this act, and at an election held on the 30th of June, 1874, the convention was approved, and delegates were chosen thereto, who assembled on the 14th of last July and framed a new constitution, the schedule of which provided for the election of an entire new set of State officers in a manner contrary to the then existing election laws of the State. On the 13th of October, 1874, this constitution, as therein provided, was submitted to the people for their approval or rejection, and according to the election returns was approved by a large majority of those qualified to vote thereon; and at the same election persons were chosen to fill all the State, county, and township offices. The governor elected in 1872 for the term of four years turned over his office to the governor chosen under the new constitution, whereupon the lieutenant-governor, also elected in 1872 for a term of four years, claiming to act as governor, and alleging that said proceedings by which the new constitution was made and a new set of officers elected were unconstitutional, illegal, and void, called upon me, as provided in section 4, Article IV, of the Constitution, to protect the State against domestic violence. As Congress is now investigating the political affairs of Arkansas, I have declined to interfere.

The whole subject of Executive interference with the affairs of a State is repugnant to public opinion, to the feelings of those who, from their official capacity, must be used in such interposition, and to him or those who must direct. Unless most clearly on the side of law, such interference becomes a crime; with the law to support it, it is condemned without a hearing. I desire, therefore, that all necessity for Executive direction in local affairs may become unnecessary and obsolete. I invite the attention, not of Congress, but of the people of the United States, to the causes and effects of these unhappy questions. Is there not a disposition on one side to magnify wrongs and outrages, and on the other side to belittle them or justify them? If public opinion could be directed to a correct survey of what is and to rebuking wrong and aiding the proper authorities in punishing it, a better state of feeling would be inculcated, and the sooner we would have that peace which would leave the States free indeed to regulate their own domestic affairs. I believe on the part of our citizens of the Southern States—the better part of them—there is a disposition to be law abiding, and to do no violence either to individuals or to the laws existing. But do they do right in ignoring the existence of violence and bloodshed in resistance to constituted authority? I sympathize with their prostrate condition, and would do all in my power to relieve them, acknowledging that in some instances they have had most trying governments to live under, and very oppressive ones in the way of taxation for nominal improvements, not giving benefits equal to the hardships imposed. But can they proclaim themselves entirely irresponsible for this condition? They can not. Violence has been rampant in some localities, and has either been justified or denied by those who could have prevented it. The theory is even raised that there is to be no further interference on the part of the General Government to protect citizens within a State where the State authorities fail to give protection. This is a great mistake. While I remain Executive all the laws of Congress and the provisions of the Constitution, including the recent amendments added thereto, will be enforced with rigor, but with regret that they should have added one jot or tittle to Executive duties or powers. Let there be fairness in the discussion of Southern questions, the advocates of both or all political parties giving honest, truthful reports of occurrences, condemning the wrong and upholding the right, and soon all will be well. Under existing conditions the negro votes the Republican ticket because he knows his friends are of that party. Many a good citizen votes the opposite, not because he agrees with the great principles of state which separate parties, but because, generally, he is opposed to negro rule. This is a most delusive cry. Treat the negro as a citizen and a voter, as he is and must remain, and soon parties will be divided, not on the color line, but on principle. Then we shall have no complaint of sectional interference. . . .

[Andrew Johnson]: With your force bill, with the authority to take away the State government of Arkansas, with the government of Louisiana usurped, with a military empire laid off, it seems as if a pretty good part of the Union has been usurped and put under the control of a dictator, and that the States North and West had better begin to look into this. It suits the purpose now to take charge of certain Southern States for the approaching presidential election. "When we get them firmly in our grip, when we have once fixed upon their necks the mailed heel of power," do you think the usurper will stop his hand? No; he will go on conquering, he will go on extending his military power until he has accomplished his purpose, and then perchance the time may come when somebody in this Hall may introduce a resolution:

Whereas great disturbance and dissatisfaction exist; for the purpose of preserving peace and harmony: Therefore,
Be it resolved, That A or B is hereby declared President—

I do not care whether you call him President or monarch or king—

for the next presidential term or "the next eight years."

What would you do? Where is the Army? Where is the Navy? Who is commander-in-chief? Who has a portion of the confederacy under his heel, the mailed heel of power, with a powerful party in the other States? What would you do? Do not all know the impotency, the weakness of an unarmed people when brought in contact with an army? The people would be powerless. Here in my place, not in a personal sense but a public one, as one of the Senators of the United States, I to-day warn this people against the approaching danger. I tell my countrymen that empire is ahead. Instead of having a free and republican government now, we have the kind of government that I

will call their attention to. I hold in my hand a volume that treats
upon the various kinds of government, defines them, and gives a
proper definition. After laying down the three principal forms of government monarchy, aristocracy, and democracy, then among the various enumerations the writer says that governments out of these three
can be divided to infinity into mixed governments of various kinds,
and one form is:

Stratocracy is a military government. This word is derived from
two Greek words which signify "army" and "power."

We have got now "army" and "power." We have got a stratocracy;
we have not got a democracy, and we have not got a republican form
of government. How far off is empire? How far off is military despotism? I warn the people of my native country and of my native State of
the danger ahead. On a former occasion, when there was great difference of opinion among us, I warned my countrymen against the dangers that were coming. I warned them against bringing on a strife and
a contest that would result in the shedding of blood and the sacrifice
of property. I warned them against that struggle which set man against
man and put his hand against the throat of a brother. Yes, the land
that gave brothers birth was drenched with the blood of brothers. I
warned my countrymen against the catastrophe that has passed and
gone. The great misfortune of my life, the deep feeling of my heart is
that it turned out to be true. I wish I had proved a false prophet. Now
today in my place I warn the people of the United States against encroachments upon, against violations of, and against the total disregard of the Constitution of the United States. Do not let us talk about
party; let us talk a little about country, for party on the one side or
the other has run this Government well-nigh to destruction. Parties
have been running the Government long enough. Let the people now
lay hold of parties and run them. Let us save the country. What is the
great cry now? It is "save the party," and so that the party is saved
all is well, the country may go. Sir, let us try to save the country and
save it in the original form of its Government as handed down to us by

the founders of the Republic. I warn my country to-day against these encroachments that are being made on the Constitution of their fathers. If there is not a return made to those great principles, those great truths which are recognized in the Constitution, I tell you this Government is overthrown and its character changed.

Let us forget, then, that we have been divided into parties; let us teach the people not opposition to the Government, as has been the case sometimes. Great clamor was once made against the Government, and it was said the Government is this, or that, or the other. O, let us make the proper distinction; the Government is good enough; the organic law is all right; speaking in general terms, and administered according to its designs, it would produce happiness and prosperity to the people and result in making us the greatest Government in the world. We should make the distinction between the Government and the administrators of the Government. Let us bring the hearts of the people up to love the Government, while they oppose a cruel, a corrupt, a perfidious, a treacherous Administration that tries to overturn and overthrow the Government, and have a common effort made to sustain the Government and eject from power its corrupt and usurping rulers.

I know that I have almost always acted with one party, and I have acted on certain principles laid down for my guide, and I expect to pursue and follow them, carry me where they may, for in the pursuit of a correct principle we can never reach a wrong conclusion. The Constitution is my guide, and I intend to follow it. When it is encroached upon according to my judgment, with all the ability that I may have I will resist the encroachment and call the attention of the country to it as well as I can.

So much then for the Louisiana portion of this question and the Arkansas portion. Now the government of Arkansas is going on, but Congress was called upon to interfere with it. Then if we could have the force bill passed all would be lovely! But there seems to have been some little doubt about it. Sheridan says the people are all banditti, and if he had a military commission the President need not disturb himself any further, for he could manage all the rest! We see the power that is asked for; we see the desire to exercise unauthorized powers. We see in every movement, in every phase, a desire to get from under the control of the people, to get from under the Constitution, which is nothing more nor less than the combined and expressed will of the people in the form of an organic law; and before it should be violated, even if it needed amendment, we should be patient and amend it in the mode and manner designated in the instrument as framed by Washington and his compatriots. . . .

PART FIVE

THE WRITING OF THE FOURTEENTH AMENDMENT

SECTION 1. All persons born or naturalized in the United States, and subject to the jurisdiction thereof, are citizens of the United States and of the State wherein they reside. No State shall make or enforce any law which shall abridge the privileges or immunities of citizens of the United States; nor shall any State deprive any person of life, liberty, or property, without due process of law; nor deny to any person within its jurisdiction the equal protection of the laws.

SECTION 2. Representatives shall be apportioned among the several States according to their respective numbers, counting the whole number of persons in each State, excluding Indians not taxed. But when the right to vote at any election for the choice of electors for President and Vice President of the United States, Representatives in Congress, the Executive and Judicial officers of a State, or the members of the Legislature thereof, is denied to any of the male inhabitants of such State, being twenty-one years of age, and citizens of the United States, or in any way abridged, except for participation in rebellion, or other crime, the basis of representation therein shall be reduced in the proportion which the number of such male citizens shall bear to the whole number of male citizens twenty-one years of age in such State.

SECTION 3. No person shall be a Senator or Representative in Congress, or elector of President and Vice President, or hold any office, civil or military, under the United States, or under any State, who, having previously taken an oath, as a member of Congress, or as an officer of the United States, or as a member of any State Legislature, or as an executive or judicial officer of any State, to support the Constitution of the United States, shall have engaged in insurrection or rebellion against the same, or given aid or comfort to the enemies thereof. But Congress may by a vote of two-thirds of each House, remove such disability.

SECTION 4. The validity of the public debt of the United States, authorized by law, including debts incurred for payment of pensions and bounties for services in suppressing insurrection or rebellion, shall not be questioned. But neither the United States nor any State shall assume or pay any debt or obligation incurred in aid of insurrection or rebellion against the United States, or any claim for the loss or emancipation of any slave; but all such debts, obligations and claims shall be held illegal and void.

SECTION 5. The Congress shall have power to enforce, by appropriate legislation, the provisions of this article.

Congressman John Armor Bingham Tells How He Made the Equal Protection Clause of the Fourteenth Amendment a Sweeping Extension of the Bill of Rights

The future leader of the House Radicals, John A. Bingham (1815-1900), was born in Mercer, Pennsylvania, the son of a carpenter. He early had to struggle for his limited education; he worked for a while as a printer. After studying law and practicing at Cadiz, Ohio, he became a Whig politician, aided by his ability as a stump speaker, especially in the "log cabin and cider" campaign for Harrison in 1840. In 1854, he was elected to Congress as an antislavery man and remained there almost continuously until 1873, when he became American minister to Japan for ten years.

Bingham, as this selection shows, was a clear, persuasive speaker, although his other speeches reveal a degree of invective worthy of his friends Stevens and Sumner. He was the center of national attention as Special Judge Advocate during the trial of Lincoln's assassins and again as a manager and dramatic closing speaker in the impeachment trial of Andrew Johnson. Most important, however, was his authorship of the famous civil rights portion of the Fourteenth Amendment, forbidding any state to abridge the privileges or immunities of citizens of the United States or to deprive any person of life, liberty, or property without due process of law or to deny to any person the equal protection of the laws. In the speech reproduced below, he not only tells the story of how he came to write this clause, but he also explains his far-reaching intent to make the Fourteenth Amendment a formula by which all of the civil rights guaranteed against the federal government in the first eight amendments were made applicable against the states as well.

As other of his speeches reveal, Bingham interpreted the protections for the freedmen and all other citizens quite broadly, very much in the spirit of Chief Justice Earl Warren's famous desegregation opinion in *Brown v. Topeka* (1954) a century later. Furthermore, following the equalitarian tradition of Charles Sumner as expressed in the Roberts case (1849), Bingham had almost certainly meant that all Americans should enjoy equal access to public facilities and all other rights of citizenship. The fullest consequences of the Bingham position in making the first eight amendments applicable to both state and federal governments appeared a century later, when Justices Hugo Black and William O. Douglas insisted that the same high procedural standards that had marked the interpretation of the Bill of Rights must be met by the states.

A sharp setback to Bingham's hopes occurred in 1883 in the Civil Rights cases, which nullified the federal Civil Rights Law of 1875. The judges decided that social discrimination in denying Negroes access to inns, public

Selection: The House speech following is taken from the *Congressional Record*, 42nd Cong., 1st Sess. (1871) Appendix, pp 83-85.

conveyances, and places of amusement did not violate the Thirteenth, Fourteenth, or Fifteenth amendments. Ahead lay the discriminatory "separate and equal" doctrine of *Plessy v. Ferguson* (1896), which had first appeared in the Roberts case when it had overcome Sumner's doctrine of "equality before the law." This growing conservatism of the Supreme Court has been attributed to the increased power of large corporations which profited as "persons" from the equal protection clause; and it has been suggested that Justice Stephen Field led the conservative shift of the 1880s as part of a general reaction against the portent of the revolutionary Paris Commune of 1871.

[John Bingham]: . . . Sir, I sat at the feet of one who, though departed this life, still lives among us in his immortal spirit, and still speaks to us from the reports of the highest judicial tribunal on earth, which he so long adorned as the Chief Justice of the Supreme Court of the United States. I took counsel, sir, of that great man, John Marshall, foremost of all the judges, in the hope that by his guidance, the amendment might be so framed that in all the hereafter, it might be accepted by the historian of the American Constitution and her Magna Charta "as the keystone of American liberty. . . ."

In reëxamining that case of Barron, Mr. Speaker, after my struggle in the House in February, 1866, to which the gentleman has alluded, I noted and apprehended as I never did before, certain words in that opinion of Marshall. Referring to the first eight articles of amendments to the Constitution of the United States, the Chief Justice said: "Had the framers of these amendments intended them to be limitations on the powers of the State governments they would have imitated the framers of the original Constitution, and have expressed that intention." Barron *vs.* The Mayor, &c., 7 Peters, 250.

Acting upon this suggestion I did imitate the framers of the original Constitution. As they had said "No State shall emit bills of credit, pass any bill of attainder, *ex post facto* law, or law impairing the obligations of contracts"; imitating their example and imitating it to the letter, I prepared the provision of the first section of the fourteenth amendment as it stands in the Constitution, as follows:

"No State shall make or enforce any law which shall abridge the privileges or immunities of the citizens of the United States, nor shall any State deprive any person of life, liberty, or property without due process of law, nor deny to any person within its jurisdiction the equal protection of the laws."

I hope the gentleman now knows why I changed the form of the amendment of February, 1866.

Mr. Speaker, that the scope and meaning of the limitations imposed by the first section [of the] fourteenth amendment of the Constitution may be more fully understood, permit me to say that the privileges and immunities of citizens of the United States, as contradistinguished from citizens of a State, are chiefly defined in the first eight amendments to the Constitution of the United States. . . .

These eight articles I have shown never were limitations upon the power of the States, until made so by the fourteenth amendment. The words of that amendment, "no State shall make or enforce any law which shall abridge the privileges or immunities of citizens of the United States," are an express prohibition upon every State of the Union, which may be enforced under existing laws of Congress, and such other laws for their better enforcement as Congress may make. . . .

Is it not clear that other and different privileges and immunities than those to which a citizen of a State was entitled are secured by the provision of the fourteenth article, that no State shall abridge the privileges and immunities of citizens of the United States, which are defined in the eight articles of amendment, and which were not limitations on the power of the States before the fourteenth amendment made them limitations?

Sir, before the ratification of the fourteenth amendment, the State could deny to any citizen the right of trial by jury, and it was done. Before that the State could abridge the freedom of the press, and it was so done in half of the States of the Union. Before that a State as in the case of the State of Illinois, could make it a crime punishable by fine and imprisonment for any citizen within her limits, in obedience to the injunction of our divine Master, to help a slave who was ready to perish; to give him shelter, or break with him his crust of bread. The validity of that State restriction upon the rights of conscience and the duty of life was affirmed, to the shame and disgrace of America, in the Supreme Court of the United States; but nevertheless affirmed in obedience to the requirements of the Constitution. (14 Howard, 19-20. Moore *vs*. The People.)

Under the Constitution as it is, not as it was, and by force of the fourteenth amendment, no State hereafter can imitate the bad example of Illinois, to which I have referred, nor can any State ever repeat the example of Georgia and send men to the penitentiary, as did that State, for teaching the Indian to read the lessons of the New Testament, to know that new evangel, "The pure in heart shall see God."

Mr. Speaker, this House may safely follow the example of the makers of the Constitution and the builders of the Republic, by passing laws for enforcing all the privileges and immunities of citizens of the United States, as guaranteed by the amended Constitution and expressly enumerated in the Constitution. Do gentlemen say that by so legislating we would strike down the rights of the State? God forbid. I believe our dual system of government essential to our national existence. That Constitution which Washington so aptly said made us one people, is essential to our nationality and essential to the protection of the rights of all the people at home and abroad. The State governments are also essential to the local administration of the law, which makes it omnipresent, visible to every man within the vast extent of the Republic, in every place, whether by the wayside or by the fireside, restraining him by its terrors from the wrong, and protecting him by its power, in the right. . . .

OPINION OF THE COURT [JUSTICE BRADLEY]

. . . The Thirteenth Amendment has respect, not to distinctions of race, or class, or color, but to slavery. The Fourteenth Amendment extends its protection to races and classes, and prohibits any State legislation which has the effect of denying to any race or class, or to any individual, the equal protection of the laws.

Now, conceding, for the sake of the argument, that the admission to an inn, a public conveyance, or a place of public amusement, on equal terms with all other citizens, is the right of every man and all classes of men, is it any more than one of those rights which the states by the Fourteenth Amendment are forbidden to deny to any person? And is the Constitution violated until the denial of the right has some State sanction or authority? Can the act of a mere individual, the owner of the inn, the public conveyance or place of amusement, refusing the accommodation, be justly regarded as imposing any badge of slavery or servitude upon the applicant, or only as inflicting an ordinary civil injury, properly cognizable by the laws of the State, and presumably subject to redress by those laws until the contrary appears?

After giving to these questions all the consideration which their importance demands, we are forced to the conclusion that such an act of refusal has nothing to do with slavery or involuntary servitude, and that if it is violative of any right of the party, his redress is to be sought under the laws of the State; or if those laws are adverse to his rights and do not protect him, his remedy will be found in the corrective legislation which Congress has adopted, or may adopt, for counteracting the effect of State laws, or State action, prohibited by the Fourteenth Amendment. It would be running the slavery argument into the ground to make it apply to every act of discrimination which a person may see fit to make as to the guests he will entertain, or as to the people he will take into his coach or cab or car, or admit to his concert or theatre, or deal with in other matters of intercourse or business. Innkeepers and public carriers, by the laws of all the States, so far as we are aware, are bound, to the extent of their facilities, to furnish proper accommodation to all unobjectionable persons who in good faith apply for them. If the laws themselves make any unjust discrimination, amenable to the prohibitions of the Fourteenth Amendment, Congress has full power to afford a remedy under that amendment and in accordance with it.

When a man has emerged from slavery, and by the aid of beneficent legislation has shaken off the inseparable concomitants of that state, there must be some stage in the progress of his elevation when he takes the rank of a mere citizen, and ceases to be the special favorite of the laws, and when his rights as a citizen, or a man, are to be protected in the ordinary modes by which other men's rights are protected. There were thousands of free colored people in this country before the abolition of slavery, enjoying all the essential rights of life, liberty and property the same as white citizens; yet no one, at that time, thought that it was any invasion of his personal status as a freeman because he was not admitted to all the privileges enjoyed by white citizens, or because he was subjected to discriminations in the enjoyment of accommodations in inns, public conveyances and places of amusement. Mere discriminations on account of race or color were not regarded as badges of slavery. If, since that time, the enjoyment of equal rights in all these respects has become established by constitutional enactment, it is not by force of the Thirteenth Amendment (which merely abolishes slavery), but by force of the Thirteenth [Fourteenth], and Fifteenth Amendments.

On the whole we are of opinion, that no countenance of authority for the passage of the law in question can be found in either the Thirteenth or Fourteenth Amendment of the Constitution; and no other ground of authority for its passage being suggested, it must necessarily be declared void, at least so far as its operation in the several States is concerned. . . .

DISSENTING OPINION [JUSTICE HARLAN]

. . . Scarcely a day passes without our seeing in this court-room citizens of the white and black races sitting side by side, watching the progress of our business. It would never occur to any one that the presence of a colored citizen in a court-house, or court-room, was an invasion of the social rights of white persons who may frequent such places. And yet, such a suggestion would be quite as sound in law—I say it with all respect—as is the suggestion that the claim of a colored citizen to use, upon the same terms as is permitted to white citizens, the accommodations of public highways, or public inns, or places of public amusement, established under the license of the law, is an invasion of the social rights of the white race. . . .

. . . I suggest, that it may become a pertinent inquiry whether Congress may, in the exertion of its power to regulate commerce among the States, enforce among passengers on public conveyances, equality of right, without regard to race, color or previous condition of servitude, if it be true—which I do not admit—that such legislation would be an interference by government with the social rights of the people.

My brethren say, that when a man has emerged from slavery, and by the aid of beneficent legislation has shaken off the inseparable concomitants of that state, there must be some stage in the progress of his elevation when he takes the rank of a mere citizen, and ceases to be the special favorite of the laws, and when his rights as a citizen, or a man, are to be protected in the ordinary modes by which other men's rights are protected. It is, I submit, scarcely just to say that the colored race has been the special favorite of the laws. The statute of 1875, now adjudged to be unconstitutional, is for the benefit of citizens of every race and color. What the nation, through Congress, has sought to accomplish in reference to that race, is—what had already been done in every State of the Union for the white race—to secure and protect rights belonging to them as freemen and citizens; nothing more. It was not deemed enough "to help the feeble up, but to support him after." The one underlying purpose of congressional legislation has been to enable the black race to take the rank of mere citizens. The difficulty has been to compel a recognition of the legal right of the black race to take the rank of citizens, and to secure the enjoyment of privileges belonging, under the law, to them as a component part of the people for whose welfare and happiness government is ordained. . . .

PART SIX

THE KU KLUX KLAN

General Nathan Bedford Forrest, Grand Wizard of the Ku Klux Klan, and General John Brown Gordon of Georgia Defend the Invisible Empire; Klan Victims Disagree

The dashing Confederate raider General Nathan B. Forrest (1821-1877) was the son of a Tennessee blacksmith who moved to Mississippi where his death threw the burden of supporting a large family upon the boy. Although only meagerly educated, Nathan Forrest rose to become a wealthy slave-trader, a real-estate promoter, and the owner of cotton plantations in both Mississippi and Arkansas. During the war, he proved himself one of the boldest and most versatile of the Confederate cavalry raiders, terrifying Union garrisons by his swift assault and his threat of no quarter to the enemy. As a brigadier general and one of the chief heroes of the Confederacy, he was chosen in 1867 by a convention from several states to be Grand Wizard of the Ku Klux Klan. His followers, at least, intended to go much further than to form a secret recreational group analogous to the Freemasons, although, as Forrest's testimony suggests, he personally fought terrorism and moved vigorously to disband the organization when it became notorious.

His fellow witness before investigating congressmen was the wealthy Atlanta insurance man General John B. Gordon (1832-1904), a much better-educated man than Forrest, who had studied at the University of Georgia, practiced law, and engaged in the development of Georgia coal mines. He won a military reputation and the rank of lieutenant general during the war, beginning as the daring head of a company of mountaineers, "the Raccoon Roughs." He was with Lee's army at Appomattox. After the war, he turned to law in Atlanta and then, after being defeated for governor by Republican R. B. Bullock, led the fight for home rule in Georgia. Gordon was commonly identified with the Klan, although his testimony suggested that he and a group of solid propertyholders had only organized a "purely peace police" to defend the community against Negro criminality. Following Reconstruction, Gordon rose rapidly in state politics, even defeating Alexander Stephens, local hero and the former Vice-President of the Confederacy, for the governorship, and eventually became a United States Senator (twice elected) and an industrial leader of the New South.

The testimony of a Negro victim of the Klan, William Coleman, is next considered. His facts are self-evident regarding the motives of the Klansmen in punishing him for Radical activity. From the same volume, pp. 482-83.

The testimony of Forrest and Gordon are from the *Reports of the Committees for the House of Representatives for Affairs in the Insurrectionary States*, 42nd Cong., 2nd Sess., 1871-72, I, 449-53.

Following this is an excerpt from the testimony of a Southern white suggesting the role of Klansmen in attacking miscegenation, very much along the lines of the second Klan of the 1920s, which was concerned with racial purity and immorality. From the same volume, pp. 558-60.

Finally there is the circumstantial account of General O. O. Howard, head of the Freedmen's Bureau, who noted to what extent his schools for the Negro had become the target of the Klan. From the *Autobiography of General O. O. Howard* (1907), pp. 374-83.

General Forrest, when examined, said:

I say to you, frankly, that I think the organization did exist in 1866 and 1867.

Question. In what portions of the country?

Answer. I do not think it existed anywhere except in Middle Tennessee. There may have been some in a small portion of West Tennessee; but if there was any, it was very scattering.

Question. Under what name is it your belief it existed at that time?

Answer. Some called them Pale Faces; some called them Ku-Klux. I believe they were under two names.

Question. Had they an officer known as a commander?

Answer. I presume they did.

Question. Was their organization military in its character?

Answer. No, sir; I think not.

Question. Were they subject to command and drill in any military form?

Answer. They were like the Loyal Leagues, and met occasionally and dispersed again. The Loyal Leagues existed about that time, and I think this was a sort of offset gotten up against the Loyal Leagues. It was in Tennessee at the time; I do not think it was general.

Question. Had it a political purpose then?

Answer. I think it had not then; it had no political purpose.

Question. You say it was organized like the Loyal Leagues, or in opposition to them?

Answer. I think it was in opposition.

Question. Was the purpose of the Loyal Leagues political?

Answer. I do not presume it was; I do not know what it was.

Question. What did you understand to be the purpose of the two organizations?

Answer. I can tell you what I think the purpose of the organization that you first spoke of was; I think it was for self-protection.

Question. You mean now what is called Ku-Klux?

Answer. Yes, sir; I think that organization arose about the time the militia were called out, and Governor Brownlow issued his proclamation stating that the troops would not be injured for what they should do to rebels; such a proclamation was issued. There was a great deal of insecurity felt by the southern people. There were a great many northern men coming down there, forming Leagues all over the country. The negroes were holding night meetings; were going about; were becoming very insolent; and the southern people all over the State were very much alarmed. I think many of the organizations did not have any name; parties organized themselves so as to be ready in case they were attacked. Ladies were ravished by some of these negroes, who were tried and put in the penitentiary, but were turned out in a few days afterward. There was a great deal of insecurity in the country, and I think this organization was got up to protect the weak, with no political intention at all.

Question. Do I understand you to say that the Loyal League organization in Tennessee countenanced or promoted crimes of the kind which you have mentioned?

Answer. I do not know that they promoted them; but those crimes were not punished; there was very little law then.

Question. Was this before the organization of the State government, or did it continue afterward?

Answer. Well, it continued so for a year afterward.

Question. How long, according to your information, did this Ku-Klux organization exist?

Answer. I think it was disorganized in the early part of 1868.

Question. Did it continue until after the presidential election?

Answer. No, sir; I think it was in the latter part of 1867, or the early part of 1868; I do not know the exact date.

Question. Where can we get the information as to the manner of its dissolution and the time of it?

Answer. I do not know where you can get it. I never got any positive information except that it was generally understood that the organization was broken up.

Question. Who were understood to belong to it?

Answer. Men of the Southern States, citizens.

Question. Did they speak to you without hesitation of the organization, as if it required no concealment?

Answer. No, sir; they did not.

Question. Did they deny or admit its existence?

Answer. They did not do either; they did not deny it or admit it. It was understood, though, among the southern people, that this organization had disbanded about the time of the nomination of candidates for President of the United States.

Question. When they proceeded to carry out the objects of the organization, did they do it in numbers, by riding in bands?

Answer. I do not know; I never saw the organization together in my life; never saw them out in any numbers, or anything of the kind.

*   *   *   *   *   *   *

Question. Were you trying to suppress the organization, or the outrages you speak of?

Answer. I was trying to suppress the outrages.

Question. Outrages committed by colored men?

Answer. By all people; my object was to keep peace.

Question. Did you want to suppress that organization?

Answer. Yes, sir; I did suppress it.

Question. How?

Answer. Had it broken up and disbanded.

Question. What influence did you exert in disbanding it?

Answer. I talked with different people that I believed were connected with it, and urged its disbandment, that it should be broken up.

Question. In the light of that statement, is it not probable that this part of the account of the interview with you is correct?

"Since its organization the Leagues have quit killing and murdering our people. There were some foolish young men who put masks on their faces, and rode over the country, frightening negroes; but orders have been issued to stop that, and it has ceased."

Answer. I never uttered such words; I did not talk to that man twenty words.

Question. You say you were trying to stop the proceedings, and that they did stop.

Answer. Yes, sir; and I think they completely stopped. I do not hear of anything of that kind now—of difficulties there—any more than I hear of them here. I think that since 1868 that organization has been disbanded. I do not think there has been any organization together; if there has been, it has been by irresponsible parties, without any organization at all.

General Gordon, when questioned on the same subject by the committee, said:

Question. What do you know of any combinations in Georgia, known as Ku-Klux, or by any other name, who have been violating the law?

Answer. I do not know anything about any Ku-Klux organization, as the papers talk about it. I have never heard of anything of that sort except in the papers and by general report; but I do know that an organization did exist in Georgia at one time. I know that in 1868—I think that was the time—I was approached and asked to attach myself to a secret organization in Georgia. I was approached by some of the very best citizens of the State—some of the most peaceable, law-abiding men, men of large property, who had large interests in the State. The object of this organization was explained to me at the time by these parties; and I want to say that I approved of it most heartily. I would approve again of a similar organization, under the same state of circumstances.

Question. Tell us about what that organization was.

Answer. The organization was simply this—nothing more and nothing less: it was an organization, a brotherhood of the property-holders, the peaceable, law-abiding citizens of the State, for self-protection. The instinct of self-protection prompted that organization; the sense of insecurity and danger, particularly in those neighborhoods where the negro population largely predominated. The reasons which led to this organization were three or four. The first and main reason was the organization of the Union League, as they called it, about which we knew nothing more than this: that the negroes would desert the plantations, and go off at night in large numbers; and on being asked where they had been, would reply, sometimes, "We have been to the muster;" sometimes, "We have been to the lodge;" sometimes, "We have been to the meeting." Those things were observed for a great length of time. We knew that the "carpet-baggers," as the people of Georgia called these men who came from a distance and had no interest at all with us; who were unknown to us entirely; who from all we could learn about them did not have any very exalted position at their homes—these men were organizing the colored people. We knew that beyond all question. We knew of certain instances where great crimes had been committed; where overseers had been driven from plantations, and the negroes had asserted their right to hold the property for their own benefit. Apprehension took possession of the entire public mind of the State. Men were in many instances afraid to go away from their homes and leave their wives and children, for fear of outrage. Rapes were already being committed in the country. There was this general organization of the black race on the one hand, and an entire disorganization of the white race on the other hand. We were afraid to have a public organization; because we supposed it would be construed at once, by the authorities at Washington, as an organization antagonistic to the Government of the United States. It was therefore necessary, in order to protect our families from outrage and preserve our own lives, to have something that we could regard as a brotherhood—a combination of the best men of the country, to act purely in self-defense, to repel the attack in case we should be attacked by these people. That was the whole object of this organization. I never heard of any disguises connected with it; we had none, very certainly. This organization, I think, extended nearly all over the State. It was, as I say, an organization purely for self-defense. It had no more politics in it than the organization of the Masons. I never heard the idea of politics suggested in connection with it.

Question. Did it have any antagonism toward either the State or the Federal Government?

Answer. None on earth—not a particle. On the contrary, it was purely a peace police organization, and I do know of some instances where it did prevent bloodshed on a large scale. I know of one case in

Albany, Georgia, where, but for the instrumentality of this organization, there would have been, beyond all doubt, a conflict, growing out of a personal difficulty between a black man and a white man. The two races gathered on each side, but this organization quelled the trouble easily and restored peace, without any violence to anybody, and without a particle of difficulty with either the black race or the white. They stopped one just as much as they did the other. This society was purely a police organization to keep the peace, to prevent disturbances in our State. That was the motive that actuated me in going into it, and that was the whole object of the organization, as explained to me by these persons who approached me. I approved of the object.

Question. You had no riding about at nights?

Answer. None on earth. I have no doubt that such things have occurred in Georgia. It is notoriously stated—I have no personal knowledge of anything of the kind, but I have reason to believe it—that disguised parties have committed outrages in Georgia; but we have discovered in some cases that these disguised parties did not belong to any particular party. We have demonstrated that beyond all question in some cases, by bringing to trial and conviction parties who belonged, for instance, to the radical party, who had in disguise committed outrages in the State. There is not a good man in Georgia who does not deplore that thing just as much as any radical deplores it. When I use the term "radical," I do not mean to reflect upon the republican party generally; but in our State a republican is a very different sort of a man from a republican generally in the Northern States. In our State republicanism means nothing in the world but creating disturbance, riot, and animosity, and filching and plundering. That is what it means in our State—nothing else; there is no politics in it. In the North the thing is very different. There men can differ in politics, and yet have the kindliest relations; in Georgia we cannot do it unless we are willing to countenance all sorts of outrages upon our people. There are genteel republicans in Georgia, who are just as safe as any one else; who travel all over the State; who occupy high positions, and are never insulted in the street, the cars, or anywhere else. If there is any organization in Georgia for the purpose of putting down republicanism there, why does it not attack the leaders of that party? It strikes me as the very highest commentary upon the law-abiding spirit of the people of Georgia that such men as I could name —men in high position who have plundered our people by the million —still live and are countenanced on the streets, have no insults offered to them. The truth is simply this: that individuals in Georgia of all parties and all colors have, I suppose, committed outrage; but such affairs have been purely personal, just as they are when they occur anywhere else in the United States. I do not believe any more crimes have been committed in Georgia than in any other community of the same number anywhere else in the country. That is my honest conviction. I do not believe that any crime has ever been committed by this organization of which I have spoken, and of which I was a member. I believe it was purely a peace police—a law-abiding concern. That was its whole object, and it never would have existed but for the apprehension in the minds of our people of a conflict in which we would have had no sympathy and no protection. We apprehended that the sympathy of the entire Government would be against us; and nothing in the world but the instinct of self-protection prompted that organization. We felt that we must at any cost protect ourselves, our homes, our wives and children from outrage. We would have preferred death rather than to have submitted to what we supposed was coming upon us. At this time I do not believe any such organization exists, or has existed for a long time. I have not heard of it for two years, I am certain.

Question. Why did it cease to exist; why did it pass away?

Answer. Well, sir, it just dissolved because the courts became generally established; and though the courts were in the hands of the opposite party, our people believed they were trying to do justice; that a general protection was extended over us. Our people thought we could get justice at the hands of these judges; though they were of the opposite party, and though negroes were on the juries, we were satisfied that in the existing condition of things we were safe. Since Governor Bullock's election I have not heard anything of that organization. I am not sure that it did not pass away with his election. It certainly has not existed since within my knowledge; and I think I would have known it if it had. I think that my position would have brought it to my knowledge if any such organization had existed for several years past. As I have stated, the only reason it has passed away is, I think, because the people felt safe. Courts were established and police regulations were generally instituted.

You must remember that we were in a state of anarchy there for a long time. We had no law but drum-head courts-martial. Our people were entirely powerless to do anything. We always felt that if the Federal troops were kept in our midst we would be protected. I want to state that with great emphasis. Our people have always felt that if the white troops of the Federal Army could have been stationed in our midst in those negro belts we would have been safe. But the troops were perhaps two hundred miles away; and before they could have been brought to our relief the whole neighborhood might have been slaughtered. We then believed that such a thing might occur on almost any night. Such was the condition of things in Georgia at that time. I do not believe that it exists now, or has existed for two years. To my certain knowledge this organization never did exist as a political organization. I do not know what may have been the case elsewhere; but very certainly there was no politics in this thing in Georgia, so far as I had anything to do with it; and I think that the organization was of the same character all over the State—probably over the South wherever it existed. We never called it Ku-Klux, and therefore I do not know anything about Ku-Klux.

Macon, Mississippi, November 6, 1871.

WILLIAM COLEMAN (colored) sworn and examined.

By the CHAIRMAN:

Question. Where do you live?

Answer. I live in Macon.

Question. How long have you lived here?

Answer. I came here about the last of April.

Question. Where did you come from?

Answer. I came from Winston County.

Question. What occasioned your coming here?

Answer. I got run by the Ku-Klux.

Question. Give the particulars to the committee.

Answer. Well, I don't know anything that I had said or done that injured any one, further than being a radical in that part of the land, and as for interrupting any one, I didn't, for I had plenty of my own of anything I wanted myself. I had done bought my land and paid for it, and I had a great deal of hogs; I had eighteen head of hogs to kill this fall. I had twelve head of sheep, and one good milk-cow, and a yearling, and the cow had a right young calf again, and I had my mule and my filly, and all of it was paid for but my mule, and I had my brother hired to pay for him. The mule cost me $65, and I had him hired out to pay for him. It was like I was getting the mule from you, and you wanting a hand to work the value of the mule out in work.

Question. Did any of the Ku-Klux come to your house?

Answer. They did.

Question. In the night-time?

Answer. They came about a half hour or more before day, as nigh as I can recollect by my brains, being frightened at their coming up in this kind of way. They were shooting and going on at me through the house, and when they busted the door open, coming in shooting, I was frightened, and I can only tell you as nigh as my recollection will afford at this time that it was about a half hour to day.

Question. What did they do to you?

Answer. None of the shot hit me, but they aimed to hit me; but I had one door just like that at the side of the house and the other at this side, and there was the chimney, and there was my bed in that corner opposite, and they came to that door first, [illustrating,] and hollered "Hallo;" bum, bum, bum, on the lock. I jumped up and said, "Hallo." Then one at the door said, "Raise a light in there." "What for; who is you?" I said. He says, "Raise a light in there, God damn you; I'll come in there and smoke my pipe in your ear." He said that just so. I said, "Is that you, uncle Davy?" Says he, "No, God damn you, it isn't uncle Dave; open this door." Says I, "I am not going to open my door to turn nobody on me that won't tell me who they are before I do it. Who are you?" He says, "God damn you, we didn't come to tell you who we are." I was peeping through the little crack in the door. I had bored a gimlet-hole about as big as that pen to put a string through, and had a latch inside so that when I had been off at work anywhere, and happened to come home at night, I could open the door without my wife having to get up, and she would put the string through the door and I would pull, and that was the way I would get in.

Question. That was the hole you looked through?

Answer. Yes, sir.

Question. What did you see?

Answer. I saw men out there standing with horns and faces on all of them, and they all had great, long, white cow-tails way down the breast. I said it was a cow-tail; it was hair, and it was right white. They told me they rode from Shiloh in two hours, and came to kill me. They shot right smart in that house before they got in, but how many times I don't know, they shot so fast outside; but when they come in, they didn't have but three loads to shoot. I know by the way they tangled about in the house they would have put it in me if they had had it. They only shot three times in the house. The men behind me had busted in through the door; both doors were busted open. By the time the fellows at the back door got in the door, these fellows at the front door busted in, and they all met in the middle of the floor, and I didn't have a thing to fight with, only a little piece of ax-handle; and when I started from the first door to the second, pieces of the door flew and met me. I jumped for a piece of ax-handle and fought them squandering about, and they were knocking about me with guns, and firing balls that cut several holes in my head. The notches is in my head now. I dashed about among them, but they knocked me down several times. Every time I would get up, they would knock me down again. I saw they were going to kill me, and I turned in and laid there after they knocked me down so many times. The last time they knocked me down I laid there a good while before I moved, and when I had strength I jumped to split through a man's legs that was standing over me, and, as I jumped, they struck at me jumping between his legs, and they struck him and he hollered, "Don't hit me, God damn you," but they done knocked him down then, but they hadn't knocked him so he couldn't talk. I jumped through and got past him. They didn't hit him a fair lick, because he was going toward them, and it struck past his head on his shoulder. If it had struck his head, it would have busted it open. I didn't catch that lick. I got up then; they had shot out the loads. I grabbed my ax-handle, and commenced fighting, and then they just took and cut me with knives. They surrounded me in the floor and tore my shirt off. They got me out on the floor; some had me by the legs and some by the arms and the neck and anywhere, just like dogs string out a coon, and they took me out to the big road before my gate and whipped me until I couldn't move or holler or do nothing, but just lay there like a log, and every lick they hit me I grunted just like a mule when he is stalled fast and whipped; that was all. They left me there for dead, and what it was done for was because I was a radical, and I didn't deny my profession anywhere and I never will. I never will vote that conservative ticket if I die.

Question. Did they tell you they whipped you because you were a radical?

Answer. They told me, "God damn you, when you meet a white man in the road lift your hat; I'll learn you, God damn you, that you are a nigger, and not to be going about like you thought yourself a white man; you calls yourself like a white man, God damn you." Here is what I put it to, because I had my filly; I had bought her to ride, not to stay in the stable, but to ride when I got ready, like you would do with your property. When I bought her I bought her for $75; she was not nigh grown; a little thing, with flaxen mane and tail, and light cream-color, and I would get on my filly on a Saturday evening. I would work until Saturday evening, but I won't work any longer for any man, for my own work or any body else, unless it is mighty urgent; then I will go on until night, but if it is nothing but work straight along, I will work until Saturday at 12 o'clock, and I will strike off there. I believe if a man does it all over the world, he can make an honest living and put his work to good use.

Question. Were you working on your own land?

Answer. Yes, sir; that I bought and paid for; $473 for it.

Question. How many men were concerned in beating you?

Answer. Eight men.

Question. Were they all disguised?

Answer. Yes, sir; every one of them. . . .

By the CHAIRMAN: [to a Southern white]

Question. The first part of your examination related to the case of Betsy Lucas, and you went on to say that a party of men went on to Jackson Cosby's, Hinton's, and Price's, all of whom lived with black women as concubines, and that they whipped the women, and directed them to leave. Did you understand how large a number of men were concerned in the purification of that locality?

Answer. I think, to the best of my recollection, there were only eight or ten; not more than ten, perhaps.

Question. By what refinement of ethics were the women whipped and the men left to go free?

Answer. Well, judge, the presumption by outsiders now is that the men were whipped and they deny it. That was the impression, that the men were whipped and they deny it. The women were whipped, and they acknowledge it. I do not know by what refinement of ethics it was done. If I had been there I should have as certainly allowed it to the rascals as the women.

Question. Did you understand that the black women say that their paramours were whipped as well as themselves?

Answer. No, sir; I never heard that they said anything about it, except that they acknowledge that they were whipped themselves.

Question. Is it not fair to presume that they would have spoken of their lovers having been whipped as well as themselves, if they had been whipped?

Answer. I suppose so, unless they were induced by their lovers to withhold the fact, because the odium which would attach to them for having been whipped for such a thing in the community would have necessarily driven them away.

Question. Were these four gentlemen whom you have named cotton planters?

Answer. When you speak of a planter, judge, the idea conveyed is of a man of extensive means. We have a sort of distinction here. When we say a farmer, we mean a man of but little means. Those men are farmers, and by saying that I mean that they are men of moderate means.

Question. Owning land and cultivating it?

Answer. Yes, sir; but only small places. I do not suppose they own over two hundred and forty acres of land.

Question. Not able, probably, to indulge in the luxury of regular wives?

Answer. O, yes, sir; there is no difficulty on that score. Our theory is in this country that a wife will support herself.

Question. In this matter of miscegenation in this part of the country, is it your information that the black women seduce the white men, or that the white men seduce the black women?

Answer. I think they are both pretty well seduced together. I do not think there is much seduction either way.

Question. Is that practice so uncommon in the country that it is thought worthy of a Ku-Klux visitation in order to correct such irregularity?

Answer. Well, living together, as I understand they were living together, is a thing that is very uncommon. I do not know any other instance within my knowledge either in this country or elsewhere. That white men and black women have frequent intercourse I have no doubt is true, but that they live together, as these parties did, is a thing of rare occurrence.

Question. That is regarded as more obnoxious than these accidental or occasional cases of sexual commerce?

Answer. Yes, sir.

Question. Is the practice itself of sexual commerce between the two races frowned upon and denounced by the community generally?

Answer. Yes, sir; that is my information, that persons of respectability denounce it of both races.

Question. In point of fact, there are a great many of the mahogany color in this community?

Answer. Yes, sir, a great many. There are, however, fewer than a person would suppose from a knowledge of the former condition of society here, though there are a good many.

Question. In the presence of the great fact that this commerce between the two races has been going on for generations here, how do you account for the severe denunciation by the democratic party against what is called negro equality?

Answer. Upon the same principle on which I would account for the fact that a man at the North will go to a house where lewd women hold themselves out for sale, and have intercourse with them, and yet refuse to introduce those women into his family. Just upon the same principle it is done.

Question. Do you think the opinion has been a sincere and well-grounded one, that the introduction of negro suffrage would tend to produce social equality among the two races?

Answer. I think that it has prevailed to a greater or less extent. The people think that the natural result of it must be in time to break down to a considerable extent that barrier which has heretofore been interposed between the two races in a social point of view.

Question. Do the southern white men apprehend any danger to their own virtue, or that their own principles will be undermined, and that they will be led to intermarry with the negroes because of the extension of equal civil, and political rights to the blacks?

Answer. I do not know of any such apprehension as that on the part of the southern men, sir.

Question. They do not apprehend that they themselves will ever be in danger of intermixing freely, socially, and sexually with the blacks?

Answer. No, sir; the apprehension seems to be this: that the conferring of the right of suffrage on the negro, and his equality before the law, and his right to all the privileges of the free schools, will in process of time bring the two races together in the school-room as children, and that in that way the principles of their children and the rising generation will eventually be more or less affected. That is the apprehension.

Question. The apprehension is founded on the fear that they will be brought together in the school-room?

Answer. Yes, sir; that this contaminating influence, as we regard it, will be brought about upon the white race in that way eventually. There is no immediate danger apprehended now.

Question. Have not the two races been raised side by side from time immemorial, under the same roof, intermingling as children, and growing up together as young men and young women?

Answer. Yes, sir.

Question. Is it supposed that the school-room will be any more dangerous to their virtue?

Answer. Yes, sir; in this way: when they mingled together heretofore the white child recognized his own superiority; he was the child of the owner, and the negro or colored child was recognized as the child of the slave. The negro himself recognized that supposed superiority, and in recognizing it showed a proper deference. When you would see the negro child and the white child at play together around the plantation, the negro child invariably gave way to the white, and the white children were often domineering in consequence.

Question. Did it not follow as a necessary result, from the fact that the one was the dominant and the other the inferior or servile race, that the negro women had not the same power of resisting the lust and temptations of the master or the master's son?

Answer. I suppose that that had a great deal to do with it.

Question. Do you not think that the dangers of sexual commerce between the two races are greatly diminished by the fact that the blacks are now free?

Answer. I think it has been very little diminished.

Question. Do you think that the blacks, as a matter of choice, would seek to intermarry with the whites?

Answer. I do.

Question. What evidence have you of that?

Answer. Just this evidence, judge, that as the black woman sought the superior, or white man, to have intercourse with him, the black man has always sought, as we understand, to have intercourse with the white woman when he could, on account of this superiority of race.

Question. I ask what evidence you have that the blacks, as a matter of choice, would seek to intermarry with the whites?

Answer. I say that the evidence of that results from this known principle existing in the minds of the negroes to seek intercourse with the superior race. That is the evidence I have.

Question. You have no idea that the white race here would ever seek to intermarry with the black race?

Answer. No, not as a class; certainly not. There are instances where white men have married black women, and where black men have married white women.

Question. Are they not so extremely rare as to be regarded as exceptional cases?

Answer. Yes, sir, they are; but I will state to you frankly that they are rare, and the more so on account of the fear of severe punishment on the part of both races. . . .

THE KU-KLUX KLAN

After Congress had overthrown President Johnson's plan and had completed the formal reconstruction of the insurrectionary States according to its own views, the political disabilities of the late Confederates deprived them of suffrage and placed the political control of these States in a new party, composed of Southern Union men, Northern men who at the end of the war settled in the South, and the negroes.

Politicians of the Republican Party hoped through this combination to keep the Southern States Republican on national issues and secure the rights of complete citizenship to the new voters.

The negroes were generally very ignorant and not wisely led, and even if they had been the wisest of rulers the opposition of the whites to being ruled by their late slaves would have been naturally very fierce.

The opposition, as yet powerless at the polls, was greatly strengthened by the course, hostile to Congress, which President Johnson had pursued, and early in 1868 began to show itself in the operations here and there of certain secret organizations. The primary object of these associations was undoubtedly political, in some places avowed to be in opposition to the Union Leagues, that favored strong national control in the South, leagues which not only took form in Northern cities but also had prototypes in the South among the Unionists and negroes.

The ex-Confederate General Forrest even claimed for the former a "benevolent and defensive" purpose. The benevolence was to be mutual aid; the defensive, ostensibly to prevent Union leagues, composed mostly of negroes, from disturbing the peace. Whatever the origin of the associations, when full grown they became a monster terrible beyond question. The oath of perpetual secrecy with the penalty of death attached to its violation, of implicit obedience to a chief or chiefs, the guarding of secrets by the obligation to slay a betrayer, and the oath of every chief to obey without hesitation the orders of some "inner circle," constituted societies which in some parts of the South came to rival the Nihilistic assassins of Russia or the inner chamber of the old Spanish Inquisition. From the numerous cases of murder and outrage perpetrated upon negroes and those who befriended them during the days of reconstruction, which were reported to my officers and were by them recorded with the different circumstances attending them, it is now clear that the main object from first to last was somehow to regain and maintain over the negro that ascendency which slavery gave, and which was being lost by emancipation, education, and suffrage.

The opposition to negro education made itself felt everywhere in a combination not to allow the freedmen any room or building in which a school might be taught. In 1865, 1866, and 1867 mobs of the baser classes at intervals and in all parts of the South occasionally burned school buildings and churches used as schools, flogged teachers or drove them away, and in a number of instances murdered them. But the better portion of the communities had not been engaged in these acts, and there was no evidence that respectable Confederate soldiers were involved in these enterprises.

Our work of establishing schools went steadily on. Early in 1868, however, was the first appearance in my Bureau school reports of an offensive secret organization. It was from Charlestown, W. Va. Our workers received a note from the "Ku-Klux Klan." Not a white family there after that could be found willing to board the excellent lady teachers. At Frostburg a male teacher was threatened with violence, the Klan having sent him notes, ordering him to depart. Loyal West Virginians, however, stood by him and he did not go. In Maryland, also, one teacher was warned and forced to leave. The Klan signed their rough document which was placed in his hand, "Ku-Klux Klan." The face of the envelope was covered with scrawls; among these were the words: "Death! Death!" By a similar method a teacher at Hawkinsville, Ga. (a colored man), was dealt with by menace and afterwards seriously wounded. The Georgia superintendent wrote that for the last three months, April, May, and June, 1868, there had been more bitterness exhibited toward all men engaged in the work of education than ever before; and there were few but had received threats, both anonymous and open. Several freedmen had abandoned their fields from fear.

The cry from Alabama was even more alarming. People from a distance could not comprehend the feeling; schoolhouses were burned, and those left standing were in danger; teachers were hated and maltreated, two being driven from their work. "The truth is," they cried, "we are in the midst of a reign of terror."

But Louisiana exceeded; Miss Jordan's school at Gretna was entered by ruffians; the walls of her room were covered with obscene pictures and language, and threats against the teacher posted; she was insulted on the ferry and in the streets, and even annoyed in such a small way as to be required to pay twice as much ferriage as the teachers in the white schools. In Markville, the Ku-Klux Klan made more open demonstrations, but always by night. They posted their documents around the town, so terrifying the colored people that they did not dare leave their homes after dark. The night schools had to be closed. At Mary and Sabine parish; at Cherryville and Rapides parish; at Washington and Opelousas; at St. Landry parish, and elsewhere in a similar way by visitations and threats the schools were shut up and the teachers driven off.

In Texas, both at Georgetown and Circleville, the schools were similarly closed out; at the latter place the school edifice was burned to the ground.

Mrs. Baldwin, the teacher at Bowling Green, Ky., was a Christian lady of agreeable manners and unusual culture, but not one of the twenty-seven loyal families of the place dared incur the odium of giving her a home. The Regulators had made themselves felt; men, professing to be gentlemen, insulted her upon the streets. Vile books and pictures were sent to her by mail; and, as a last resort, she was threatened with assassination if she was found in the city at the expiration of five days. Many other schools had to be maintained under military guard; five school buildings in Kentucky were burned about that time.

Of course such conduct, bad as it seemed for the community, could not properly be charged to any of the people beyond those who were guilty of the barbarous acts, or those who, in their blindness of prejudice, sustained them. It became evident in studying the letters and communications which reached me, usually cautiously written, so as not to anger the whites around them if they should happen to be published, that in the early summer of 1868, the former irregular and local hostility to freedmen's schools had taken on a new strength. It involved in its meshes Unionists and well-to-do industrious negroes, as well as teachers and scholars. Further examples will illustrate the procedure: On May 16th, L. S. Frost, a white teacher in Tennessee, was taken at night from his room by a mob of disguised young men and carried to a field near by, men choking and beating him all the way; they were flourishing their pistols over his head, and threatening to kill him instantly if he did not cease resisting. They made him promise to leave town the next morning. They then blackened his face and portions of his body with a composition of spirits of turpentine, lamp-black, and tar, and released him. About a dozen persons were engaged in the outrage, some of whom were recognized by Mr. Frost.

John Dunlap, a teacher educated in Ohio, was in July, 1868, in charge of a colored school at Shelbyville, Tenn. On Independence Day, about ten o'clock at night, a body of Ku-Klux, some fifty strong, masked, armed with pistols and bearing an emblem resembling the bleeding heart of a man, were paraded in front of his house. When he presented himself, they gave him commands which he resisted. They fired through his window, made him surrender his pistol, caused him to mount, and escorted him to the public square. Then they seized and secured a prominent colored man, James Franklin. Proceeding with the regularity of soldiers, a captain commanding, they marched their victims across the Duck River, where, dismounting, with something like a leathern thong or strap they first flogged Franklin, each man giving him five blows. After that, taking Dunlap to another place, with the same parade, they performed the same operation, badly lacerating his body. After directing him to leave the city the next day, they released him. Dunlap not at once complying with their demand, they served upon him a formal notice, sent in the form of an unstamped letter through the post office, ordering him to leave by July 15th, or he would be burned to death. Dunlap thereupon went to Nashville and remained two months. Then he came back. He was visited again after his return, but was now prepared with a guard. While the Ku-Klux were hallooing that they "wanted Dunlap and fried meat" and were approaching his residence, the guard fired upon them. The band retreated and did not appear in Shelbyville again.

A school building was burned at Carthage, Tenn., by incendiaries; and at Somerville, Saulsbury, Pocahontas, and in numerous other country places the schools were completely broken up by insults and shameful outrages perpetrated upon the teachers.

The outcropping of cruelties in portions of Louisiana showed by the persons who were chosen as victims that the effort of the secret organization was particularly political. On July 28, 1868, William Cooper, a white Unionist, came to our agent in the parish of Franklin. He was severely wounded, having been shot in his own house near Girard Station; a freedman named Prince was killed in the same parish, and all the teachers were so terrified by such demonstrations as to stop teaching.

In the preceding April a good teacher, Frank Sinclair, had been slain in Ouachita, and other helpers there were so put in jeopardy of their lives that they could only teach secretly in the cabins.

At many points in the State were these "bands of desperadoes formed in secret organization, styling themselves the Ku-Klux Klan." They shot and hung colored men. Their lifeless bodies were found, but the secrets were so well kept that no guilty parties could be discovered. In some places negroes were taken out and whipped (as a rule by night) and there was no clew to the perpetrators. Even United States agents dared not hold a public meeting in that region—a gathering at night of negroes at any place would be regarded with suspicion by the whites and result in outrage and suffering to the blacks.

The aspect of society in Arkansas in the summer and fall of 1868 presented similar combined secret planning and movement. Lawlessness, rowdyism, and depredations in some parts of the State for a while ran riot. Union men were driven from their homes and freedmen subjected to the grossest maltreatment. In Crittenden county, Mr. E. G. Barker, our Bureau agent, was shot and severely wounded, August 12, 1868. An attempt to assassinate him at Hamburg, Ashley county, two years before had failed to end his life, but the wounds received had caused him the loss of an arm.

The secret bodies had different names in different localities. They appeared as "Regulators," "White Caps," "Pale Faces," "Knights of the White Camellia," and "Ku-Klux" or "Ku-Klux Klan." General Forrest testified before the Congressional Committee that his estimate of their numbers in Tennessee alone exceeded 40,000.

The latter part of the year 1868, before the election of General Grant for his first term, these murderous secret societies reached their greatest activity. Even the country hamlets in the neighborhood of Chattanooga, which city always after the war abounded in Union men and late Union soldiers, were boldly visited by this strange horde. They came upon one commodious schoolhouse in the country and burned it to the ground; but the persistent teacher, a colored youth, though threatened by the Ku-Klux Klan with violence and death if he did not yield to their commands, made himself a brush arbor and there continued his school to the end of the term. Before the November election (the freedmen's first national suffrage) the Ku-Klux, armed and masked as usual, at night paraded the streets of several cities, and filled the freedmen with terror. Similar detachments boldly roamed over large districts of country outside of the cities.

At Rock Spring, Ky., the Ku-Klux, estimated fifty strong, came at ten o'clock at night, seized the teacher, James Davis, a native of the place, an able and respected colored man, and ordered him to leave the country. His fine school building was reduced to ashes.

On October 21, 1868, a host of these "Regulators" set upon a negro assembly at Cadiz, which a Bureau messenger, Mr. P. S. Reeves, was visiting and addressing. The Regulators stoned the building and dispersed the negroes. Some of the rush shouted after Mr. Reeves: "Kill the scalawag!" "Shoot the Yankee!" This was done while he was finding his way to the hotel. He halted and faced them. They then "surrounded him, thrust their pistols into his face, beat him, kicked him," and after abusing him for a while ordered him to run for his life. This time, by what he called a quick walk, he reached the hotel. A larger mob surrounded the public house and could only be appeased by his promise to leave town the next morning.

After the election, for a time, the excessive wrath abated. From my point of observation, the two months of 1868 that followed the Presidential election and the first six in the next year, 1869, were quite free from the Ku-Klux raids.

During the last half of 1869, however, there was a quickening of the secret pulse. In the northern part of Alabama, along the border between Alabama and Tennessee, now and then there was "trouble between the races." "But," said our representative, "this is attributed to incursions of Ku-Klux coming from Tennessee where, in remote localities, the organization is kept up for political effect, rather than for the bitter strife of former years." But Tennessee herself was at this time comparatively clear of any active operations of the Ku-Klux Klan. From Kentucky, however, a teacher who had a remarkably good school about ten miles from Bowling Green wrote: "The Ku-Klux Klan came one night and told me if I did not break up my school they would kill me." The teacher obeyed. He reported that the white people said that this action by the Ku-Klux was had because "the niggers there were getting too smart."

North Carolina, that had made such good progress in every way under our systematic work, began in some of its counties to be infested during the latter half of 1869. "There was for a time a suspension of schools in a number of districts." Our inspector wrote that it was "owing to the influence of certain lawless bands." Teachers became frightened, and, under the threats of violence printed on placards and put upon doors and fence posts, it was deemed best to obey the dread-inspiring foes that, many or few, were magnified by excited imaginations into multitudes. The marauders went in bands, always masked, usually in small squads, each squad having from five to ten in number. One of our best North Carolina workers near the close of this bitter year, 1869, had in his communication from his district, consisting of Rowan, Iredell, Davie, and Yadkin counties, these sad words: "Our situation is now more painful than it has ever been since we took up this notable cause of the freedmen. I mind my own business as closely as I can, but know no safety of life or property."

South Carolina showed some eruptions of the same nature as late as December 24, 1869. A gentleman of good standing was building a large school structure at Newberry, S. C., for the education of the children of the freed people. He was visited by armed men and driven from the hotel where he was boarding, and a young lady teacher at the same place, sent by the Methodists from Vermont, was subjected to the meanest sort of insults and persecutions.

Georgia, too, in this time of comparative quiet, furnished some instances of the action of the secret bands. In about half of the State "Ku-Klux Klans," armed, disguised, roaming through country districts, committed their atrocious outrages. . . .

PART SEVEN

CARPETBAG RECONSTRUCTION

Edward King, Journalist and Novelist, Views the Honest Carpetbag Regime of Governor Adelbert Ames of Mississippi

Another distinguished New England writer who visited the Radical states was Edward King (1848-1896), a Massachusetts-born member of the editorial staff of the influential and antislavery *Springfield Republican*. His chance to cover the South came in 1874 when he was sent by his friend, the editor of *Scribner's Monthly*, to report upon the effects of the war on the South. Unlike the later observers of the 1870s, he still saw many virtues in the Republican regimes, especially in that of Governor Adelbert Ames of Mississippi, an idealistic New England reformer who had been a military governor of the state and still managed to attract many conservative voters. Ames defeated his "Scalawag" rival for the governership, James L. Alcorn, who would not go as far as Ames in helping the freedman or in pursuing racial equality. (Alcorn was a former slaveholder, a Confederate brigadier general, a Unionist going back to his Kentucky days as a disciple of Henry Clay. Alcorn, instead of following President Johnson's policy when he entered the Mississippi legislature, decided that the strategy of the future lay in adopting the Republican line, cooperating with the Radicals, and in utilizing the Negro vote to win power. Though he did become governor in 1869 and United States Senator shortly thereafter, he was unwilling to enforce social equality or support mixed schools.)

Edward King discovered the Louisiana literary maverick George Washington Cable, who was an outspoken white champion of the Negro against the "perpetual alienation" imposed on the race. Within the next decade, this local-colorist would attract international attention for his sketches of the New Orleans Creoles and octoroons. King had persuaded Cable to publish his stories in *Scribner's*.

King's articles appear in *The Great South* (1875), from which this excerpt is taken, pp. 315-16.

. . . There are some negroes who are exceedingly capable, and none of those immediately attached to the Government at Jackson are incapable. In the Legislature there are now and then negroes who are ignorant; but of late both branches have been freer from this curse than have those of Louisiana or South Carolina.

A visit to the Capitol showed me that the negroes, who form considerably more than half the population of Mississippi, had certainly secured a fair share of the offices. Colored men act as officials or assistants in the offices of the Auditor, the Secretary of State, the Public Library, the Commissioner of Emigration, and the Superintendent of Public Instruction. The Secretary of State, who has some negro blood in his veins, is the natural son of a well-known Mississippian of the old *régime*, formerly engaged in the politics of his State; and the Speaker of the House of Representatives at the last session was a black man. The blacks who went and came from the Governor's office seemed very intelligent, and some of them entered into general conversation in an interesting manner.

The present Governor, ex-United States Senator Adelbert Ames, was four years Military Governor of Mississippi, and knows the temper of both whites and blacks in the State very well. To his military *régime* succeeded the Government of Mr. Alcorn, now United States Senator from Mississippi, and when Mr. Alcorn was sent to the senate, Lieutenant-Governor Powers took his place. Alcorn, returning from the Senate last year, contested the Governor's chair with Ames, but, not succeeding in a re-election, returned to Washington. At the outset of Governor Ames' civil administration, which began recently, he affirmed his determination to redeem the Republican party in that section from the charge of corruption, and the Legislature has taken measures to second his laudable resolve.

Mississippi's State debt is but little—some three millions; she was fortunate enough not to have any credit in the markets of the world when reconstruction began and therefore escaped a good many financial dangers. Her repudiation of her honest indebtedness, years ago, did her infinite harm, and it would be wise to take up that debt, and pay it in future. Part of the money at present owed by the State is due the schools. The State tax is not large; it is the city and county taxation which is oppressive, but that is mainly because of the straitened circumstances of the people.

The vicious system of issuing State warrants has been for some time pursued, but a bill was passed at the last legislative session, funding all these warrants; which had the effect of bringing them up at once from sixty to eighty cents. A new law also requires that all taxes be paid in greenbacks. The State paper has, at times since reconstruction, been sold on the street in Jackson at forty per cent below par. The return to a cash basis will, it is estimated, save twenty-five per cent in the cost of government alone. A general movement in favor of "retrenchment and reform" on the part of the dominant party is manifest, the natural result of which will be the restoration of the State's credit. Governor Ames is firm in his measures, and is not surrounded, to judge from a brief look at them, with men who are inclined to misuse their opportunities.

The State Superintendent of Education informed me that there are about 75,000 children now in attendance upon the State schools, fully 50,000 of whom are colored. He believed that there was at the time of my visit $1,000,000 worth of school property owned in the State, which proved a great advance since the war. In counties mainly Democratic in sentiment, there is formidable opposition to anything like a public school system, but in those where Republican or negro officials dominate, schools are readily kept open and fully attended. The Superintendent said that he had in only one case endeavored to insist upon mixed schools, and that was in a county where the white teachers had refused to teach negro students. He had found it necessary to inform those teachers that, in that case, they must not attempt to keep the black children from the white schools, since he was determined that they should receive instruction.

The school fund is quite large; there are normal schools at Holly Springs and Tougaloo; and the blacks have founded a university named after Ex-Governor and Senator Alcorn. It occupies the site of the old Oakland College near Rodney, on the Mississippi River, and receives an annual appropriation of $50,000.

A successful university has also been in operation in Tougaloo for several years. First-class teachers for the public schools are very much needed. Large numbers of very good private schools are maintained in the State by those citizens who still disbelieve in free public tuition.

The University of Mississippi at Oxford, an old and well managed institution, exclusively patronized by whites, receives, as does Alcorn University, an annual subsidy of $50,000 from the State, and its average attendance is fully equal to that before the war. It has been properly fostered and nourished by the Republican Government, and the motley adventurers in South Carolina might learn a lesson in justice and impartiality from the party in power in Mississippi.

As soon as the funds devoted by the State to educational purposes are paid in greenbacks, or, in other words, when the evil system of "warrants" is thoroughly extinct, Mississippi will make sterling progress in education, and, in proportion, will grow in thrift, wealth and importance.

Jackson has two flourishing newspapers, *The Pilot* being the Republican, and *The Clarion* the Democratic organ. Socially, the town has always been one of high rank in the South, although some of the rougher Mississippian element has at times been manifest in that section. The residence once occupied by Mr. Yerger, who killed the military Mayor of Jackson, shortly after the close of the war, because that Mayor had insisted upon the collection of certain taxes is still pointed out to visitors. There are many charming drives in the town; a little beyond it, the roads are rough and the country is wild. A garrison is maintained at Jackson, and now and then the intervention of United States authority is necessary to quell disturbances in interior districts.

The State has made efforts to secure immigration, but, like many other Southern commonwealths, finds it impossible to compete with the North-west. . . .

Edward Alfred Pollard, Former Proslavery Writer, Praises the Merits of the Freedman

When *Lippincott's Magazine* encouraged Southerners to present their sec-
tion of the country, they invited pieces from two proslavery men of note,
George Fitzhugh, author of *Sociology for the South* (1854), and Edward
Pollard (1831-1872), former editor of the *Richmond Examiner,* with which
Fitzhugh had also been associated. During the war, Pollard had attacked
Jefferson Davis as unfit for office and blamed him for the defeat of the
Confederacy. He also became a foe of the Ku Klux Klan and had written
sympathetically of the Negro in *Black Diamonds Gathered in the Darkey
Homes of the South* (1859). However, he opposed Radical Reconstruction
when he supported Horace Greeley's candidacy for President in 1872. This
article reflects a remarkable pro-Negro position for the South, especially
for a strong proslavery man in former years.

From Edward Pollard, "The Negro in the South," *Lippincott's Magazine* V
(1870), 383-91.

The writer has to confess that he was educated in that common school of opinion in the South that always insisted on regarding the Negro as specifically inferior to the white man—a lower order of human being, who was indebted for what he had of civilization to the tuition of slavery, and who, taken from that tuition, was bound to retrograde and to relapse into barbarism and helplessness. The writer was even advanced in this school. He had been fond of writing his opinions on the subject—that the negro was an inferior species of humanity; that by the employment of his imitative faculties he had obtained his *maximum* of civilization in the condition of slavery; and that to emancipate him would be to put him on the high road to ruin. Educated thus to disesteem the negro, yet always having a compassionate interest in him—admiring in him his extraordinary qualities of humor and tenderness, indulging a number of poetic fancies in him, grown by education and habit sentimental toward him, yet constantly insisting that he was a poor, intellectually helpless creature, who never could get along outside the leading-strings of slavery—the writer was prepared to witness with pity what the whole South arranged itself to see—the misfortune and inevitable decline of the negro from the moment his emancipation was declared.

The South has seen no such thing. Whatever may be the vanity of opinion which compels men to persist in error, or yet more frequently to be silent under conviction, the writer comes sharply before the public with this confession: that his former views of the negro were wrong, that the results of emancipation especially have been the reverse of his expectations—a surprise the force of which he can neither resist nor contain. So keen has been that surprise that from the very intensity of it the writer is moved to communicate it to the public. He feels more like exclaiming, "A discovery! than writing in any more deliberate mood of the proofs he has obtained concerning

the new condition of the negro. It is that this singularly questionable
creature has shown a capacity for education that has astonished none
more than his former masters; that he has given proofs of good citizenship which are constantly increasing; that his development since
emancipation is a standing surprise to candid observers among the
Southern whites themselves; that his condition since then has been on
the whole that of progress, and in the face of difficulties that would
soon have tested and broken down that progress had it been factitious
or dishonest; and that, so far from being a stationary barbarian or a
hopeless retrograde, the formerly despised black man promises to become a true follower of the highest civilization, a new object of interest to the world, and an exemplary citizen of the South.

Every year since the conclusion of the war I have been in different parts of the South; I have conversed with all classes of people
there; I have enjoyed the conditions of a good observer. I have
observed the remarkable good order in civil life which the negro has
maintained since the day he was emancipated; I have seen that he
is sober, law-abiding—that he has gone into his new condition with an
adaptation little less than wonderful; I have witnessed the zeal with
which the black people are availing themselves of the schools and
means of education; I have observed in Southern cities the animated daily routes of their children to the schools; I have noticed
the industry of the negro—its steady, *undeniable* increase in the
South; I have wondered at the remarkable thrift by which he has
obtained from his scanty wages not only a livelihood, but a degree
of comfort and a decency of dress such as he had never known before; I have been pleased to see his manifestations of self-respect,
the pride shown in dress and manners; and, above all, I have
found in him a sense of importance and responsibility conceived
from the idea that he is on trial before the world. The results of
these observations I have put against the weight of a theory that
had formerly persuaded me of the hopeless defect of the negro,
and his worthlessness as a subject for intellectual experiment—the
old ultra slaveholders' theory that negroes without masters are can-

nibals all; and the consequence is simply that I have decided to follow after the evidence of my eyes rather than to pursue farther the ingenuity of speculations.

On the conclusion of the war the emancipation of the negro was regarded by the Southern people as chief among the terrors that were to be inflicted upon them by the loss of struggle. It had been habitually painted as the most dreadful feature in that death's-head of "Subjugation" which for years had been held up in Confederate newspapers to nerve to desperation the arms of the South. The common representation was, that the negro, wild and intoxicated by a change of condition so sudden and vast would be no longer manageable) that he would go through the South murdering and plundering, taking revenge on his former taskmasters; or that, less violent, he would die and rot in the byways, a nuisance and an eyesore, until his own vices had consumed him, or until the animosity of race had expunged him from the face of the earth. How have all these raw-head-and-bloody-bones stories now disappeared, even from the imagination of the South! The negro has been seen to accept his great, and sudden gift of liberty with a sobriety and a moderation that history will be surprised to record, since it is without example, so far as I know, of a people thus surprised by a change of condition as radical as can be possibly imagined, whose fortune did not hurry them into some excesses. What of promise there was in the negro was immediately shown when he accepted without violence, and even without vanity, the gift of his freedom; going into his new place with a facility of adaptation at which we have not yet ceased to wonder, taking up with quiet thankfulness his new career; and even so little disturbed by the conceit of his new condition that to-day it is the common testimony in the South that the white people suffer no more from the insolence of the blacks than they did in the days of slavery. History owes here an extraordinary tribute to the negro for his conduct on an occasion so trying. He has accepted his liberty with a self-possession, a decorum and a facility that some of the most cultivated and polite nations might envy in an emergency where such good fortune had beeen imposed upon them. The promise which he has given in conduct so wise and moderate I believe he is now fulfilling by his steady improvement in his new condition; and that, too, in the face of difficulties which have put his capacities of developing himself to the severest test. In short, the negro in the South is fulfilling the expectations of his friends; surprising those who, wishing him well, had yet pitifully distrusted him in his new career; and giving the very best answers to his detractors in those quiet proofs of progress which make but little noise of self-assertion, but against which no misrepresentation, no matter how violent and persistent, can long prevail.

There are some large, appreciable facts in the condition of the negro in the South which go to check the too common habit of the newspapers to make unproved, reckless assertions concerning him. They afford some light on a subject which covers an extensive ground, which has but few statistical guides, and on which a speculative class of writers, taking advantage of the supposed absence of any facts capable of proof, have imagined that they might impose almost anything upon the credulity of the public. Thus I have been repeatedly told in a loose way that the negro in the South will not work, that he is hopelessly lazy, that his idea of freedom is to live without labor, etc. This is a common charge against the negro: it is easily made in general terms, but happily the assertion may be brought under the dominion of some general facts which go to test its truth, and to show that prejudice and exaggeration have dictated this reproach.

There is some flippancy about this reproach which has at last become tiresome. Nor are the sources from which it commonly comes very highly recommended to us for the qualities of censorship. There are, I regret yet dare to say, many thousands of lazy white persons in the South, loafing on street corners and drinking whisky, perpetually talking of "enterprise" coming down South—as if said enterprise was something to be brought to them in a box and opened in their midst—the day Virginia is admitted into the Union, or some other event happens, who are exceedingly ready and apt to declaim on the laziness of the "cussed niggers." Now I do not believe that the negro is, or ever will be a model of industry. His temperament is tropical. But I do say that, notwithstanding his disadvantages (and they are many) the negro has shown since his emancipation an industry that is extraordinary; that is constantly, daily increasing, both in volume and discipline, that has supplied him with comforts that he never knew before; that has enabled him to build churches and to found charitable institutions of his own; that has kept him better clothed than he was in his former condition; and that exhibits its results to-day in the vast bulk of the agricultural products of the South.

There are two facts which furnish a curious commentary on the reproach that the negro is deficient in industry, or that he has declined in this respect since his release from his former condition:

1. How can we account for the fact that there has been no considerable falling off in the volume of production in the South—on the contrary, an increase under many heads—on the supposition that the negro has decreased in industry?—for it must be admitted that accessions of labor in the South from abroad that is, other than the negro—have been wholly inconsiderable. Again, another common detraction of the negro (and one made curiously enough, by the very same writers who have reproached him for indolence) is, that he is dying out, that his numbers have been fearfully diminished by mortality incident to his emancipation; and so these theorists, anxious to degrade the negro on every possible plea, are plunged into the inconsistency that, if his race is really the victim of such fearful mortality, then the industry which it has shown in yet keeping up the average of Southern production is one that deserves wonderful acknowledgment and praise. The fact is, both of these hypotheses—that of the decline of the negro in industry and that of his disappearance through death and disease—are false and an example of those inconsistencies and absurdities into which men fall who are anxious, from incomplete observation or from the haste of prejudice, to construct theories, without attention to the great facts which underlie the details and limit the area of speculation.

2. The second significant fact which I wish to bring before the reader is the appearance, for the first time in the history of the Southern negro, of a considerable migratory movement. Within recent months there has been a movement of the negroes, by tens of

thousands from Virginia to other fields of labor, and the indications are of a column of emigration from the lands where the cereals are cultivated, and where wages are low, pushed down into the "black belt" extending from the Sea Islands of South Carolina to the trans-Mississippi borders of Louisiana. The movement is one of vast economical importance and does not appear yet to have drawn sufficent attention from what few thoughtful men remain among the legislators and publicists of Virginia. But I propose to regard it here only in the single aspect of a striking, vivid proof of the negro's desire for work, which has enabled him to overcome what is notoriously the strongest characteristic of his race—an attachment to local associations; and as an indication also of a moral enterprise wholly inconsistent with the theory of his tendency to barbarism. We may, at least, see now that the negro is not content to starve or to rot wherever fortune has placed him: emigration such as he has undertaken is an incident of civilization: it has required calculation and a strength of purpose which barbarians could scarcely be expected to have, for twenty thousand Virginia negroes to leave their scanty and narrow homes, going out not as mere adventurers and vagabonds, but as cheerful and organized bands of laborers.

The difficulty, as I have observed it in the South, is not so much that the negroes will not work, as that they are not very ready or very cheerful to work where they think their wages either insufficient or precarious. And it must be admitted that there are some grounds of complaint in this respect. The wages of farm-hands in Virginia are eight to ten dollars a month, and out of this the laborer has to provide clothing for himself, pay doctors' bills and support all the non-producing members of the family, paying house-rent for them as they are but seldom allowed to reside on the farm where he is employed. This is a hard life, and not calculated to impart much cheerfulness to the laborer—to make him quite as *glad* to work as some of his philosophic censors would have him to appear. How the negro nerves himself to such ill-paid labor, how he works so generally under conditions so hard, is rather the wonder; and I must confess to admiration of the resolute industry which thus makes the best of the situation, and does whatever the hands find to do. The results which he achieves out of these scanty wages are yet more wonderful, and indicate a careful and exacting economy which those who have been fond of thinking the black man improvident and careless of his money will find it very difficult to explain. In the town of Lynchburg, Virginia, the negroes have built out of contributions among themselves a Methodist church which cost thirteen thousand dollars. The writer was present when their house of worship was dedicated: there was a congregation of about two thousand colored people, and it was inexpressibly touching to notice what neatness of attire they had all struggled to attain and what a fine, hopeful appearance they presented—not even one of the little children of the Sunday-school (who by the way, sung from their printed hymn-books) putting in a draggled appearance. Where do they get their clothes from? In the days of slavery, it is well known by those who have visited the plantations, negroes were frequently found (and sometimes in circumstances of embarrassment when ladies were present) who were not presentable on account of the imperfect cover of their nakedness: there might have been a shirt wanting, or there might have been *only* a shirt, or there might have been indecent glimpses through the rents. Now, every one who has lately traveled in the South will testify that instances are very rare where a negro makes any indecent exhibition from imperfect clothing; and this improvement in dress will especially strike one familiar with the former rags of slavery. This may be a small circumstance in itself, but it is a large one when we measure it against the means of the negro laborer; and it is eloquent alike of the economy and thrift which enable him, and the self-respect which prompts him, to make such an appearance in the world. . . .

Robert Somers, Scottish Journalist Takes an Optimistic View of Sharecropping in Tennessee

A rather fresh note in the interpretation of the postwar South was struck by the eminent editor of Glasgow's *North British Daily Mail* and also the *Morning Journal,* Robert Somers (1822-1891). He had long investigated social, economic, and political questions at first hand in Britain and published his studies of the Scottish poor laws, monetary questions, commerce, education, and labor. As a versatile journalist and writer, he was later to publish a historical romance, *The Martyr of Glencree.*

He spent six months in the South investigating the effect of wartime changes on economic conditions. His observations given here of the allegedly pleasant effects of sharecropping upon the freedman have also been made by other contemporaries for this period.

From Somers' interesting book, which has come to be regarded as authoritative, *The Southern States of America* (London and New York, 1871), pages 126-29.

TENNESSEE SHARECROPPERS

Jones is one of the greatest founders of towns in America. The present borough of Jones must be the tenth or eleventh of the same name that have already passed under my observation without provoking a remark; but having wandered here more than once in quest of the postmaster, I may as well, were it only in respect to Jones, make a note of it.

Jonesboro' consists of ten houses, two of which—neat little frame stores—are in course of erection, and cause the people in the neighborhood to say, when they meet to tell and hear the news, that Jonesboro' is building up rapidly. The ten houses are so arranged as to form a large square, of which the track and depôt of the Memphis and Charleston Railroad is one of the sides, with wings of streets from the corners to the right and left. The ten houses of Jonesboro' are disposed, as may be judged, with considerable effect. There are merchants in Jonesboro'—grocery, hardware, and dry goods—and one always finds half a dozen well-bred horses hitched in the square, and twice as many mules, saddled or waggoned, and either way, having the art of standing still without the hitching process which, despite its "cruelty to animals," appears to be one of the institutions of the United States. Bullock teams crawl about with cotton or timber to the depôt; strong mounted men come and go, calling for the postmaster, with an air as if it were of little or no consequence whether they found him or not; and negroes are always dropping in on mules or afoot with little bags full of something, which they carry into the stores, and carry out again mostly empty. There are rich plantations round Jonesboro', but close on the other side of the railway track there are three or four thousand acres of as good and pretty land as one could wish to see, from which every vestige of fence and housing was stripped during the war, and all trace of cultivation has now disappeared; and how the taxes on it are paid no one seems to know or care.

But a great uproar arises in one of the ten houses which on being looked at, differs from all the rest, and has the appearance simply of an elongated caravan, raised on little pedestals of red brick that might be mistaken for wheels. The riot in the caravan at length bursts out through one of the ends in a rabble of men—backways, sideways, foreways, and on all fours pell-mell—yelling and whooping, throwing off their coats, squaring and drawing pistols at each other, and in a very high state of animal excitement. The scene was rather alarming; but I was assured by an "intelligent negro" that it was only a little bad whisky, the gas of which in the head must get off in this way every now and then, and that no harm would arise. Nor did there; for, though some shots were fired, nobody was killed or wounded, and in a few minutes afterwards the combatants were embracing one another in the most tender and affectionate manner possible, and in a minute or two more had all, greatly sobered and relieved, slouched back into the caravan. The bacchanalians were white men, of the class of "croppers," who had been trying their luck during the year in a crop of cotton on the waste and semi-ruined plantations about, and were taking the fall out of it in this fashion.

The planters who come to Jonesboro', though not in the most cheery mood just now, are men who take a philosophical and busi-ness-like view of their affairs and of the whole situation of the South. The fall of cotton does not profoundly disconcert them, for the rapidly enlarging crop had prepared them for a descending scale of prices, and the war in Europe is referred to as accounting in some measure for the depth and suddenness of the present decline. There is an opinion in the Northern States that the Southern cotton-growers are an inert, unskilful race. There could hardly be a greater mistake; and the idea that cotton can be grown, and the resources of the soil developed, more successfully than by the men who have been studying and practising these matters all their days, must be discarded as a vain hallucination. One requires only to meet the cotton-planters of the South, and to note the energy with which they act, and the care and diligence they apply to their affairs, to feel that strangers coming in to farm, welcomed as they would be, must be largely indebted to the knowledge and experience of the residents long engaged in the agricultural pursuits of the country. The emancipation of the slaves is accepted with remarkable equanimity when one considers the overturn of personal fortune and all the bitterness of the war with which it was associated; and an expression of gladness to have now done with slavery and to have touched some common ground of civilization, is often heard. But what the planters are disposed to complain of is that, while they have lost their slaves, they have not got free labourers in any sense common either in the Northern States or in Europe; and looking round here at Jonesboro', after a calm and wide survey, one cannot but think that the New England manufacturer and the Old England farmer must be equally astonished at a recital of the relations of land, capital and labour as they exist on the cotton plantations of the Southern States. The wages of the negroes, if such a term can be applied to a mode of remuneration so unusual and anomalous, consist, as I have often indicated, of one-half the crop of corn and cotton, the only crops in reality produced. This system of share and share alike betwixt the planter and the negro I have found to prevail so generally that any other form of contract is but the exception. The negro, on the semi-communistic basis thus established, finds his own rations; but as these are supplied to him by the planter, or by the planter's notes of credit on the merchants in Jonesboro', and as much more sometimes as he thinks he needs by the merchants on his own credit, from the 1st of January onward through the year, in anticipation of crops which are not marketable till the end of December, he can lose nothing by the failure or deficient outcome of the crops, and is always sure of his subsistence. As a permanent economic relation this would be startling anywhere betwixt any classes of men brought together in the business of life. Applied to agriculture in any other part of the world, it would be deemed outrageously absurd. But this is only a part of the "privileges" (a much more accurate term than "wages") of the negro field hand. In addition to half of the crops, he has a free cottage of the kind he seems to like, and the windows of which he or his wife persistently nail up; he has abundance of wood from the planter's estate for fuel and for building his corn cribs and other outhouses, with teams to draw it from the forest; he is allowed to keep hogs, and milch cows, and young cattle, which roam and feed with the same right of pasture as the hogs and cattle of the planter, free of all charge; he has the same right of hunting and shooting, with quite as many facilities for exercising the right as anybody else—and he has his dogs and guns, though, as far as I have discovered, he provides himself with these by purchase or some other form of conquest. Though entitled to one-half the crops, yet he is not required to contribute any portion of the seed, nor is he called upon to pay any part of the taxes on the plantation. The only direct tax on the negro is a poll-tax, which is wholly set apart for the education of his children, and which I find to be everywhere in arrear, and in some places in a hopeless chaos of non-payment. Yet, while thus freed from the burden of taxation, the negro has, up to this period of "reconstruction" enjoyed a monopoly of representation, and has had all legislative and executive power moulded to his will by Governors, Senators, and Deputies, who have either been his tools, or of whom he himself has been the dupe. For five years past, the negroes have been King, Lords, and Commons, and something more, in the Southern States.

But, to come back to the economic condition of the plantations, the negro field-hand, with his right of half-crop privileges as described, who works with ordinary diligence, looking only to his own pocket, and gets his crops forward and gathered in due time, is at liberty to go to other plantations to pick cotton, in doing which he may make from two to two and a half dollars a day. For every piece of work outside the crop he does even on his own plantation he must be paid a dollar a day. It may be clearing ditches, or splitting rails or anything that is just as essential to the crops as the two-inch ploughing and hoeing in which he shambles away his time, but for all this kind of work he must be paid a dollar a day. While the landowner is busy keeping accounts betwixt himself and his negro hands, ginning their cotton for them, doing all the marketing of produce and supplies of which they have the lion's share, and has hardly a day he can call his own, the "hands" may be earning a dollar a day from him for work which is quite as much theirs as his.

Yet the negroes, with all their superabounding privilege on the cotton field, make little of it. A ploughman or a herd in the old country would not exchange his lot for theirs, as it stands and as it appears in all external circumstances. They are almost all in debt; few are able at the end of the year to square accounts with "the merchant"; and it is rarely the planter can point with pride, and with the conscious joy of recording his own profit, to a freedman who, as the result of the year's toil, will have a hundred or two dollars to the good. The soul is often crushed out of labour by penury and oppression. Here a soul cannot begin to be infused into it through the sheer excess of privilege and licence with which it is surrounded.

Edwin De Leon Takes an Optimistic View of the Southern Mills and Cheap Labor in the New South

Edwin De Leon was one among many observers of the South who wrote for *Harper's Magazine*. Unlike other critics, he took a rather favorable view of the hiring of women and children in the cotton mills and the paternalistic labor system used for white workers. As the selection indicates, the Southern industrialist was rightly optimistic in his expectations for local industry based on cheap labor and lower transportation costs due to the accessibility of cotton supplies. Within a generation, the Southern cotton mill was to outstrip that of New England in total output.

From Edwin De Leon, "The New South," *Harper's Magazine* XLVIII (1873-1874), pp. 406-22.

. . . Even from Louisiana comes a confirmation of the statements already given as to the greater cheapness of labor South. One of the leading stockholders of the Louisiana Manufacturing Company having visited, in the interest of his company, the prominent factories of the North this summer, thus testifies:

"The particular class of labor required by cotton factories is *cheaper here* than in any of the manufacturing districts of the North. This I know from actual personal investigation. Mr. Meigs, our superintendent, a Northern man, uses this language in his report of the condition of the mill 31st January, 1872. After recommending the erection of dwellings contiguous to the mills for the workmen, he says: 'From my experience, I believe that the proposed dwellings can rapidly be filled with a most desirable class of employees, whose *unusual adaptation* to the manufacturing life my three months' experience here has confirmed me in affirming. They are intelligent, apt to learn, polite, active, cheerful, and willing to an unusual degree. Applicants for employment are increasing. If you can give us houses for these applicants, you will very soon have as desirable a class of operatives as can be found *on this* or on the *other side of the Atlantic.*' " This is a Northern expert's opinion.

Another report says : "In respect to labor, we can get large numbers of boys and girls from the orphan asylums and charitable institutions in the cities. There is no demand for that class of labor, consequently it is cheap. Lane's Mill, in New Orleans, has but twenty-five looms, yet has proved very profitable. The class of osnaburgs it turns out are in great local demand, and sold at the highest rates, equal to the Northern prices for a similar article."

To a direct question asked this Louisiana manufacturer the following explicit and interesting answer was given: "I have a statement of a Georgia mill showing a clear annual profit of twenty-five per cent. Why, when you reflect on the advantages we possess over the people of the North, is it not astonishing that Southern men can be found stupid enough to talk about the South being unable to compete with the North in manufacturing cotton goods, and newspapers silly or wicked enough to propagate such absurd fallacies?"

Question. "Then your great experience and long study of the subject convince you that the South should turn her attention to manufacturing?"

Answer. "If we desire to renew our progress to wealth and power, we must resort to other agencies of production, and not limit our industry and enterprise to one single interest. We have regained our ascendancy in the cultivation of superior cotton; but we never can regain that of which we so long boasted—the monopoly of its production. Every fact in my experience teaches me that we must look to manufactures as one of the great agencies for the acquisition of wealth. That the South ought to be, and must be, a manufacturing region is the natural conclusion that I draw from a knowledge of its actual resources and superior advantages for that form of productive labor."

These are weighty words and wise ones, and the experience of every man who has looked into the development of this new labor at the South confirms the correctness of the conclusions arrived at, and put with equal precision and force. The "Bourbons," as he terms them, at the South are by no means confined to the political class, of which there are rare fossil specimens, but are also to be freely found in the fields as well as in the cities and towns.

Question. "Can we successfully compete with Northern manufactories?"

Answer. "Haven't I just told you that the osnaburgs made in the Lane Mill command the same prices as those made at the North, and are bought in preference, as being of better make? Why shouldn't we be able successfully to compete with them? We can buy cotton here at *two cents* a pound *less* than they can. Our mill uses the loose cotton purchased from the presses at two cents less per pound than the cost of the cotton bought for Northern consumption. The supply of this is always equal to the demand, for the presses last year turned out 20,000 bales. We can buy Pittsburg coal, delivered on the river's bank, in front of our factory, at less than the cost of anthracite to Northern mills. Add to these our immunity from the heavy freight and insurance charges paid to get the goods to market, as well as to secure the raw material, and the demonstration is clear why the North will not be able to compete with us. During the war New Jersey became famous for its manufactories. To-day the mill of Mr. Nicodemus *is the only one* in operation there. Now what is the cause of this? Our Bourbon friends will hardly credit the statement, but they were *forced to close their doors by the success of the Georgia mills;* and to-day many of the original proprietors of the Northern mills may be found successfully conducting, or interested in, similar establishments in Georgia. They told me last summer that they could run a mill in the South at twenty per cent less cost than in New Jersey. We have also an immense advantage in fuel."

With reference to the general appearance of these factory hands, personal observation convinces me that the popular prejudice as to the unhealthiness of this kind of labor, under proper restrictions and with proper surroundings, is erroneous. The women and boys, though certainly not as florid and fresh-looking as the lads and lasses who spend all their time in the open air, or pursue that healthiest of all avocations, the pastoral or agricultural life, look strong and healthy, and are quite jolly when they leave the mill at six o'clock in the afternoon. Their hours of work are usually from 7 A.M. to 6 P.M., with an interval at mid-day of half an hour for dinner. Attached to some of the mills are residences for the operatives, but in the majority of instances they board themselves, thus avoiding some of the supposed demoralizing efforts of colonization. Thus far it is certain that no moral miasma has been generated in the South by the introduction of this species of labor. The additional comforts provided for the family by the utilization of the formerly idle hands of the women and children can be readily appreciated. Nor is the education of the latter neglected, as night schools supply the loss of daily tuition; and their labor is so light in the factories as not to incapacitate them from attending night school, when sufficiently ambitious to aspire to improvement. The rate of wages, though less than the Northern, in consequence of superior cheapness of living South, is more remunerative. Women can earn an average of thirty dollars per month, and children about half as much, which is more than sufficient for a support. For experts higher wages are given, these being the rates for unskilled labor. The Southern factories are built with a view to hygiene, are well ventilated, clean, and with plenty of light, and, under good management, have no causes at work apparently to injure health. The confinement and fatigue are by no means greater than, or even equal to, those to be encountered in the usual employments of people compelled to earn their daily bread by the daily labor of their hands. The avoidance of intermixture of the two sexes in the factories obviates the chances of immorality. Upon the whole the system works well in the South thus far, and seems to give general satisfaction.

What a Northern manufacturing town can do for its population, the typical New York town of Cohoes, on the Hudson, will show. It is a manufacturing place altogether. Its 20,000 inhabitants live on or off the manufacturing establishments that make it up. The Harmony (cotton) Mills pay out in monthly wages $80,000, the knitting-mills (woolen), $69,000: iron manufactories, $37,000; pin, bobbin, cement, and furniture factories swelling the aggregate of monthly wages to $200,000. Of its inhabitants fully 15,000 are employed in the various manufacturing establishments alluded to, and about three-fifths of this number are women and children. There are 5000 operatives in the Harmony Mills alone, owned by William Garner, of New York, and two others, who have a smaller interest, and live there. Even more than Lowell is this a model manufacturing town, and the South might have some like it.

Next in importance is the lumber business, which, as before stated, is being rapidly transferred to the South—the pine region of Georgia, Alabama, Mississippi, and Florida furnishing immense supplies for a universal and increasing want. Years ago the hardy Maine lumbermen were in the habit of making annual winter raids on the Southern Atlantic coast in Georgia, penetrating sometimes into the interior; but since the war Northern energy and capital have poured into Alabama and Florida, and great mills with all the modern improved machinery have been erected, and the somewhat harsh music of the saw now sends it echoes through the sylvan solitudes which but recently resounded only to the cries of wild beasts. Florida has become one of the great centres of this new development, and both in her eastern portion, bordering on the Atlantic, and in her western, on the Gulf, sends forth annually immense quantities of hewn and sawed timber to the North and to Europe. A brief statement of what is doing at one point only in the vicinity of Pensacola and Perdido Bay, and on the Black Water River, in the same neighborhood, will give a faint idea of the rapid growth and great proportions this industry is attaining.

During the war the few saw-mills in this neighborhood were either burned down or the owners so impoverished as to be unable to work them. The city of Pensacola was itself deserted, after having been partially burned down. Its inhabitants fled away to Alabama, where they settled, and the place was absolutely deserted: so much so that the weeds grew up densely in the streets, and became the haunts of the foxes and the wild turkeys. This state of things continued for two years after the war. Then the scattered fugitives began to return, bringing back new recruits with them, and strove manfully to recuperate their shattered fortunes Some of the more energetic among them turned their attention to the saw-mills and the lumber trade; and commencing on the Black Water, in a small way at first, soon accumulated sufficient profits to expand their business and enlarge the limits of their operations. Mr. Simpson, of Pensacola, was one of the most energetic and successful of these pioneers, and still controls and owns the largest of the Bagdad Mills, on the Black Water. He is now a rich man, and in his neighborhood are three new mills, all, like his own, built or rebuilt since the war. There are also other mills on the Escambia, as well as a very fine one (the Molino) midway between Pensacola and Montgomery, Alabama. . . .

William H. Gray, Arkansas Negro Politician, Argues for Negro Suffrage as a Guarantee Against Injustice

Here is a view of a Negro political convention in Arkansas which reflects the intelligent, articulate William H. Gray as a spokesman for his race and a realistic analyst of the importance of Negro suffrage in protecting his people.

From "Arkansas," *The American Annual Cyclopedia: 1868,* p. 34.

. . . William H. Gray, a negro, and delegate to the convention from Phillips County, rose and spoke as follows:

"It appears to me, the gentleman has read the history of this country to little purpose. When the Constitution was framed, in every State but South Carolina free negroes were allowed to vote. Under British rule this class was free, and he interpreted that 'we the people' in the preamble to the Constitution, meant all the people of every color. The mistake of that period was that these free negroes were not represented *in propria persona* in that constitutional convention, but by the Anglo-Saxon. Congress is now correcting that mistake. The right of franchise is due the negroes, bought by the blood of forty thousand of their race shed in three wars. The troubles now on the country are the result of the bad exercise of the elective franchise by unintelligent whites, the 'poor whites' of the South. I could duplicate every negro who cannot read and write, whose name is on the list of registered voters, with a white man equally ignorant. The gentleman can claim to be a friend of the negro, but I do not desire to be looked upon in the light of a client. The Government has made a solemn convenant with the negro to vest him with the right of franchise if he would throw his weight in the balance in favor of the Union and bare his breast to the storm of bullets; and I am convinced that it would not go back on itself. There are thirty-two million whites to four million blacks in the country, and there need be no fear of negro domination. The State laws do not protect the negro in his rights, as they forbade their entrance into the State. [Action of loyal convention of '64.] I am not willing to trust the rights of my people with the white men, as they have not preserved those of their own race, in neglecting to provide them with the means of education. The Declaration of Independence declared all men born free and equal, and I demand the enforcement of that guarantee made to my forefathers, to every one of each race, who had fought for it. The constitution which this ordinance would reënact is not satisfactory, as it is blurred all over with the word 'white.' Under it one hundred and eleven thousand beings who live in the State have no rights which white men are bound to respect. My people might be ignorant, but I believe, with Jefferson, that ignorance is no measure of a man's rights. Slavery has been abolished, but it left my people in a condition of peonage or caste worse than slavery, which had its humane masters. White people should look to their own ancestry; they should recollect that women were disposed of on James River, in the early settlement of the country, as wives, at the price of two hundred pounds of tobacco. When we have had eight hundred years as the whites to enlighten ourselves, it will be time enough to pronounce us incapable of civilization and enlightenment. The last election showed that we were intelligent enough to vote in a solid mass with the party that would give us our rights, and that too in the face of the influence of the intelligence and wealth of the State, and in face of threats to take the bread from our very mouths. I have no antipathy toward the whites; I would drop the curtain of oblivion on the sod which contains the bones of my oppressed and wronged ancestors for two hundred and fifty years. Give us the franchise, and if we do not exercise it properly you have the numbers to take it away from us. It would be impossible for the negro to get justice in a State whereof he was not a full citizen. The prejudices of the entire court would be against him. I do not expect the negro to take possession of the government; I want the franchise given him as an incentive to work to educate his children. I do not desire to discuss the question of the inferiority of races. Unpleasant truths must then be told; history tells us of your white ancestors who lived on the acorns which dropped from the oaks of Dodona, and then worshipped the tree as a God. I call upon all men who would see justice done, to meet this question fairly, and fear not to record their votes."

In the session of January 29th, he said: "Negroes vote in Ohio and Massachusetts, and in the latter State are elected to high office by rich white men." He had found more prejudice against his race among the Yankees; and if they did him a kind act, they did not seem to do it with the generous spirit of Southern men. He could get nearer the latter: he had been raised with them. He was the sorrier on this account that they had refused him the rights which would make him a man, as the former were willing to do. He wanted this a white man's government, and wanted them to do the legislating as they had the intelligence and wealth; but he wanted the power to protect himself against unfriendly legislation. Justice should be like the Egyptian statue, blind and recognizing no color. . . .

W. W. D. Turner, Alabama Negro Politician, Defends the Importance of the Negro Vote and the Radical Policy

At the 1867 Alabama Convention of freedmen, W. W. D. Turner showed why the Negro had only the alternative of supporting Radical policies, but was willing to consider any reasonable offer made by the Southern conservatives. The exchange over racial reconciliation is interesting, although readers may question the historicity and realism of the arguments given by the Confederate officer.

From "Alabama," *The American Annual Cyclopedia: 1872*, pp. 18-20.

. . . Public meetings now began to be held by the freedmen to appoint delegates to a State convention at Mobile on May 1st. At Opelika a body of some three hundred assembled from the adjacent country to take into consideration the propriety of sending delegates to the convention. At their invitation, Colonel Swearingen made an address explaining to them fully their new relations toward the white inhabitants. He said their interests were identical, and they should be united in a common effort to promote the welfare and prosperity of the State. Upon its political and social prosperity depended the welfare of the freedmen. Several freedmen subsequently spoke, one of whom told those present that they were yet in their infancy so far as freedom was concerned. As they were ignorant of the real object of the convention at Mobile, it behooved them to be cautious what steps were taken toward sending delegates. They had much to learn yet, and were liable to be misled by evil and designing men.

In other towns freedmen's meetings were also held, but the numbers in attendance were generally small. In Mobile, on April 17th, in the evening, a meeting of the freedmen was held. The chairman, W. W. D. Turner, on taking his seat, addressed the meeting. The substance of his remarks was of a general nature:

That it would seem as if they were in an auction establishment; they were up to be knocked down to the highest bidder; they knew their rights, and would call upon the law to defend them in the exercise of those rights; they supported and were a portion of the Republican Radical party, and if the Southern party that would meet on Friday night would offer them better terms than the former they would go and join it. The speaker then alluded to the late case respecting the colored people riding in the cars, and claimed that it was their inalienable and undeniable right to ride in those cars under the law of the land. It was a contest between the prejudices of the people and the Civil Rights Bill, and the latter must overcome the former.

The colored people claimed to have a knowledge of their rights as citizens; they were fools as scholars, but they had been well instructed in their rights. They meant, not only to enjoy the privileges of the ballot-box, but claimed also the right to sit in the jury box when the lives or liberties of their mothers, daughters, wives, and sisters were at stake. Although the colored people were no scholars, they were not going to send any fools to represent them—either at Montgomery or in Congress. Three-fourths of the white men of Alabama were very ignorant. At the salt-works, at which he was employed as a slave during the war, there were three white men, not one of whom could read or write his own name, and he, a slave, had to do all the work for them, and had to read and answer all the letters that his master would send from England to his overseer. The reason he mentioned this was because he wished to show that the mass of ignorant white men who had voted heretofore have not sent ignorant numskulls to Congress, and neither would the colored people.

They had not the educated men among themselves to send, but they would send representatives from among their white friends who were to be depended upon, and who had the ability and the will to look after their interests, and in the mean time they would educate their own people up to the proper point.

A prominent government official had told him that the negroes did not owe their enfranchisement to Abraham Lincoln; that they did not owe it to Congress or to the Northern abolitionists, but that they owed it to the fact that it was inflicted as a punishment on the people of the South for its rebellion. This same official had asked for the negro vote on the ground of being an old soldier. Now, he would say to this official that if the negro was not indebted to Congress, the abolitionists, or Abraham Lincoln, neither were they indebted to the old soldier, and they could not vote for him, as he was one of those who held that enfranchisement was one of the worst things that ever happened to the negro race and to the South; some people held that they were little better than monkeys; now, whether they were monkeys or men, they knew who their friends were, and they would never elevate to power their enemies—the men who held their enfranchisement to be a mistake.

The resolutions adopted by the meeting were as follows:

Whereas, In the present disorganized condition of the Southern States, and more especially of the State of Alabama, it behooves every citizen who loves liberty, law and order, and peace, and tranquillity of society, to interest himself and to use his every effort to the accomplishment of the work of reorganization: Therefore,

1. *Be it resolved by the Union men of Mobile in mass meeting assembled,* That our everlasting thanks are due the Thirty-ninth Congress of the United States for its untiring efforts in the passage of such reconstruction measures as it has in its wisdom seen proper to enact.

2. *Resolved,* That as Republican Union men we will maintain the principles of the great Republican party in the support of the best interests of the common country, and to the end that peace, harmony, and prosperity may again be fully restored to the nation.

3. *Resolved,* That in Generals Pope and Swayne we have the utmost confidence, and that we fully indorse their action thus far in the work of reconstruction, and hopefully trust that the result of their labor in the great and arduous duties imposed on them as military rulers over the people will result in a satisfactory success.

4. *Resolved,* That we believe that the present condition of the country requires that every Union man should ally himself to the great Republican party; that it having been chief in the salvation of the country, we may properly look to it for the country's protection.

5. *Resolved,* That we recognize no distinctions, either political or civil, existing either in law or fact, made or to be made on account of race, color, or previous condition, including the rights of suffrage, holding any office within the gift of the people and of sitting in the jury-box.

So much disturbance grew out of the attempt of the colored people at this time to ride in the street railroad cars, that the municipal authorities of Mobile called the attention of the commandant of the Freedmen's Bureau to the dispute. In advance of any decision of the question by competent legal or military authority, and in the absence of instructions, he advised the freedmen to abstain from any action tending to produce riot or commotion dangerous to the peace or security of the city; he advised them to seek legal redress whenever prevented from riding. Suits were subsequently commenced against the president of the railroad company in the Federal Commissioners' Court, which required him to appear before the United States Circuit Court. . . .

The only colored speaker on the occasion said:

FELLOW-CITIZENS: I feel my incapacity to-night to speak, after hearing the eloquence of those preceding me. I received an invitation from the white citizens of Mobile to speak for the purpose of reconciling our races—the black to the white—to extend the hand of fellowship. You have heard the resolutions. You are with us, and I believe are sincere in what they promise. It is my duty to accept the offer of reconstruction when it is extended in behalf of peace to our common country. Let us remove the past from our bosoms, and reconcile ourselves and positions together. I am certain that my race cannot be satisfied unless granted all the rights allowed by the law and by that flag. The resolutions read to you to-night guarantee every thing. Can you expect any more? If you do, I would like to know where you are going to get it. I am delighted in placing myself upon this platform, and in doing this I am doing my duty to my God and my country. We want to do what is right. We believe white men will also do what is right.

The next speaker was a late Confederate officer during the war. He said:

It is the first time for seven long years that we sit—and at first we sat with diffidence—under the "old flag," and I cannot deny that my feelings are rather of a strange nature. Looking back to the past, I remembered the day (the 10th day of January, 1861) when I hauled down that flag from its proud staff in Fort St. Philip, and thought then that another flag would soon spread its ample folds over the Southern soil.

But that flag is no more. It has gone down in a cloud of glory—no more to float even over the deserted graves of our departed heroes—one more of the bright constellations in the broad canopy of that firmament where great warriors are made demigods.

But I did not come here to-night to tell you, men of Alabama, that my heart was with you—for you well know that as far as that heart can go, it never will cease beating for what is held dear and sacred to you. But I came here to speak to those of our new fellow-citizens, who are now seeking the light of truth.

It is said that two races now stand in open antagonism to each other—that the colored man is the natural enemy of the white man, and, hereafter, no communion of interests, feelings, and past associations, can fill the gulf which divides them.

But who is it that says so? Is it the Federal soldier who fought for the freedom of that race? Is it even the political leader whose eloquence stirred up the North and West to the rescue of that race? No; it is none of these. It is not even the intelligent and educated men of that class, for I now stand on the very spot where one of them, Mr.

Trenier, disclaimed those disorganizing principles, and eloquently vindicated the cause of truth and reason.

Why, then, should there be any strife between us? Why should not our gods be their gods—our happiness be their happiness? Has any thing happened which should break up concert of action, harmony, and concord in the great—the main objects of life—the pursuit of happiness?

Where can that happiness spring from? Is it from the midst of a community divided against itself, or from one blessed with peace and harmony?

In what particular have our relations changed? In what case have our interests in the general welfare been divided? Is not to-day the colored man as essential to our prosperity as he was before?

Is not our soil calling for the energetic efforts of his sinewy arms? Can we, in fact, live without him? But while we want his labor he wants our lands, our capital, our industry, our influence in the commerce and finances of the world.

And if, coming down from those higher functions in society, we descend to our domestic relations, where do we find that those relations are changed?

Does not the intelligent freedman know that neither he nor we are accountable to God for the condition in which we were respectively born?

Does he not know that, for generations past, the institution of slavery had been forced upon us by the avarice, the love of power of the North? Does he not know that to-day we have in him the same implicit faith and reliance we had before?

Louisiana's State Superintendent of Schools Attributes Current School Problems Partly to the Hostility of Whites to Mixed Schools

This brief extract from the Louisiana School Superintendent's report for 1872 during the period of Radical rule suggests the conflicts that arose over mixed schools. In 1874 a New Orleans mob attacked a mixed high school and drove out Negroes and even those suspected of having any Negro blood. Awakened to a sense of guilt over Southern race relations, George Washington Cable, a Confederate veteran and the future distinguished short-story writer, protested to two New Orleans newspapers in September 1875: "Parents who have had their children nourished by Negro nurses cannot logically object to those being taught by a polite and competent mulatto." He recalled that white children had always played freely with slave children and said that mixed schools did not prevent anyone from choosing his companions freely (quoted in George W. Cable, *The Negro Question* [1958 edition by Arlin Turner]).

From "Louisiana," *Report of the Secretary of the Interior* (Washington, 1872), II, pp. 195-96.

EVILS OF ENFORCING THE MIXED SCHOOLS

[Louisiana State Superintendent of Schools]:
"There is probably no other State in the Union where the work of popular education, by a system of free schools, is conducted under the disadvantages which are encountered in Louisiana. Not only have we, in common with some sister States, to build the whole system anew, and to do this in the face of that general apathy, rising at times to positive antagonism, which prevails in the Gulf States, but that provision of our constitution which forbids the establishing of public schools from which any child shall be rejected on account of race, color, or previous condition, excites a determined opposition on the part of many who would otherwise co-operate in the opening of schools and in the raising of funds for their support.

"Justice to our division superintendents requires that, in estimating what has been done by them, this fact should be borne in mind.

OFFICIALS DENIED DISCRETIONARY POWER

"Neither the division superintendents nor the boards of school directors are allowed, under the law, the least discretionary power, and because of that constitutional provision, to which reference has been made, the sympathies of thousands are alienated who might otherwise be expected to co-operate with us, and the weight of their influence is often thrown against the establishment of any schools whatever in the districts where they reside.

ANTAGONISM AROUSED — OFFICIALS OSTRACISED

"Even further than this: where persons of character have been willing to accept the position of school directors, from a desire to extend the advantages of education, they have, in many instances, been deterred from accepting the trust by the apprehension of persecution, and even social ostracism, on the part of the opponents of the law.

FACTS TO BE MET

"It were irrational to overlook the fact that this active antagonism of so large a portion of the white population of the State is a formidable hindrance to our school-work. However unreasonable it may be shown to be, and unworthy the intelligence of the age, its undeniable existence and influence must be taken into account in any estimate of past progress or of future prospects. The noblest vessel, however ably managed, makes but slow progress when forced to contend with both wind and tide. Such has been the position of those intrusted with the school-work in this State, and such it continues to be, with but little promise of a speedy alteration. What has been accomplished has been in the face of difficulties nowhere else experienced, and, at many points, in defiance of a sleepless opposition.

FULLER POWERS NEEDED BY SUPERINTENDENTS

"A corrective for the last-named difficulty would be found in empowering the division superintendent to establish schools where, after a reasonable time for action, a parish board fails in performing its duties. The lack of direct power in our higher school officers greatly lessens their efficiency, inasmuch as it renders their most vigorous exertions liable to be neutralized by the apathy or timidity of the boards through whom alone they can act. With power given the division superintendent to act in case of the failure of a parish board in its duty, he may be justly held responsible for the opening of a school in every ward district of his division. . . .

CAUSES OF FAILURE

"To render this presumption reasonable, however, several things must be previously determined. They to whom this power is intrusted must be imbued with a sense of the value of education; they must be capable of administering the system so far as it devolves on them, and be willing to devote to the public good the time and labor which the administration of the law requires and, finally, they must be in sympathy with the system itself. Should either of these pre-existent conditions be wanting, the ward district system contains within itself the elements of failure. A district will not voluntarily tax itself to support a system it dislikes. A community deficient in intelligence will manifest no zeal for education, and people struggling for the necessaries of life will feel little disposed to devote themselves to gratuitous labors for the public.

COLORED CITIZENS WILLING BUT INCAPACITATED

"The recently emancipated citizens of Louisiana constitute the portion of our people who sympathize most with our public-school system. Struggling upward to the light after generations of bondage, oppression, and enforced ignorance, the instances are rare in which the necessary qualifications for this delicate and important office are found to exist among them, and as they are generally compelled to employ their entire energies in securing the necessaries of life, they have no time to bestow on a work which offers no material compensation.

WHITE CITIZENS OPPOSED TO MIXED SCHOOLS

"The older white citizens of the State are, as a body, possessed of ample intelligence and leisure to act in the work of popular education, but a majority of them are decidedly averse to a system of instruction which makes no distinction on account of race, color, or previous condition, and as these two classes constitute the bulk of the people of the State, successful results from the ward district system are problematical at the best. In those sections of the State where an active, intelligent, and courageous leadership could be secured, good results have been obtained; but in other sections, where these requisites were unattainable, the system has proved a failure. . . ."

PART EIGHT

TWO VIEWS OF SOUTH CAROLINA RECONSTRUCTION

"A South Carolinian" Explains the Southern View Regarding Radical Policy

It is rather surprising that the *Atlantic Monthly* editors, who were encouraging articles on Reconstruction from the Southern view, should have considered this essay as unusually frank and hence requiring anonymity. It expresses commonly voiced conservative objections to the operation of the Carpetbag system in South Carolina and elsewhere. Compare this with Daniel Chamberlain's essay (pp. 255-273).

From "A South Carolinian," "The Political Condition of South Carolina," *The Atlantic Monthly*, XXXIX (1877), 177-94.

[THE editors of The Atlantic Monthly have received from a South Carolina contributor the following paper, to the striking statements of which the fact that the writer is by birth, education, traditions, associations, and residence a Southerner ought to give additional value. Their interest in the present political juncture it is believed will amply justify the devotion of these pages to them. The writer's name is withheld for obvious reasons.]

The appearance of the Northern armies in the South during the late war was everywhere hailed with rejoicings by the negroes, and on the full achievement of their liberty through the defeat of the South their exultation was unbounded. The carpet-baggers came here in the army, in the service of the Freedmen's Bureau, and as agents of Northern churches and benevolent associations. They at once took the negro by the hand, and told him that the Northerners had freed him and intended to keep him free, give him property, and educate his children. The negro listened eagerly, and, well knowing his old masters were anything but satisfied with the new order of things, blindly followed the guidance of his new friends. Supplies were distributed, colored schools were founded, and the blacks were induced to leave the white churches and worship apart. Many colored men from the North, superior to their Southern brethren in culture, also came to help on the work.

A few of the carpet-baggers were pure men, zealots and philanthropists; but many were dishonest, adventurers who had left their country for their country's good. Reconstruction came. The enfranchised freedmen were utterly at sea in politics; they needed leaders. The Southern whites refused the opportunity, though it is doubtful if they could have secured it, with scorn. The carpet-baggers seized it. Their authority over the blacks was already assured, but to make it doubly sure the Union Leagues were established. Every negro joined them, and was awed by their mystic rites. Free political use was also made of the churches. The negro went to the polls, took a ballot from a carpet-bag friend, and without looking at it (with reason, for he could not read) dropped it in the box. He did not know what voting meant; he had only a vague though all-absorbing idea that it would bring him great good and avert great evil.

The constitutional convention of this State was held early in 1868. It was composed of carpet-baggers, scalawags (native white republicans), and a moiety of the brightest field-hands, ignorant of the alphabet. A constitution was framed—with a bill of rights pre-fixed which would have made Calhoun gasp and satisfied Jefferson and Sumner themselves—with clauses by which the State that orig-inated nullification and secession is officiously made to declare that its citizens owe paramount allegiance to the constitution and govern-ment of the United States, and that the "State shall ever remain a member of the American Union; and all attempts, from whatever source or upon whatever pretext, to dissolve the said Union shall be resisted with the whole power of the State."

The constitution was adopted and the first legislature and ad-ministration were chosen. The composition of the legislature was like that of the convention; the governor, attorney-general, and state treasurer were carpet-baggers; the lieutenant-governor and secretary of state were negroes; the house selected a scalawag for speaker. Then began those fantastic tricks which for six years made the government of South Carolina the worst mockery of the name ever seen on earth. In the legislature no bills, unless of a purely legal character, could be passed without bribery, and by bribery any bill whatever could be passed. A formidable lobby sprang up, and presently organized depredations were commenced on the public; I will merely summarize the main performances. In the cases of the Greenville and Columbia Railroad and the Blue Ridge Railroad, the State had guaranteed railroad bonds to the extent of $6,000,000, reserving mortgages on the roads sufficient to cover the amount. Rings composed of carpet-baggers and native speculators paid the legislature to enact laws by which the State released her mortgages, still retaining her liability for the $6,000,000, and authorized the roads to pledge their property anew. In the case of the bank of the State, whose notes the State was bound to redeem, fraudulent notes to the amount of $750,000 were approved and assumed. The state-house was gorgeously fitted out: there were clocks at $480, mirrors at $750, and chandeliers at $650 apiece; elegant toilet sets were placed in the rooms of officials; there were two hundred fine porcelain spittoons at eight dollars apiece; and costly carpets, mirrors, sofas, etc., under the pretense of fitting up committee rooms, were furnished members for their apartments at boarding-houses. The real debt thus incurred was $50,000, but the contractor by sharing the spoil procured an appropriation of $95,000. Contingent funds became a notorious leak in the treasury; during the six years preceding 1875 they aggregated $376,000. During the same years the expenses incurred for the public printing ran up to the astounding figure of $1,104,000. During 1871, 1872, and 1873, they amounted to $900,000, or a thousand dollars a day. . . .

The officials in Columbia grew fabulously rich. Men, white and black, of no property went there, and, with no perceivable or conceivable means of honest living beyond a moderate official salary, would soon build palatial residences and support landaulets and blooded horses worth more than their pay for a year. The state administration exceeded the legislature in corruption. They made stupendous over-issues when an issue of bonds was authorized, and pocketed the proceeds. In connection with the financial agency in New York, they perpetrated some of the boldest swindles that were undertaken. A commission had been appointed to buy $700,000 worth of lands to sell to freedmen, who met with difficulty at first in persuading their old owners to sell them land. This commission, by charging the State five or six times as much as they paid for lands, succeeded in stealing over a half million of dollars. The treasury was annually rifled of the taxes till it became bankrupt.

The executive of South Carolina has unusual powers. With the approval of the senate he appoints the justices of the peace (called trial-justices here), county auditors, county treasurers, and many other local officers. The appointees for six years were corrupt whites, or equally corrupt and far more ignorant blacks, all rabid partisans.

The colored justices could rarely read or write, and sent out their warrants signed with cross-marks. These officers were paid by fees, and were eager to listen to trivial complaints against whites, or to stir up litigation. The treasurers of the counties were often in default; and as they owed their appointment generally to the state senator from their county, they were compelled to supply him with the public funds whenever he called for them. The local officers elected by the people were on a par with the appointees of the governor.

To make matters worse, the fountains of justice were corrupted. The supreme court was composed of one carpet-bagger, one scalawag, and one negro. The circuit courts, however, were not degraded. There were only two or three white or colored republicans competent to exercise judicial functions; and the whites, it was well understood, would not allow a perversion of power in this direction. So native white lawyers were generally selected for circuit judges—men who, retaining their honesty, would consent to keep quiet on politics, or openly profess republicanism. But to offset this there were juries composed chiefly of illiterate and degraded negroes, who thought their only duty was to find no bill or not guilty in all cases of blacks prosecuted by whites. Negro felons sent to the penitentiary were pardoned out by the wholesale. The highest number of prisoners in the penitentiary at Columbia (our only state prison) at any one time since the war has been four hundred and eighty. Yet in 1870 two hundred and five convicts there confined were pardoned. Pardons were granted as freely to men sentenced to serve for life or a term of years as to felons of a less degree of guilt. Negro convicts were generally pardoned, for political purposes, but money could obtain pardons for undeserving whites.

The demoralization became inconceivable. Larceny was universal. If a man hung up his coat at one end of a field, before he could plow to the other end and back it was stolen. Cows turned loose to browse came home milked dry. Live stock of all kinds was killed in the woods in the day-time. Cotton was picked from the fields at night, and corn "slip-shucked." Gardens and orchards were stripped, and water-melons actually became a rarity on white men's tables. Burglary, especially of smoke-houses and barns, was common. Everybody had dogs and guns, and thousands kept watch at night over their property.

In short, from 1868 to 1874 inclusive, the government of South Carolina was a grand carnival of crime and debauchery. After a year or so, the oppression grew so grinding that in many counties Ku-Klux Klans were organized. But their excesses soon carried the score over on the other side, and drew down the just indignation of the national government. They existed chiefly in counties where the whites outnumbered the negroes, and which had escaped the ravages of the war.

All these matters were aggravated by the management of the state militia. The militia officers appointed by the governors were all blacks, and the negro population eagerly enlisted. The whites scornfully refused to enlist under colored officers. The governor had power to receive any organization of private individuals, as part of the militia; but if he refused them, it was made highly penal to continue the organization. In several places the whites formed companies of their own, and offered themselves to the governor, who invariably refused them, and caused them to disband; but for the negro militia, one thousand Winchester and nineteen thousand Springfield rifles, with plenty of ammunition, were purchased. Armed with these, they drilled in a manner highly insulting and alarming to the whites. The military companies were used to tickle the negro's taste for martial pomp, and keep the negro vote consolidated.

It is now time to contemplate the other side of the picture.

For years after the fall of the Confederacy the people could not hear a renewal of war mentioned without a shudder. Politics fell into abhorrence. The leaders of secession lost their influence. We had been told that the Yankees would back up against the North Pole before they would fight; that one man could drink all the blood which would be shed. But the North had warred promptly, aggressively, and successfully, and rivers of blood had run; consequently, the commands of the North were obeyed, the ordinance of secession was repealed, the constitutional amendment abolishing slavery was ratified, reconstruction was not resisted. The old leaders, indeed, were not disposed to submit. They bitterly protested against the enfranchisement of the freedmen, railed at the military government and the constitutional convention, tried to stir up enthusiasm for Seymour and Blair and a white-line democratic state ticket in 1868, and in every manner to rouse up the people; but their exertions were but ill-seconded. There were state conventions of the democracy, indeed; but it is a remarkable fact that, for nearly eleven years after the war, there were, except here and there, no democratic primaries—precinct clubs—in South Carolina. Efforts were repeatedly made to form them, but the people would not join them, or, having joined, attend. It became the custom to elect delegates to the state conventions by calling mass-meetings of the county democracy at the county courthouse. These meetings elected the delegates, or made county nominations. Their only attendants, generally, were ten or a dozen gentlemen who had been our statesmen before the war.

The people regretted their defeat, and looked with hostility on both the emancipation and the enfranchisement of their slaves. The war and its results had cost them blood, property, and liberty; "But," said they, "it's no use trying to resist the current; the North is too strong for us, and is bound to have its way." To the solicitations of their more sanguine leaders they replied, "You have misled us once; we will be more prudent in the future." The course of President Johnson inspired them with hopes, but these fled when the unity of the North was perceived. The prospect of electing Seymour animated them to some extent, but events soon chilled them again. For years, voting was regarded as a mournful and onerous farce, and thousands refrained from it.

Even the new *régime*, with all its horrors, was submitted to, the sporadic outbreaks of the Ku-Klux forming the one exception. The leaders tried a change of tactics. In 1870 they dubbed the state democracy the Citizens' Reform Party, and, in the hope of catching part of the negro vote, nominated a Northern-born republican resident for governor, who accepted because dissatisfied with the party corruption. They hoped through success to make a step towards regaining power. But the negroes remained solid, and the regular republican ticket was again elected. The leaders of the whites now acquiesced in the do-nothing policy. For four years the whites kept almost altogether out of politics. The nomination of Greeley, indeed, excited their hopes powerfully at first, but his election was soon perceived to be impossible. No state ticket was run in 1872. There were two republican tickets in the field: the regular nominees supported by the corrupt element—and consequently the bulk —of the party, and a bolting ticket supported by some republican leaders, with their followers, who were in favor of reform. The few whites who turned out to vote for Greeley also voted for the bolting candidates, who, however, were defeated. The tax-paying democrats met once or twice after this to consult over their grievances, but confined themselves to temperate remonstrances, petitions, and nonpartisan investigations.

In the election of 1874 there was again a split among the republicans. The party convention nominated a ticket at the head of which was Mr. Daniel H. Chamberlain, for governor. He was supposed to be corrupt, as he had been attorney-general and a member of various important commissions at the time when corruption was greatest. The honest element again bolted. The whites met in convention, and resolved to support the bolting ticket. In return the bolters divided many local nominations with the democrats. The whites almost to a man voted for the bolting candidates,—county, legislative, and state,—although many of them (even the nominee for lieutenant-governor) were colored; so desperate at last had they become under governmental oppression. Mr. Chamberlain and the other regular candidates for state officers were elected; but the bolters and democrats elected about two fifths of the legislature.

The whites now expected the oppression to be redoubled. But when Mr. Chamberlain was installed, a curious spectacle was presented. He had made the usual promises of reform on the stump, amidst the smiles of his supporters, who had nominated him because they thought him a congenial spirit. He now announced that he had spoken in earnest. He made wholesale removals of the corrupt officers appointed by his predecessors, and replaced them by honest and competent men, in large part democrats. The corrupt schemes of the legislature were relentlessly vetoed. It was as bad as any preceding body, and elected two infamous men as circuit judges. Terrible excitement arose, which the governor quieted by refusing to commission the judges on a legal quibble; and by his threatening to veto the usual extortionate tax-bill, the most reasonable one known since 1867 was procured. The corrupt regular republicans went into vehement opposition to the governor, while the bolters and the democrats rallied to sustain his vetoes.

The reforms in justice, however, were most widely, deeply, and immediately felt. The wholesale pardoning at once stopped; the penitentiary began to fill up; good jury commissioners (the executive names them), who would select decent blacks for jurors and give the whites half the panels, were appointed. The whites began to take interest in the courts, and to look with less disfavor on colored jurors; the corrupt justices walked the plank by scores; a great decrease of crime was perceptible in a few months; race hatred greatly subsided. It is impossible to express the immense feeling of relief experienced at the restoration of confidence in the government.

The whites were unable to make too much of their savior. He was admitted into the most aristocratic society. He was elected orator by the colleges, called on by fashionable associations to respond to toasts, and lionized everywhere. The white leaders and the papers called loudly for his reëlection, and though the corrupt element of his party were determined to nominate another man or bolt should he carry the convention, a large section was in favor of renominating him. The whites shuddered at the terrible ordeal they had gone through, and seemed ready to recognize the rights of the negro and do anything in the way of compromise to avert such evil in the future. In several municipal elections (noticeably in Charleston) mixed tickets, half democrats and half blacks or republicans, were elected. It seemed as if a political millennium were about to dawn.

The motives of the governor have been variously construed. The belief became common that he was a pure man and had been slandered in the past. Many, however, believed him to be talented, ambitious, and unscrupulous; declaring that he had been a corruptionist while it suited his designs, but that on becoming governor he had determined to turn over to the whites, get socially recognized, procure an election to the United States Senate, and go there with such a powerful Southern support behind him that he could play an important part in national politics. This is the belief of the whites at present. Governor Chamberlain is a cold, elegant man, a graduate of Yale, and a lawyer. He is a student of comparative literature, and is thoroughly familiar with the course of modern thought. Some cultivated men in the State say that he went with the current till he gained power to control it; that then, out of pure love of political science, he undertook to bring about a reconciliation between the races and solve the great problem of Southern reconstruction and harmony. That he has ambition they do not deny; but they look on it as the ambition of a statesman, not of a politician. They recall the cold, judge-like neutrality with which he presided over the people. He did not truckle to the whites, as has been charged. He associated with them professedly as a republican, but avoided insulting their prejudices. He always gave the blacks strict justice. In his appointments he preferred republicans, when fit ones could be found; but where none were fit, he would select democrats.

The governor of South Carolina is elected every two years. Mr. Chamberlain was elected in November, 1874, simultaneously with the democratic national House of Representatives. The election of that house was hailed with thanksgiving in South Carolina, as an indication that the North had determined to protest against the oppression of the Southern whites by their old slaves and the carpetbaggers. But, after a time, the fact began to attract attention that a majority of the democratic congressmen were Southerners, and many of those Southerners ex-Confederate generals. A wild hope seized our old political leaders that the palmy *ante-bellum* times were about to return, that the democracy was again to control the national government, and that the South was again to rule the councils of the democracy. Every Southern State was now democratic except South Carolina and Louisiana, and Louisiana was on the verge of a change. Even Mississippi, than which only South Carolina was worse Africanized, had been carried by the white-liners. Good gov-

ernment, indeed, was now restored in our State and by their assistance could be maintained. But it was not a government under
their own auspices, or those of the democratic party; and while it
continued they could hope neither to be heard at Washington nor
to practice their cherished traditions at home.

From the beginning of 1876 they set themselves to the task of
arousing the people. A violent cry was raised against the governor,
and the whites were called on to follow the example of their brethren in the other Southern States. Social pressure was brought to
bear, an energetic canvass begun, and newspapers were brought up
or new ones founded; for the main body of the whites were still disposed to hesitate. "We had better wait," said they, "and see how
things go in the North. If the democrats carry the elections there
in November, and get control of the national government, why, of
course, we can rise up and throw off republican rule in the State. But
we have a good government now, and had best let well-enough alone,
for fear our old oppression might be re-established." But the work
went on. At the Fort Moultrie centennial thousands of Confederate
soldiers, once more under arms, were paraded before the people of
the State. Wade Hampton was their captain. Hot Southern speeches
were made, and the troops in attendance from Georgia, disgusted
at the unwonted spectacle of negroes in office, rode rough-shod
over the colored police of Charleston. Mr. Tilden had just been
nominated at St. Louis, and the brilliant prospects of electing him
were triumphantly paraded. Then came race conflicts: the killing
of a colored legislator in Darlington County, the lynching of two
negroes in Marlboro' and six in Edgefield, and finally the Hamburg
massacre. This last and the governor's action concerning it were followed by appeals to the whites, made with all the old vehemence of
Carolinians. Everybody was urged to buy arms; rifle clubs and
mounted companies were everywhere formed, the young men being
cheered on to join them; and the old system of browbeating and
challenging all non-conformists to the duello was vigorously put in
operation.

The whites in the old Ku-Klux counties, where the negroes are
in the minority, turned over *en masse* to the revolutionary policy;

in the other counties they held back for a long time, discouraging violence as inexpedient, as likely to hurt Tilden in the North, as being, in short, *premature*. But gradually they half fell, were half driven, into line; though not all; for when the state democratic convention met on August 15th there was still a powerful minority (about two-fifths) in favor of postponing action until it should be seen what the republicans would do about Chamberlain. It is useless to say, however, that the majority carried their point. General Wade Hampton, the Murat of the Confederacy, in whom are strikingly crystallized all the arrogant old plantation qualities of the South, was nominated for governor with a corresponding ticket. It was determined to carry the State by the method known as the Mississippi Plan.

I will merely summarize the means used; I was in the State during the whole campaign, and know whereof I speak. The plan was, first, to arouse the white population to secession or nullification madness; next, to get as many negroes as possible to vote the democratic ticket, and prevent as many as possible from voting the republican; and finally, to put such a face on their doings as to work no harm to the democratic cause outside the State.

In the first matter they thoroughly succeeded. General Hampton, an orator of no mean order, an accomplished gentleman sprung from the best Carolina stock, our greatest and most celebrated soldier, in company with numerous other ex-Confederate generals and officers (among whom were some from other States, including Toombs, Hill, and Gordon), began a systematic canvass of the State, speaking at every county town and at other places of size. Such delirium as they aroused can be paralleled only by itself even in this delirious State. Their whole tour was a vast triumphal procession; at every depot they were received by a tremendous concourse of citizens and escorts of cavalry. Their meetings drew the whole white population, male and female (for the ladies turned out by tens of thousands to greet and listen to the heroic Hampton), for scores of miles around, and had to be held invariably in the open air. They were preceded by processions of the rifle clubs, mounted and on foot, miles in length, marching amidst the strains of music and the booming of cannon; at night there were torchlight processions equally imposing. The speakers aroused in thousands the memories of old, and called on their hearers to redeem the grand old State and restore it to its ancient place of honor in the republic. The wildest cheering followed. The enthusiasm, as Confederate veterans pressed forward to wring their old general's hand was indescribable. Large columns of mounted men escorted the canvassers from place to place while off the railroad. They were entertained at the houses of leading citizens, held receptions attended by all the wealth, intelligence, and brilliance of the community, and used all the vast social power they possessed to help on the work.

Besides this, the fearful memories of the ante-Chamberlain days were revived. The governor's participation in them was maliciously asserted. The acknowledged fact that the mass of the negroes had opposed his reforms was skillfully paraded. His attempts to secure United States troops were denounced as a damning outrage; "South Carolina should be ruled by South Carolinians" was repeated from mountain to sea-board.

The work of buying arms and organizing democratic primaries and rifle clubs was energetically pushed on, till every democrat in the State had a gun and was enrolled in a primary, and three fourths of the whites belonged to the military. The ostracism and dragooning of all who hung back was carried to the last extreme, until the whites were as consolidated as in 1860.

The negroes saw these portentous movements; they saw the soldiery drilling, and every white man spending hours daily at the target. Rumors of Hamburg* reached them. Their former masters urgently importuned them to vote for Hampton. Every republican meeting was interrupted by armed multitudes of democrats, half the time demanded for democratic speakers, the republican orators jeered at, interrupted, vilely insulted, and hissed down, while the intruding speakers plainly announced that the whites were going to carry the election at all hazards and that the negroes had better

* The Hamburg, S.C., Riot of July 8, 1876, involved the killing of seven Negroes and one white, and was caused by a conservative attempt to disarm a Negro militia company. After Governor Chamberlain denounced this as a massacre, he lost many of his Democratic supporters. [Ed.]

vote the democratic ticket to save themselves trouble. Long lines of cavalry were kept constantly parading and proved particularly effective. Then another holocaust took place at Ellenton, and was talked about by the whites all over the State in the presence of the negroes. The whites, furthermore, suddenly assumed a dictatorial demeanor in their daily intercourse with the colored people, knocked them down or shot them on the slightest provocation, and by free use of menaces prevented indictments. Prominent republicans, white and colored, were threatened with ambuscades or followed by crowds of bullies if they left towns to canvass in the country; the negroes and white republicans were insulted on the streets; if troublesome, they were forced into fights by bravoes or picked off by "chance" shots during the course of pretended drunken rows got up near them. Terrorism soon reigned supreme.

To conceal these things systematic deception was used. Hundreds of false affidavits were procured, charging the negroes with aggression at both Hamburg and Ellenton, and justifying the whites in everything, even in the murder of prisoners; the responsibility for every deed of democratic violence was fixed on republicans; reconciliation to the results of the war was loudly professed. For over a month hardly any negroes turned democrats, yet large accessions were triumphantly claimed in the papers; ten colored democrats were nominated for the legislature in counties sure to go republican; the negro majority, which the last census gives as thirty-five thousand (seventy-five thousand white voters and one hundred and ten thousand colored), was boldly asserted to be only ten or fifteen thousand; and the judges (mostly democratic whites who had professed republicanism, or consented to preserve silence) were induced to declare for Hampton and *Hayes* (the latter for effect North), and denounce Chamberlain; *though a few months before, each and every one of them had been the very loudest supporters he had in the State.*

So few colored men joined the democratic clubs during the earlier weeks of the campaign that, to make the matter sure, there came proposals in the press and resolutions by the precinct and rifle clubs to employ no colored republicans as laborers, and to give no patronage to republican brick-layers, blacksmiths, carpenters, hack-men, market-men, etc., when democratic negroes were accessible. Thousands of republicans at once had ruin or democracy staring them in the face as alternatives; and hundreds of them finally began to turn.

For election day a *coup d'état* was contemplated. The members of the rifle clubs informally agreed among themselves to guard the polls and systematically patrol the public roads in a menacing manner, so as to frighten off the negroes and keep them at home.

But suddenly the governor came out with his proclamation. In the earlier part of his administration he had accepted ten or a dozen rifle clubs as militia; but the hundreds that had been organized since the opening of the campaign had asked no permission and were clearly illegal. So he ordered them to disband, and (as commander-in-chief) he disbanded those he had accepted, they too having been turned into political machines. The papers announced a day or two beforehand that the order was to be issued, and added, falsely and maliciously, that the arms of the clubs would also be demanded, although private property, each member having purchased his own gun. It would have taken but a wave of Hampton's hand to cause a frightful outbreak; but he counseled submission, especially when the president's proclamation came out, as the more expedient course, and the clubs ceased drilling and parading, though, of course, retaining their arms; it would have taken but a drum beat to make most of them fall into ranks. Then United States troops were poured into the State, and a garrison was stationed at every important town. The interference with republican meetings was immediately stopped.

When the democrats first began their demonstrations the negroes were cowed all over the State. They kept remarkably quiet, and it seemed as if their old fear of their masters would so reassert itself as soon to force them into the democratic ranks. But after a while, in some of the counties where they predominate—noticeably Charleston, Darlington, and Orangeburg—they became intensely excited at what they judged this evident blow at their liberty. They purchased guns and ammunition as fast as they were able, burnished the arms the State had given them, had broken or rusty weapons repaired, got knives, clubs, and torches ready, consulted together secretly, and evinced a stern determination to resist aggression to the death. They furthermore, alarmed at the daily defections from their ranks on account of work taken from republicans, began in the most fearful manner to maltreat and intimidate every colored man who gave promise of turning democrat. The excitement over this matter in Charleston resulted in a terrible riot, during which the city for one night and practically for several days was in the hands of black savages, who shot or beat every white who appeared on the streets. Indignant at the breaking up of their meetings by democratic soldiery, they began to attend armed. The bloody collision at Cainhoys was the consequence of this policy. After the arrival of the garrisons, the negroes all over the State broke out into extravagant expressions of joy and thanksgiving, appeared under arms on every occasion, and acted in the most alarming manner everywhere. Their orators advised them to cut the throats of white women and children, if the shot gun policy were continued, and to apply the torch to the dwelling of any man who discharged them on account of politics. In a week or two the increase of crime was positively appalling. The whites had conjured up a spirit which threatened to tear them in pieces.

The republican convention met on the 12th of September. Governor Chamberlain used all his official power and personal influence to pack it with his adherents and the honest element of the party; but the corrupt element was in the majority. The governor was a candidate for renomination, and he urged as candidates for the other high offices men of acknowledged integrity and uprightness. But so bitterly had the corruptionists come to hate him that they made a violent onslaught on him; and although they knew that without his interference the whites would out-Mississippi Mississippi in the election, they gave him plainly to understand that they must no longer be trodden on by him. That it was necessary to success to renominate him they bitterly admitted; but beyond this they resolutely refused to go. The governor had either to stoop, or to turn over the State to the strongest and fiercest spirits of the section which had tried to tear the Union asunder. A compromise was effected, and the governor was renominated; a few of the highest officers were given to his adherents, and the rest were given to the corruptest men in the corrupt section of the party. It was a sorry ticket; but, thanks to his efforts, it was the best put forward by the party convention since reconstruction. Similar compromises in the nominations were effected afterwards in many localities; but in a majority of counties the corruptionists broke out in open rebellion, put up their own men, and refused to give the Chamberlainites a showing; and the Chamberlainites and Mr. Chamberlain acquiesced.

The coming of the troops was a terrible backset for the democrats; but they had gone too far to recede. The troops were loudly welcomed, and their gentlemanly West Point officers entertained at formal but polite dinners to keep up appearances; although the furious deportment of the negroes soon made the whites, now unorganized, *really* glad that the troops were among them to prevent overt violence. A day of prayer and fasting for democratic success was appointed by the central committee of the party, and, at their request, religious services with the same object (an unknown thing) were held in every church—even Episcopal and Catholic— in the State. The "preference policy" was sternly pursued. Thousands of colored republicans lost their situations. Negro tenants (republican) were everywhere warned to leave. On trying to rent new lands they were coldly asked, "Are you going to vote for Hampton?" Republican craftsmen were everywhere idle. The papers and orators unintermittingly declared that every democrat should make it his duty to secure at least one negro to vote for Hampton, by fair means or foul, and watch him deposit his ballot. This was the famous "one man apiece" policy. In consequence, all the whites, especially gentlemen of property emulated each other in purchasing voters. Thousands of negroes had liens on their crops released, land rented them at nothing, supplies promised for next year, or money paid them outright in consideration of their turning democrats, or of staying away from the polls. In consequence of the discharge of colored laborers, the torch began its terrible work all over the country, and the whites were compelled to keep watch over their property at night. The streets of every village were patrolled. All the more bravely did the whites face the torch, all the more zealously did they work, after the significance of the democratic victory in Indiana began to appear. It was well known that the republican party there had made the issue on the "bloody shirt" and the "solid South," and on that issue had been defeated. Grant was furiously denounced from one end of the State to the other, and the people loudly called on to aid in electing a democratic president who would keep his hands off the South in the future. And the leaders, thinking everything was going for Tilden and the democrats, became absolutely frantic with the desire, which had been strong enough before, to participate in the victory, to get back to Washington, and to restore Palmetto ascendency in the national councils.

As the election day approached, there were signs that the republicans, frightened at the immense depletion of their strength, would attempt performances in repeating unparalleled in the history of elections; and the democrats began on all sides to say that if the republicans tried that game the democrats should try it too. The rowdies and fire-eaters among the lower classes of whites were worked up with the notion, and made ready for anything.

The election passed off amid terrible excitement, but, on the whole, peaceably. United States troops were posted at a large proportion of the polls and places where trouble or overt intimidation was apprehended, and were called on frequently to repress incipient tumults. Both parties turned out in full force, and stayed at the polls all day. Guns were brought by both parties, and concealed in houses near many polls, but the troops would not allow any to be shown. The whites, though, to a man, wore pistols as usual, as did all the negroes, few in number, who had been able to buy them. In Barnwell County, however, the ballot-box at a rural poll in a negro section, where no troops were posted, was fired on by an unknown party (supposed of course to be whites) from a neighboring swamp, and a stampede occurred. The poll was closed. Afterwards the managers reopened it in an adjoining place, and the negroes were rallied, inspired with mob courage, and deposited 2027 votes. The democrats afterwards protested against the counting of these votes. In Charleston County the colored militia turned out at rural polls under arms, stood on guard near such as had no troops near them, and prevented scores of colored democrats from voting, or intimidated them into "voting right."

The election itself was one of the grandest farces ever seen. In counties where the negroes had terrorized affairs, streams of colored republicans poured from poll to poll all day, voting everywhere. The largest vote ever cast before in Charleston County had been twenty thousand. Yet on election day, although three or four thousand negroes were bribed or led by fear of starvation to refrain from voting, and although five or six hundred who did vote cast the democratic ticket, the total vote thrown reached the amazing figure of 23,891 and the county went republican by 6391 votes—six thousand having been the average majority in the past. In counties terrorized by the whites, white bravoes rode from poll to poll, and voted time and again. Hundreds of Georgians and North Carolinians crossed the borders and joined in the work. In Edgefield County the influx of Georgians and the repeating were simply tremendous. The total number of voters in that county, according to the recent state census (*which was denounced as exaggerating the population by the democratic press*, because the census-takers were paid by a fee of five cents for every name recorded instead of by a salary), is 7122, and the county has always, hitherto, gone republican by one thousand votes; yet, although a thousand negroes certainly, and an unknown number above that, were induced by money or fear of starvation to refrain from voting, the total number of votes cast was 9289, and the democrats carried the county by the astounding and tell-tale majority of 3225! Similarly startling in most of the counties were the changes as compared with the census or past elections. Every democrat with whom I have talked since election day has something of this sort to say: "Why, the negroes at my precinct repeated and voted their minors on a tremendous scale; for their total vote was almost as high as ever before, although we kept away fifty or sixty from voting and got about a dozen to vote with us. Why, I carried one negro to the polls myself, and saw him put in his ballot all right, and his two brothers stayed at home all day, for I told them if they voted against us I would turn them off."

The ballots were undoubtedly counted fairly at the polls. Through Governor Chamberlain's influence, one democrat and two republicans had been appointed managers at every precinct. The board of county canvassers, appointed to aggregate the returns for each county, was similarly composed. But in compiling the vote they made some changes of the precinct returns; for instance, the names of some candidates of each party had been misspelt on the tickets by county printers, and in several cases candidates running for certain offices had by mistake received votes for other offices. . . .

The hostility with which the whites regarded the enfranchisement of the negro has made itself felt in the sternest ostracism of Southerners who have turned republican, even if they were sincere and shunned office. In this State the negro legislature is called the menagerie, and is never referred to without a malediction. It is true that the whites have at times (noticeably in 1874) voted for negroes for office, and even high office; but it was done only to escape confiscation. Large numbers of irreconcilables refused outright to do it, and were secretly admired by those who yielded, and openly applauded by the ladies. When the bolters in 1874 spoke at one time of nominating a negro for governor, the only daily journal then in Charleston, the leading democratic paper of the State and the South, said that South Carolinians might contrive to put up with a colored lieutenant-governor, but could not stomach a colored executive; there was a line which might God forbid they should ever pass.

Colored politicians, who can be distinguished by their shiny, dressy appearance, have always been held in detestation; their appearance is the signal for wrathful silence, scowls, and derisive winks; if one of them, in the open air, passes a group of young white men, either silence falls on them till he is past, or they burst into laughter and jeer him as long as he remains in sight.

The intimidation and killing of negroes during election campaigns is a lamentable but significant sign. Negro citizenship rests solely on the very insecure support of United States bayonets; in this matter, again, the whites are guided by expediency alone. Whenever they dare, the whites in the Southern States will disfranchise the negro outright and by law; and in the meanwhile they will, in States they control, practically disfranchise him. For instance, the negro always evades paying taxes—even a poll-tax—as long as he can, and is notoriously given to roost-liftings, stealing cotton by night, killing hogs, etc., in the woods; accordingly, I am not surprised to see that in Georgia non-payment of taxes—even the poll-tax—is made to disfranchise a voter, that half the negroes are already disfranchised for non-payment, and that every man in Alabama convicted of larceny is disfranchised. White employers object to their hands taking time to vote, and one discharged for this reason cannot obtain reëmployment. Young bravoes turn out upon election day, and jeer at, bully, or force negroes coming to vote into fights. In some riotous districts of Georgia, which the democrats now carry by the significant majority of eighty thousand, not a negro vote is polled; the increase of the democratic majority in Alabama since the State fell into democratic hands is well known. In Georgia there are no colored state officers, not even constables or police, and a negro has not been summoned to serve on a jury there for years; there is only one colored man in the legislature. An educational qualification, which is loudly clamored for in some Southern States, would disfranchise ninety-five negroes out of a hundred; and though many poor whites would murmur at such a measure, the fire-eaters would quickly bring them round by a judicious use of the cane and the pistol. So I should not be surprised to see that plan adopted in the Southern States before long.

The whites, I believe, will never attempt to reënslave the negro, even should they get out of the Union, or the North refuse to interfere. The matter is often in people's minds, as may be judged by the recurrence of such remarks as "I wonder what will be the end of this thing?" "What must we do with the negro?" etc. But reënslavement presents great difficulties and dangers. The negroes would resist it to the death: kill women and children, use the torch freely, flee to the swamps, and thence sally out to fight and ravage, so dearly have they come to prize their liberty. And even should they be ultimately subjected, there would be daily and nightly outbreaks, keeping the whites in constant suspense. But it is unmistakable that the inexpediency, not the wrong of the measure, would constitute the obstacle. The whites clearly regard subordination in all things as the natural condition of the negro.

Should the North ever grant free play, or a separation occur, I should look for the whites to go as far as they dare in restricting colored liberty by black codes or detached laws, without actually reestablishing personal servitude. For instance, from the irritation felt in consequence of the stealing and selling of cotton at night, and their incursions into chicken, meat, and potato houses, and barns, we may expect negroes to be prohibited from stirring from home at night after some curfew hour, save under patrol or police regulations. From the animosity evinced towards their Union Leagues, political clubs, mass-meetings, etc., we may look for the prohibition of all colored assemblages; their churches would probably be put under police espionage, to prevent the discussion of political themes. From the great irritation felt at colored men who support their wives in idleness, or send their children (needed to work on the plantation) to school, we should anticipate stringent vagrant laws, and laws forbidding colored children to attend school during work hours, if at all. From the exasperating disposition of the negro to quit employers before his time is out, and to work unsteadily while employed, we may predict laws prescribing the manner in which they shall hire themselves (perhaps requiring strict contracts, holding them to labor for stated periods at stated wages), severely punishing idleness *and making the violations of contract by a negro a penal offense.* Bills of that purport have been introduced into the Georgia legislature, and voted down as premature. Finally, from the delight with which the killing of a negro leader is hailed who shows any signs of becoming "dangerous" through his intelligence or culture, it is easy to foresee that whites would be lightly punished (if juries would ever convict them) for crimes against blacks, while the criminal law would be severe on black offenders, and convictions easy.

The Union Leagues gave the negroes their first notions of parliamentary law and debating. They were encouraged to attend courts as spectators, were inducted into jury and militia service, and their prominent men were elevated to office. For several years—until 1872—in this State they unresistingly followed the guidance of their white friends. There was little debate at their meetings, and most measures were passed unanimously. On juries, in the legislature, etc., they were sheepish, quiet, awkward, and docile. But gradually they began to pick up hints and to see things for themselves. They became ambitious for office and distinction, acquired confidence, joined in debate, and criticised the measures proposed by their white leaders; and for a few years past they have been growing the most irrepressible democrats it is possible to conceive. They delight in attending, either to mingle in or to look on at, all sorts of assemblages,—church services and meetings, political clubs and conventions, mass-meetings, the courts,—as well as to serve on juries or in the militia. They are astonishingly quick at imitation, and are a mere second edition of the whites. At their gatherings all have something to say, and all are up at once. They have a free flow of language, and their older men exhibit a practical, get-at-the-facts disposition (narrow-minded of necessity, yet intense from that very circumstance) which is a near approach to that sterling English quality, hard common sense. They are to the last degree good-humored unless persistently opposed, when they become excited, demonstrative, and violent, in both demeanor and language. While they are speaking, their orators are subjected to all kinds of interruptions,—questions, impertinences, points of order, etc. Consequently much disorder prevails at their meetings. In the legislature knives and pistols have been drawn, and members have been expelled for disorderly conduct.

The negroes undoubtedly have a genius for intriguing. They understand all the arts of the lobby. They are quick with points of order—tack on riders, hurry jobs through under the previous question, etc. They understand well how to make corporations pay for bills, and candidates for nominations. Rings are well known in their politics. They have gerrymandered the congressional districts so as to deprive the whites of two representatives they might fairly elect. To insure the elections, they have refused to pass laws providing for registration, as the constitution directs; and under this safe-guard (every voter being allowed to vote at any precinct whatever in his county, if he swears that he is voting for the first time) they have rivaled in repeating any feats of Tammany or Philadelphia roughs. Charleston County has been chiefly the theatre of these deeds. Negroes in swarms go voting from poll to poll in the country, and then enter the city and vote at several precincts there. Negroes do this all over the State on a smaller scale, and they frequently cross from county to county to vote; while the voting, or attempts to vote, of boys under twenty-one is notorious. Until 1874 their managers also proved themselves adepts in packing ballot-boxes, or in manipulating returns; such frauds being easily detected by keeping lists of how many negroes and how many whites voted, the voting having generally been on the color line. The meetings of bolting republicans are frequently packed by regulars, their orators hissed, resolutions voted down, and their opposite carried.

The negroes moreover are as intolerant of opposition as the whites. They expel from the church, ostracize, and, if they can, mob and kill all of their own, though not of the white race, who would turn democrats; and they have done so ever since the war. The women are worse than the men, refusing to talk to or marry a renegade, and aiding in mobbing him. They treat bolting republicans in the same way. But in some counties the bolters at times, happening to outnumber the regulars, have proceeded to reverse the game, and intimidate the regulars into conformity. Charleston County for many years has had two republican factions waging relentless mob war on each other, the division originating in the rivalry of two noted white leaders. When a negro does turn democrat, he surpasses the most rabid fire-eater in violence, and on every occasion delights to banter, insult, or bully republican negroes, if white men are near to protect him.

On national questions the negroes, as is well known, implicitly follow the dictation of Northern republicans; but in home matters they are more independent. For three or four years they have displayed great dissatisfaction with their white leaders. "Our votes keep the party in power," they say, "and we ought to have the offices." In consequence, many white leaders have been discarded, and those who yet retain prominence have had to use money and official patronage freely to retain their influence. Out of about one hundred and twenty-five republicans in the two legislative houses last session, about one hundred and ten were colored. I speak from memory, but am substantially correct.

The negroes have been accused of being easily led by demagogues; but they really rule the demagogues, not the demagogues them. Let the politicians do anything which is distasteful, and opponents spring up in every quarter. They are extremely jealous of any one's assuming to dictate to them. They are impatient of trespasses and domiciliary visits to a degree only exceeded by the English races, and often resist search-warrants. They also resist arrests, and have to be vigorously clubbed. One thing, though, must be mentioned. Their fear of being reënslaved offers a means by which dexterous politicians can often impose on them. If you can prove to their satisfaction that any measure will tend to give the whites any advantage over them, it is instantly quashed and its opposite forthwith carried, *nem con.* The intense love the negro has acquired for liberty was conspicuously manifested in the recent canvass, when it became apparent that the whites were determined to carry the election on the Mississippi Plan, and, as the negroes thought, rob them of liberty. As to the negro's capacity for government, I must say frankly that he is no more fit for it than a crowd of Irish roughs picked up promiscuously in the streets of a Northern city.

A South Carolinian

Ex-Carpetbagger and Ex-Governor Daniel H. Chamberlain Concludes in 1901 that Radical Reconstruction Was "A Frightful Experiment" Doomed to Failure

The *Atlantic Monthly*, especially active in soliciting articles on Reconstruction, received a most surprising hostile verdict on it from the former Republican Governor of South Carolina, Daniel H. Chamberlain (1835-1907), technically a Carpetbagger because of his Northern and Radical affiliations but always respected for his probity. His antecedents would have suggested other opinions: he was born in Massachusetts, was a distinguished graduate of Yale and a student of the Harvard Law School before entering practice as a lawyer, and became an excellent officer at the head of a Negro regiment during the war.

After the war he visited a friend in South Carolina, where he tried unsuccessfully to operate a cotton plantation. However, he did succeed in Republican politics in the state, first as attorney-general and then in 1872-1874 as governor. Despite the well-known political corruption in South Carolina, Chamberlain remained free of any taint of jobbery, while economizing on public expenditures and reforming the tax system, thereby winning over many conservative Democrats as well as the biracial Republicans to his programs. But he was firm in protecting Negroes during the race riots, and Democrats cooled toward him and moved over to the cause of the conservative Wade Hampton and the Red Shirts. In 1876, the state was torn between the rival claims of Chamberlain and Hampton to the governorship, but President Hayes' withdrawal of federal troops forced Governor Chamberlain to yield.

The essay should be carefully compared with the estimates of Chamberlain given by "A South Carolinian" in the preceding selection. They are by no means antithetical, despite contrasting social philosophies. Chamberlain, thoroughly disillusioned, speaks of the "unreasoning antipathy" of the Radicals, although he considers Johnson's policy "fatuous." He thinks of Reconstruction as a "frightful experiment" of well-intentioned but misguided philanthropists, while the Radicals appear motivated by "hate, revenge, greed, lust for power." Most interesting is his suggestion that Congress should have tried to work with the "natural leaders" of the South and thus achieve more lasting results. This hindsight judgment is open to debate even on the basis of Chamberlain's own experience. Did he actually get the cooperation of the conservatives or were they using him as the least painful alternative, considering Northern power? Certainly his low opinion of the Negro resembles that of the anonymous "South Carolinian." Most puzzling of all is the fact that Chamberlain was writing in this vein in 1901,

From Daniel H. Chamberlain, "Reconstruction in South Carolina," *Atlantic Monthly*, LXXXVII (1901), 473-84.

a year when Negro lynchings in the South was reaching over a hundred annually and when the current "natural leaders" of the South were the Negrophobes Tillman, Vardaman, and other so-called demagogues. Grandfather clauses, white primaries, a rigid legalized Jim Crow system that swept the Southern statute books, and the decline of vocational and educational opportunities for Negroes were evident. Yet Chamberlain's interpretation of Reconstruction became the textbook version and was at that time espoused by the Columbia University "revisionists" as well as by ex-Confederate sentimentalists.

The Civil War of 1861-65 (the term is used here for convenience, though it lacks perfect accuracy) was conducted in substantial or reasonable accordance with the settled rules of war; and at its close there was a large measure of liberal feeling on the part of the North toward the South, notwithstanding the murder of Mr. Lincoln. This feeling viewed the struggle as one in which both sides were sincere and patriotic (the word is used of design, but in its high and broad meaning), in which both sides were equally brave and devoted; as well as one which had come to pass quite naturally, from causes which were far deeper than politics or even than slavery. While the victorious section was enjoying the first or early sense of success, sentiments of liberality, of concord, readiness to look forward to better relations, not backward to old quarrels, statesmanlike plans or suggestions of reunion, and restoration of old associations, widely prevailed.

Two main causes now came into operation to disturb this tendency and course of feeling and events. The first of these was the existence at the North, on the part of a strenuous, ardent, vigorous minority, of a deep-seated, long-maturing, highly-developed distrust of the South; a sentiment resting partly on moral antagonism to slavery, but chiefly on a feeling of dread or hatred of those who had brought on a destructive, and, worst of all, a causeless or unnecessary war. Not all of those who belonged to this class are to be described so mildly. Some, it may be said, if not many, were really moved by an unreasoning antipathy toward those whom they had so long denounced as slaveholders and rebels. Slavery abolished and rebellion subdued, their occupation was gone; and still they could not adjust themselves to a new order of things.

The other great cause of reaction from the friendly and conciliatory spirit which was the first result of the victory for the Union was the conduct of the South itself. Beaten in arms and impoverished, stripped of slavery, the white South found solace, or saw relief, if not recompense, in harsh treatment of the emancipated negroes, in laws, in business, and in social relations. The effect of this folly was decisive at the North. But added to this was the fatuous course of President Johnson, to whom the South, not unnaturally, gave warm support.

Out of these adverse conditions came reconstruction. Its inception and development into policy and law were not the results or dictates of sober judgment of what was best; least of all were they inspired by statesmanlike forecast, or the teachings of philosophy or history. The writer has recently turned over anew the congressional discussions, in 1866 and 1867, of reconstruction, the South, and especially the negro question, some large part of which he heard at first-hand. It is, for by far the greater part, melancholy reading,—shocking in its crudeness and disregard of facts and actualities, amazing for the confident levity of tone on the part of the leading advocates of the reconstruction acts of 1867, and for its narrowly partisan spirit. Confidence here rose easily into prophecy, and the country was assured of a peaceful, prosperous South, with negro loyalty forever at the helm. The white South was helpless. The black South was equal to all the needs of the hour: ignorant, to be sure, but loyal; inexperienced, but, with the ballot as its teacher and inspiration, capable of assuring good government. Hardly anywhere else in recorded debates can be found so surprising a revelation of the blindness of partisan zeal as these discussions disclose. But it may now be clear to all, as it was then clear to some, that underneath all the avowed motives and all the open arguments lay a deeper cause than all others,—the will and determination to secure party ascendency and control at the South and in the nation through the negro vote. If this is a hard saying, let any one now ask himself, or ask the public, if it is possibly credible that the reconstruction acts would have been passed if the negro vote had been believed to be Democratic.

True views of the situation—views sound, enlightened, and statesmanlike—were not wanting even then. Mr. Lincoln had presented such views; but above all other men in the whole land, Governor Andrew, of Massachusetts, in his farewell address to the Massachusetts legislature, January 2, 1866, discussed with elaboration the Southern situation, and urged views and suggested policies which will mark him always in our annals, at least with the highest minds, as a true, prescient, and lofty statesman, versed in the past and able to prejudge the future. His valedictory address is veritably prophetic,—as prophetic as it is politic and practical. With this great word resounding through the country, the last excuse for reconstruction as actually fixed upon is swept away; for it could no longer be held, as it had been said by the more timid or doubtful, that the whole business was a groping in the dark, without light or leading. Sentiment carried the day, sentiment of the lower kind,—hate, revenge, greed, lust of power.

It is, however, necessary at this point to be just. Not all who bore part in fixing the terms of reconstruction were ignoble or ignorant. Among them were many unselfish doctrinaires, humanitarians, and idealists of fine type. Among them, too, were men who ranked as statesmen, who in other fields had well earned the name, but who now were overborne or overpersuaded. Back of all these, however, were the party leaders, who moved on, driving the reluctant, crushing and ostracizing the doubtful, brutally riding down those who dared to oppose.

Governor Andrew's argument and policy may be briefly stated. Three great, flashing apothegms summarize it: (1) Prosecute peace as vigorously as we have prosecuted war. (2) Inflict no humiliation, require no humiliation, of the South. (3) Enlist the sympathy and services of "the natural leaders" of the South in the work of reconstruction. To the oft-repeated dictum that those who had ruled the South so long and rigorously—its natural leaders—could not be trusted with this work, Andrew pointed out, with prophetic insight, that these men, if not accepted as friends, would resume their leadership as enemies. Such a vision of the future, such a clear annunciation of truth and fact, fell on blind and impatient or angry minds. The most radical of ante-bellum and war Republicans, the greatest of all our war governors, was struck from the list of party leaders, and reconstruction proceeded apace on other lines and under other leaders. The writer recalls almost numberless interviews on reconstruction with Republican leaders at Washington, especially in the winter of 1866-67, and the summer and fall of the latter year, and particularly with the late Oliver P. Morton. Mr. Morton shared to some large degree with Mr.

Thaddeus Stevens the leadership in this enterprise. Against the two combined, no policy could gain even consideration. With Mr. Stevens no argument was possible. His mind was fixed, proof against facts or reason that suggested other views. Mere personal self-respect limited the writer's intercourse with him to one brief conversation. Not one of these leaders had seen the South, or studied it at first-hand. Not one of them professed or cared to know more. They had made up their minds once for all, and they wished only to push on with their predetermined policy. The one descriptive feature, the one overshadowing item, of their policy was, as has been said, negro suffrage, loyalty under a black skin at the helm,—a policy which, like other historical policies of "Thorough," like the policy of Strafford and Laud, whence the fitting word has come, brooked no opposition or delay, and halted for no arguments or obstacles whilst these leaders led. The personal knowledge of the writer warrants him in stating that eyes were never blinder to facts, minds never more ruthlessly set upon a policy, than were Stevens and Morton on putting the white South under the heel of the black South. Again it is necessary to say that not all eminent Republican leaders shared these sentiments, though they acquiesced in the policy. Mr. Sumner, it shall be said, did not, and, strange perhaps to add, Mr. Blaine did not; but both submitted, and even advocated the acts of 1867.

Reconstruction thus conceived, thus developed, thus expounded, was put to test in South Carolina in the winter of 1867-68. Passed, as these acts were, in lofty disregard of the feelings or interest of the whites of the South, the first crucial test they met was of course the attitude of those who were thus disregarded. The first force or element to be reckoned with was the element left out of the account. The property, the education and intelligence, the experience in self-government and public affairs, in this state, were of course wholly with its white population. Numbers alone were with the rest. The first registration of voters in South Carolina under the reconstruction acts, in October, 1867, gave a total of 125,328 persons eligible to vote, of whom 46,346 were whites, and 78,982 were blacks or colored, or a ratio of about 3 to 5. Upon the question of holding a constitutional convention, the first question prescribed by the acts for decision, the total vote in November, 1867, was 71,807,—130 whites and 68,876 colored voting *pro,* and 2801 *contra.* Of the members of the convention, 34 were whites and 63 colored. It did not contain one Democrat or one white man who had had high standing in the state previously. By this convention a constitution was framed, made up entirely of excerpts from other state constitutions, but yet a fairly good constitution in all its most important provisions. It continued in force, with a few rather unimportant changes, until 1897. State officers, under this constitution, and a legislature were elected in April, 1868, and the new government went into operation in July, 1868. In the first legislature under reconstruction, the Senate, numbering 33 members, contained 9 colored and 24 whites, of whom 7 only were Democrats. The House of Representatives numbered 124, of whom 48 were whites and 76 colored, only 14 being Democrats. The whole legislature was thus composed of 72 whites and 85 colored, with a total of 21 Democrats to 136 Republicans, or a ratio of nearly 3 to 20.

Truth here requires it to be said that the abstention of the whites from coöperation at this stage of reconstruction was voluntary and willful. The election for members of the convention went by default so far as they were concerned. They might, by voting solidly, and by the use of cajolery and flattery, such as they later did use, or by grosser arts, from which at last they did not shrink, have won an influential if not a controlling voice. All this is clear and certain; but the fact only shows the recklessness with which the sponsors of reconstruction went ahead. Such abnegation of lifelong sentiments or prejudices, such absolute reversal of themselves, as such a line of conduct required, was possible; but decent statesmanship does not build on possibilities. The question should have been, not, Is such conduct on the part of the whites possible? but, Is it to be expected? No man can say less than that it was to the last degree improbable; it would hardly be too much to say it was morally impossible. Alone of all prominent men in the state, Wade Hampton in 1868 publicly advised coöperation with the negroes in elections, but his advice passed unheeded.

But it is not true that Stevens or Morton counted on such coöperation of the whites, or cared for it. It was an after-thought to claim it; a retort to those who uttered reproaches as the scheme of reconstruction gradually showed its vanity and impossibility. It cannot be too confidently asserted that from 1867 to 1872 nothing would have been more unwelcome to the leaders of reconstruction at Washington than the knowledge that the whites of South Carolina were gaining influence over the blacks, or were helping to make laws, or were holding office. The writer knows his ground here; and there is available written evidence in abundance to avouch all his statements and opinions,—evidence, too, which will sometime be given to the world.

No view of the situation in South Carolina in these years would be accurate or complete which did not call to mind the peculiar political or party condition of the white or Democratic population. For fully ten years, if not twenty, prior to 1850, Mr. Calhoun's immense personality, strenuous leadership, and unquestionably representative views and policies dominated the state,—dominated it to the complete effacement and disappearance of all other leaders or leadership. This influence projected itself forward, and controlled the thought of the state until 1860, as truly as in the lifetime of Calhoun. American political history, for its first century, will record no other instance of individual supremacy over a high-spirited, ambitious, politics-loving community such as the career of Calhoun presents. Nor was his influence in the smallest degree factitious or adventitious. It was simply the result of the application of a stern will, prodigious industry, sleepless but not selfish ambition, and the very highest order of ability to the leadership of a political cause. Calhoun led South Carolina till the outbreak of the war, if not through the war. At the close of the war and at the date of the reconstruction acts, new leadership in political thought and action was necessary; but South Carolina then had no leaders. Not only had she no trained party or political leaders; she had no men of single commanding influence. The most influential men of the state were the heroes of the war, who, though many of them able and public-spirited, were none of them greatly experienced in public affairs. The state had its full share of able men, an especially able bar, great numbers of planters and business men who had the old-time training in politics, but no man who could to any great degree mould public opinion or control party action. This fact—and it is referred to

here only as a fact—was significant of much. In consequence, the Democratic or white party merely drifted, rudderless and at haphazard, from 1867 to 1874, the critical years of reconstruction.

Here, as at all points in this paper, the writer intends to speak with moderation of spirit and entire frankness. He thinks he can do justice to all parties and persons who took active part in reconstruction, though himself an actor, at times somewhat prominent. It will be for others to judge whether he has succeeded, as he has tried to do, in laying aside prejudices or feelings naturally developed by his activity in these scenes, so that he can see the men and events of those days objectively and disinterestedly.

It is now plain to all that reconstruction under the acts of 1867 was, at any rate, a frightful experiment, which never could have given a real statesman who learned or knew the facts the smallest hope of success. Government, self-government, the care of common public interests by the people themselves, is not so easy or simple a task as not to require a modicum of experience as well as a modicum of mental and moral character. In the mass of 78,000 colored voters in South Carolina in 1867, what elements or forces could have existed that made for good government? Ought it not to have been as clear then as it is now that good government, or even tolerable administration, could not be had from such an aggregation of ignorance and inexperience and incapacity? Is it not, has it not always been, as true in government as in physics, *ex nihilo nihil fit?*

Added to this obvious discouragement and impossibility in South Carolina was the fact that these 78,000 colored voters were distinctly and of design pitted against 46,000 whites, who held all the property, education, and public experience of the state. It is not less than shocking to think of such odds, such inevitable disaster. Yet it was deliberately planned and eagerly welcomed at Washington, and calmly accepted by the party throughout the country. What Republican voice was heard against it?

But the cup of adverse conditions was not yet full. To this feast of reconstruction, this dance of reunion, rushed hundreds, even thousands, of white and colored men from the North, who had almost as little experience of public affairs as the negroes of the South; and it

must be added that, as a class, they were not morally the equals of the negroes of the South. The story at this point is threadbare; but it must be again said in this review that the Northern adventurers at once sprang to the front, and kept to the front from 1867 to 1874. To them the negro deferred with a natural docility. He felt that they represented the powers at Washington, as they often did, and his obedience was easily secured and held. Are Stevens and Morton and their applauding supporters chargeable with countenancing these men? Not by express, direct terms; but they are justly chargeable with opening the doors to them, and not casting them off when their true character was perfectly known. So ingrained was the disregard of Southern Democrats in all affairs that concerned the political control at the South, so inflexible was the determination of officials and leaders at Washington to keep the heel on the neck, that hardly one high Republican authority could be appealed to for discountenance of the class referred to. To this tide of folly, and worse, President Grant persistently yielded; while one noble exception must be noted, the gallant and true Benjamin H. Bristow, of Kentucky, as Solicitor-General, Attorney-General, and Secretary of the Treasury.

The quick, sure result was of course misgovernment. Let a few statistics tell the tale. Before the war, the average expense of the annual session of the legislature in South Carolina did not exceed $20,000. For the six years following reconstruction the average annual expense was over $320,000, the expense of the session of 1871 alone being $617,000. The total legislative expenses for the six years were $2,339,-000.

The average annual cost of public printing in Massachusetts for the last ten years has been $131,000; for the year 1899 it was $139,000, and this included much costly printing never dreamed of in South Carolina in those days. In reconstructed South Carolina the cost of public printing for the first six years was $1,104,000,—an annual average of $184,000, the cost for the single year 1871-72 being $348,-000.

The total public debt of South Carolina at the beginning of reconstruction was less than $1,000,000. At the end of the year 1872, five years later, the direct public debt amounted to over $17,500,000. For

all this increase the state had not a single public improvement of any sort to show; and of this debt over $5,950,000 had been formally repudiated by the party and the men who had created the debt, and received and handled its proceeds.

Prior to reconstruction, contingent funds were absolutely unknown in South Carolina; a contingent fund, as known under reconstruction, being a sum of money which a public officer is allowed to draw and expend without accountability. During the first six years of reconstruction the contingent funds in South Carolina amounted to $376,000.

These are pecuniary results, but they tell a moral tale. No such results could be possible except where public and private virtue was well-nigh extinct; nor could they exist alone. In fact, they were only one salient effect or phase of a wide reign of corruption and general misrule. Public offices were objects of vulgar, commonplace bargain and sale. Justice in the lower and higher courts was bought and sold; or rather, those who sat in the seats nominally of justice made traffic of their judicial powers. State militia on a vast scale was organized and equipped in 1870 and 1871 solely from the negroes, arms and legal organization being denied the White Democrats. No branch of the public service escaped the pollution. One typical and concrete example must suffice here. In the counties of South Carolina there is a school commissioner whose powers and duties cover the choice of all teachers of the public schools, their examination for employment or promotion, the issue of warrants for installments of their salary, and, in general, all the powers and duties usually devolved on the highest school officer in a given area of territory. In one of the counties of South Carolina, during the years 1874 and 1875, the school commissioner was a negro of the deepest hue and most pronounced type, who could neither read nor write even his own name; and his name appeared always on official documents in another's handwriting, with the legend "his ✕ mark." He was as corrupt, too, as he was ignorant. Now, what course a county in Massachusetts or other Northern state would take under such an infliction the writer does not venture to say. He is only certain no Northern community would stand it. The people of this county, one morning, found their chief school officer dead in the highway from a gunshot. Such incidents must lead, will lead, in any intelligent community, to deeds of violence. The famous and infamous Ku-Klux Klan of 1870 was an organized attempt to overawe and drive from office Republican state officers, and especially negroes. It was brutal and murderous to the last degree, being from first to last in the hands almost exclusively of the lower stratum of the white population. Yet it was symptomatic of a dreadful disease,—the gangrene of incapacity, dishonesty, and corruption in public office. No excuse can be framed for its outrages, but its causes were plain. Any observer who cared to see could see that it flourished where corruption and incapacity had climbed into power, and withered where the reverse was the case.

Gradually, under the spur of public wrongs and misrule, political party remedies began to be used by the Democrats,—a word practically synonymous with whites, as Republican was with negroes,—and in 1872 a Democratic canvass was made for state officers. In 1874 the Democrats united with a section of disaffected Republicans in a canvass, in which the Republican candidate for governor received 80,-000 votes, and the Democratic candidate 68,000. Still no great or preëminent leader of the Democratic party forces had appeared. In 1874, under the stress of fear of consequences, symptoms of which were then clear, the Republican party, by some of its leaders, and some part of its rank and file, undertook a somewhat systematic effort for "reform within the party." For the next two years the struggle went determinedly on, with varying success. Two facts or incidents will illustrate the flow and ebb of reform here. Early in 1875, a notorious, corrupt negro, who had long led the negroes in one of the strongest Republican sections of the state, put himself up as a candidate for judge of the chief (Charleston) circuit of the state. The reform forces barely succeeded in defeating him. Other conflicts from time to time arose, and it was only by a close union of the Democrats in the legislature, and the free and constant use of the executive power of veto, that the reform party was saved from overthrow and rout—no less than nineteen vetoes being given to leading legislative measures by the governor in a single session. When the legislature assembled for the session of 1875-76, the reform and anti-reform forces were nearly equally matched; the former including all the Democratic members of the legislature, who were in turn heartily backed by the Democratic party of the state.

A decisive test of strength soon came. As the event of this test marks accurately the turning point in the fortunes of reconstruction in South Carolina under the congressional plan of 1867, the story must be here told with care and some degree of fullness. December 15, 1875, occurred an election by the legislature of six circuit or *nisi prius* judges for the several circuits into which the state was then divided. On the night preceding the election a secret caucus of the negro members of the legislature was held, instigated, organized, and led by the most adroit as well as the ablest negro in the state, one Robert B. Elliott, formerly of Boston. At this caucus, an oath was sworn by every member to support all nominations made by the caucus for the judge-ships. The caucus proceeded to make nominations, choosing for the two most important circuits—Charleston and Sumter—a negro, Whipper, and a white man, F. J. Moses. Not till the legislature was ready to meet on the following day did the fact of this caucus become known. Every man nominated was elected. The storm now broke over the heads of the conspirators in fury. The laugh which for a long time greeted remonstrance died away, and men asked one another what could be done. The governor at once took his stand, undoubtedly a novel and extreme stand; but, like all decent men who saw the situation at first-hand, he probably felt that sometimes in politics, as in other things, "new occasions teach new duties." He publicly announced his determination to refuse to issue commissions to Whipper and Moses. The wrath of the conspirators rose high, but the white citizens strongly backed the executive, and no commissions were ever issued. The sequel was that, after much loud boasting of their courage on the part of Whipper and Moses, they quailed, like the craven cowards they were, before the determination of the people, and never took another step to enforce their claim to office.

At this precise point came the parting of ways between the governor and his Republican supporters, on the one hand, and his white Democratic supporters, on the other hand, in their common reform struggle. It seems dramatic, almost tragic, that, in a matter of so much importance to South Carolina, hearts equally earnest and honest, as we may now believe, and minds equally free and clear, saw in the same event, and that event a signal triumph over the powers of misrule by the allied forces of the reformers, totally different meanings and significance. To the Republican reformers it seemed a splendid vindication of their policy and belief,—that all that was needed was a union of the forces of intelligence and honesty against the common enemy; to the Democratic reformers, on the other hand, it seemed a final and crowning proof that the forces of misrule were too strong to be overcome by ordinary, peaceful methods. Less cannot be said here than that, as is usual, there was truth in both views. There were, no doubt, many searchings of heart in the ranks of each division of the reformers. One eminent and devoted reformer, who felt compelled to go with the Democrats, has left on record an expression of his feelings, in quoting the words of Sir William Waller to his friend and antagonist in the English Civil War of 1640: "That great God who is the searcher of my heart knows with what a sad sense I go upon this service, and with what a perfect hatred I detest this war without an enemy. . . . But we are both upon the stage, and must act such parts as are assigned us in this tragedy." It was the feeling of many before the contest had opened or passed to the stage of hard fighting.

Pause must be made here long enough to set before an uninformed reader the array of forces for this contest, so significant to South Carolina, and so characteristic and illustrative of the inevitable results of reconstruction on the lines of 1867. It has been remarked that South Carolina had no great leader or leaders after Mr. Calhoun. This was true until 1876, but not later. Great new occasions usually bring leaders. At the head of the Democratic forces in South Carolina, in June, 1876, appeared General Wade Hampton, known only, one might say, till then, except locally, as a distinguished Confederate cavalry officer. He had led the life of a planter on a large scale, and possessed well-developed powers and habits of command. Totally unlike Calhoun, Hampton's strength of leadership lay, not in intellectual or oratorical superiority, but in high and forceful character, perfect courage, and real devotion to what he conceived to be the welfare of South Carolina. Not even Calhoun's leadership was at any time more absolute, unquestioned, and enthusiastic than Hampton's in 1876; and it was justly so from the Democratic point of view, for he was unselfish, resolute, level-headed, and determined. He was for the hour a true "natural leader;" and he led with consummate mingled prudence and aggressiveness.

The progress of the canvass developed, as must have been apprehended by all who saw or studied the situation, not only into violence of words and manner, but into breaches of the peace, interference with public meetings called by one party, and latterly into wide-spread riots. The chapter need not be retold. The concealments of the canvass on these points have long been remitted, with the occasion which called for them. It is not now denied, but admitted and claimed, by the successful party, that the canvass was systematically conducted with the view to find occasions to apply force and violence. The occasions came, and the methods adopted had their perfect work. The result is known, but must be stated here for historical purposes purely. By a system of violence and coercion ranging through all possible grades, from urgent persuasion to mob violence and plentiful murders, the election was won by the Democrats. The historian here is no longer compelled to spell out his verdict from a wide induction of facts; he need only accept the assertions, even the vaunts, of many of the leading figures in the canvass since the canvass was closed.

Is there anything to be said by way of verdict upon the whole passage? Yes; plainly this, at least,—that the drama or tragedy lay potentially, from the first, in the reconstruction policy of Morton and Stevens. The latent fire there concealed was blown to flame by the conduct of affairs in South Carolina under the inspiration, if not direction, of Republican leaders at Washington. No proper or serious efforts were ever made there to ward off or prevent the conflict. Till October, 1876, no doubt seemed to enter the minds of Republican politicians that the brute force of numbers would win, as it had won. Cries of distress, shouts of encouragement, promises of reward for the party in South Carolina, now burdened the mails and kept telegraph wires hot. Managers of the Republican national canvass vied with one another in the extravagance of hopes and promises sent to South Carolina. But the forces aroused by ten years of vassalage of white to black, and eight years of corruption and plunder and misrule, moved on to their end till the end was fully reached.

It has often been asked, Could not the end—freedom from negro domination and its consequent misrule—have been reached by other more lawful and more peaceful methods? Into speculations of this kind it is not worth while to venture. One thing may be said with confidence,—the whites of South Carolina in 1876 believed no other methods or means would avail. Their course was guided by this belief. Mr. Hallam declares that "nothing is more necessary, in reaching historical conclusions, than knowledge of the motives avowed and apparently effective in the minds of the parties to controversies." The vowed motives of the whites in the struggle of 1876 are fully recorded. Are there any evidences that these motives were simulated or affected? The policy adopted and carried out does not discredit the existence and force of these motives. The campaign of 1876 was conducted as if it were a life-or-death combat.

Finally, the more serious, most serious, question has often been raised: conceding the wrongs suffered and the hopelessness of relief by other methods, was this campaign warranted? Different answers will be given by different moralists and casuists. To the writer, the question does not seem of first or great importance. What is certain is that a people of force, pride, and intelligence, driven, as the white people of South Carolina believed they were in 1876, to choose between violence and lawlessness for a time, and misrule for all time, will infallibly choose the former.

The overthrow of Republican or negro rule in South Carolina in 1876 was root-and-branch work. The fabric so long and laboriously built up fell in a day. Where was fancied to be strength was found only weakness. The vauntings were turned to cringings of terror. Poltroons and perjurers made haste to confess; robbers came forward to disgorge, intent only on personal safety; and the world saw an old phenomenon repeated,—the essential and ineradicable cowardice and servility of conscious wrongdoers. The avalanche caught the innocent with the guilty, the patriot and reformer with the corruptionist, the bribe-giver and bribe-taker. It could not be otherwise; it has never been otherwise in such convulsions.

The historian who studies this crowning event of reconstruction in South Carolina will be sure to meet or to raise the question, Why did Republican reformers there adhere to the Republican party in 1876? The answer to this is easy. They were, most of them, trained in another school than South Carolina. Resort to violence and bloodshed was not in their list of possible remedies for political wrongs or abuses. They were ready to risk or to lose their own lives in a contest for good government; they were not ready to take the lives or shed the blood of others for any political cause not involving actual physical self-defense.

A close or interested student of reconstruction will doubtless ask, In the light of retrospect and the disillusionment of later events, does it seem that good government could have been reached in South Carolina by a continuance of the union of a part—the reforming part—of the Republican party and the whole body of Democrats in the state? Speculation and reflection have been and will be expended on this question, for to some degree it touches a vital moral point. It has already been said that on this question the two wings—Republican and Democratic—of the reformers of 1874-76 held opposite opinions. It must be conceded that, unfortunately but inevitably, into the decision of the question in 1876 purely party considerations entered strongly. It would be vain for either side to deny it. Republican reformers were party men; so were Democratic reformers. Personal ambitions, also, played their usual part—a large one. Instigations to a strict Republican party contest came freely from Washington. On the other hand, Mr. Tilden, who was made to bear in those days so heavy a load of responsibility for everything amiss in the eyes of his party opponents, was specially charged—a charge still current among the uninformed or the victims of ancient party prejudices—with influencing the Democratic party in South Carolina in this crisis to enter on a party canvass on the lines of violence and fraud. The writer thinks he now knows the charge to be unfounded; that, on the contrary, if Mr. Tilden's influence was felt at all, it was in the direction of a canvass for state officers and the legislature on non-partisan lines, and in any event a peaceful and lawful canvass. If there is any interest still attaching to the writer's own view, he is quite ready now to say that he feels sure there was no possibility of securing permanent good government in South Carolina through Republican influences. If the canvass of 1876 had resulted in the success of the Republican party, that party could not, for want of materials, even when aided by the Democratic minority, have given pure or competent administration. The vast preponderance of ignorance and incapacity in that party, aside from downright dishonesty, made it impossible. An experienced or observant eye can see the causes. The canvass on purely party lines in 1876 necessarily threw Republican reformers and Republican rascals again into friendly contact and alliance. Success would have given redoubled power to leaders who had been temporarily discredited or set aside; the flood gates of misrule would have been reopened; and, as was said by one of the leaders of reform when Whipper and Moses were elected judges, "a terrible crevasse of misgovernment and public debauchery" would have again opened. The real truth is, hard as it may be to accept it, that the elements put in combination by the reconstruction scheme of Stevens and Morton were irretrievably bad, and could never have resulted, except temporarily or in desperate moments, in government fit to be endured. As Macaulay's old Puritan sang in after years of Naseby, so may now sing a veteran survivor of reconstruction in South Carolina:—

"Oh! evil was the root, and bitter was the fruit,
    And crimson was the juice of the vintage that we trod."

There is an important inquiry still to be noticed and answered: How did the victors use their victory? The just answer seems to be, "Not altogether well," but emphatically, "As well as could have been expected,"—as well as the lot and nature of humanity probably permit. Some unfair, unjust, merely angry blows were struck after the victory was won. For the rest, forbearance and oblivion were the rule. Good government, the avowed aim, was fully secured. Economy succeeded extravagance; judicial integrity and ability succeeded profligacy and ignorance on the bench; all the conditions of public welfare were restored.

Of secondary results, it is hardly necessary to this review and picture of reconstruction in South Carolina to speak; but it would be an impressive warning for other like cases if it were added that the methods of 1876 have left scars and wounds which generations of time cannot efface or heal. The appeal for the truth of this remark may be safely made to the most ardent defender of those methods. The price of what was gained in 1876 will long remain unliquidated. No part of it can ever be remitted. The laws of human society, not written in statute books, proclaim that wrong and wrong methods are self-propagating. Long before Shakespeare told it, it was true, even from the foundation of the moral order:—

> "We but teach
> Bloody instructions, which, being taught, return
> To plague the inventor; this even-handed justice
> Commends the ingredients of our poison'd chalice
> To our own lips."

Every present citizen of South Carolina knows, and those who are truthful and frank will confess, that the ballot debauched in 1876 remains debauched; the violence taught then remains now, if not in the same, in other forms; the defiance of law learned then in what was called a good cause survives in the horrid orgies and degradation of lynchings.

The chapter of recent events covered by this paper is made up largely of the record of mistakes and crimes followed by the sure, unvarying retributions which all history teaches are the early or late result of evil courses in nations and states as well as in individuals. To whom, humanly speaking, are these woes and wastes chargeable? The answer must be, to those who devised and put in operation the congressional scheme of reconstruction,—to their unspeakable folly, their blind party greed, their insensate attempt to reverse the laws which control human society.

The designed plan of this paper does not extend to any discussion of the always grave topic of the condition and prospects of the negro race in South Carolina and the South. It has abundantly appeared in what has already been written that that race was used as the tool of heartless partisan leaders. As in all such cases, the tool was cast aside when its use was ended. Who can look on the picture,—the negro enslaved by physical chains for some two centuries and a half, then bodily lifted into freedom by other hands than his own, next mercilessly exploited for the benefit of a political party, and heartlessly abandoned when the scheme had failed,—what heart of stone, we say, would not be touched by these undeserved miseries, these woeful misfortunes, of the negro of the United States?

What had the negro to show after 1876 for his sufferings? Merely the paper right to vote,—a right which he had no earthly power or capacity to use or to defend; while, with smug faces, with hypocritic sighs and upturned eyeballs, the *soi-disant* philanthropists and charitymongers of the North looked on the negro from afar, giving him only an occasional charge to still stand by the grand old party that had set him free! To all who feel a real solicitude for the welfare of the Southern negro, it ought to be said that the conditions of his welfare lie in reversing at all points the spirit and policy of reconstruction which brought on him this Iliad of woes. Philanthropy without wisdom is always dangerous. Disregard of actual conditions is never wise. The negro depends for his welfare, not on the North, but on the South; not on strangers, however friendly or sympathetic or generous in bestowing bounty, but on his white neighbors and employers. Whatever can be done to promote good relations between him and his actual neighbors will be well done; whatever is done which tends otherwise will be ill done. By industry and thrift the negro can secure all he needs, both of livelihood and of education; whatever is given him gratuitously promotes idleness and unthrift. With all emphasis let it be said and known—and the writer's knowledge confirms the saying, as will like knowledge acquired by any honest and clear-sighted person—that the negro at the South is not, in the mass or individually, the proper object of charity.

And of his education let a word be said. Education is, no one disputes or doubts, essential to the welfare of a free or self-governing community. The negro in his present situation is not an exception to the rule. But what sort of education does he need? Primarily, and in nine hundred and ninety-nine cases out of one thousand, he does not need, in any proper sense of the words, literary, scientific, or what we call the higher education. It is not too much to say that, up to this time, a great amount of money and effort has been worse than wasted on such education, or attempts at such education, of the negro. To an appreciable extent, it has been a positive evil to him. Give him, or rather stimulate him to provide for himself, education suited to his condition: to wit, abundant training in the three R's; and after that, skill in handicraft, in simple manual labor of all kinds, which it is his lot to do—lot fixed not by us, but by powers above us. If there be aspiring spirits in the race, capable of better things, this is the soil from which they may rise, rather than from hotbeds or forcing grounds,—the so-called negro colleges and universities now existing in the South. Beyond this, let the negro be taught, early and late, in schools and everywhere, thrift, pecuniary prudence and foresight, the duty, the foremost duty, of getting homes, property, land, or whatever constitutes wealth in his community. Above all things, let him be taught that his so-called rights depend on himself alone. Tell him, compel him by iteration to know, that no race or people has ever yet long had freedom unless it was won and kept by itself; won and kept by courage, by intelligence, by vigilance, by prudence. Having done this, let Northern purses be closed; let sympathy and bounty be bestowed, if anywhere, upon far less favored toilers nearer home, and leave the negro to work out his own welfare, unhelped and unhindered. If these simple methods are adopted and rigorously observed, the negro problem at our South will tend toward solution, and the flood of ills flowing from reconstruction as imposed from without will at last be stayed; and they can be stayed in no other ways. Constitutional limits of aid by legislation have already been reached and overpassed. Rights, to be secure, must, in the last resort, rest on stronger supports than constitutions, statutes, or enrolled parchments. Self-government under constitutions presupposes a firm determination, and mental, moral and physical capacity, ready and equal to the defense of rights. Neither the negro nor the white man can have them on other terms.

PART NINE

THE END OF RECONSTRUCTION

Charles Nordhoff, Northern Journalist, Finds Racial Progress in Louisiana, If Not in Georgia, But He Opposes Federal Intervention

Among the more enlightened observers of the South in 1875—a year when the old antislavery men were having second thoughts about Radical Reconstruction—was Charles Nordhoff (1830-1901), correspondent for the New York *Herald*. At five, he had migrated with his parents from his native Prussia to Cincinnati, became a printer, served three years in the United States Navy, and then used these experiences and his self-education to write four books on seafaring life, mostly sketches. At the outbreak of the Civil War, he became the managing editor of the influential New York *Evening Post* and followed a strong pro-Union policy. He wrote books on the war, the freedmen, and labor. Keenly interested in social history, he published *Communistic Societies of the U.S.* (1875) based on observation. In 1874, he emulated Frederick Law Olmsted, the journalist interpreter of the Cotton Kingdom, by traveling through the South; this was at a time when the conservatives were gaining rapidly in "redeeming" the Radical-controlled legislatures. He had necessarily to rely upon informants for the alleged facts of overwhelming Carpetbag corruption and the urgent necessity of withdrawing federal troops from the South. However, where Nordhoff is more obviously writing from first-hand observations, as in this selection, he is much more optimistic about the progress both freedmen and white Southerners were then making. It seems clear that he is trying to be objective; but he does reflect the newer anti-Radical defeatism of 1875. Most valuable, however, is his economic analysis.

From Charles Nordhoff, *The Cotton States in the Spring and Summer of 1875* (New York, 1876), pp. 68-73, 106-11.

. . . Many of the whites indeed, would vote to make General Grant President for life and Louisiana a province, because as a very respectable and intelligent man said to me but the other day, "In that case we should at least have equal protection, and could appeal direct to Caesar for justice, and against robbery." It is not pleasant to hear such words from an American citizen.

The only sure remedy, I am persuaded, lies in the absolute non-interference of the Federal power. If today it were known that the Federal Government would not interfere in the affairs of Louisiana on any account except for rebellion against the Federal Government, the influence of those Republicans who sincerely desire good government would be increased a hundred-fold. They would be able to extinguish at once the power of the colored demagogues; for the negro dares to be politically corrupt only because he profoundly believes that the Federal arm will protect him in his acts; he has always seen it do so. Take away the constant menace of Federal interference, and the whole body of corruptionists will at once sink out of sight, as they did in Arkansas.

Nor do I believe that any serious disorder would happen in the State. The good people would know that they could hope to control the government by fair and peaceable means, and would have its help in controlling the disorderly whites. There is not the least disposition to fall into trouble with the Federal power. There is no hostility to the Union or the Government. The negro laborers are too valuable to be abused; for free labor is a very great and universally acknowledged success.

The spirit of Louisiana is not bad; he who says it is has, I do not hesitate to assert, some bad motive.

There are a few parishes, like Franklin, where human life is held cheap, where ruffians rule, and where one might, without exaggeration, say that, under the careless sway of the Republicans rulers, outlaws have mastered society. But even in these parishes, of which there are but two or three at most, no one pretends that murder is practiced for political purposes.

Franklin, for instance, was the refuge of deserters and outlaws during the war; it is thinly populated, contains but few blacks, and, I think, from what I have heard from both Democrats and Republicans, it has substantially no law except that of the pistol and knife. "The people are getting very tired of it," said a Democrat to me. "Property is unsalable; nobody goes there; and they would welcome law and order if they could get it."

I said there were perhaps two or three such parishes, but I know of only this one. Its condition is probably worse than that of some of the coal counties of Pennsylvania, but not much worse. Neither Warmouth nor Kellogg has done any thing to improve it.

But the great body of the white people of the State are good citizens, and they have learned a terribly severe lesson of the importance of justice, peace, and order in the last ten years. They have learned to respect the rights of the negro, and they and the blacks ought to be trusted with self-government. There is no other way to reform abuses in the State; and, what is still more important, a continuance of the Federal protectorate will speedily result in making life intolerable even to the white Republicans, or, at least, to that part of them who have property in the State; for, as I pointed out before, it is the worse class of colored demagogues who are now coming to the surface to take command.

The agricultural industry of Louisiana divides itself broadly in two parts—sugar and cotton. The upper part of the State is mainly engaged in cotton-culture; the lower, in the production of sugar. But, as in some of the northern and western parishes stock-raising is also practiced, so on the low alluvial lands intersected by the Mississippi, the Atchafalaya, and the numerous bayous which lead out of these streams, rice is a considerable and profitable crop as well as sugar; and latterly the small planters begin to set out orange orchards, the few orchards now in bearing being very profitable. This tree requires ten years in this climate to come into full bearing, and is liable while young to be cut down by frost. It is not a sure crop here, is subject to the scale insect, and the orange-planter needs to select with some care the site of his orchard, and to seek protection against the cold north winds of the spring season. But the tree bears well, and has much less care than it should have; and the crop finds a very ready sale for cash, the orchardist usually, I hear, selling his fruit on the tree, and at a gross valuation made when the oranges are ripening. The flowers, also, have a market value.

A few large sugar-planters are beginning the systematic culture of the orange; and where the situation is favorable to the tree, it makes a very profitable crop. At twelve years after planting it should yield one thousand dollars an acre, with a trifling cost for cultivation and care.

Along the river or the bayou there is usually a strip of land from half a mile to a mile deep; back of that come forest and swamp, and beyond that, probably, the face of another bayou. The land is flat, but falls a little from the river toward the swamp; so that when a rise of the waters comes, the plantation is overflowed from the back first, unless, of course, the levee in front breaks. Many plantations have a back as well as a front levee, and often you see a pumping wheel and engine, which are needed to get rid of the rain-water. They say of Florida that the water is so close to the surface that you may dig down anywhere two feet deep and go a-fishing; and these sugar and rice lands are at this season not much drier. The banks of the stream are fringed with live-oaks, and in the shade of these the plantation-house is usually placed, with the sugar-house near-by, and the cottages of the laborers beyond that. On some of the bayous which are quite narrow, the plantation lines extend on both sides, and the fields are connected with the sugar-house by floating bridges, which are swung to one side to allow a steamboat to pass. On the Mississippi the high levees partly conceal the buildings, and from the deck of a steamboat the view of roof-lines above the levee gives the landscape a very quaint appearance.

In many places rice is the crop of the small farmers—men with one hundred or two hundred acres of land. It requires less capital than sugar, and is sufficiently profitable. It depends, of course, on the waters rising sufficiently high to flood the land at the proper time. To

accomplish this, flooding ditches are cut, and water is let in through
the levee by simple flood-gates. About Point à la Hache such ditches
and gates are found at intervals of every few hundred feet for miles of
the river-front. In a good season the yield, I am told, is from twelve to
fifteen barrels per acre, which ought to bring five dollars per barrel.
The expense is about twenty dollars per acre, which includes taking
off the crop. In some parts the people continue to cut it with a sickle,
and I have seen it threshed out by driving horses over it in a large
circle. But reapers and steam-threshers are coming into use and the
rice country has always mills to which the farmers take their rice to
get it hulled. In the rice-fields the colored laborer receives one dollar a
day, and feeds himself.

In some places, as on the Atchafalaya and about Grand Lake, live-
oak timber is cut and shipped to different parts of the world. One of
the important petty industries of Lower Louisiana is the collection of
the moss which hangs in long festoons from all the trees, particularly
from the oak. Negroes and white men alike devote themselves to this,
and the quantity brought to New Orleans annually is quite large. On
the sugar-plantations, when fire-wood is cut the moss is usually the
perquisite of the colored men, and they understand how to prepare it
for market, and make some pocket money in this way.

Sugar, however, is the main crop of Southern Louisiana. Various
causes make it just now a precarious crop; and sugar-plantations in
some of the best locations in the State could be bought in the spring of
1875 for less money than the machinery of the sugar-houses cost. I
was surprised to find that a large number of Northern and Northwestern men have come down here since the war, and bought sugar-estates.
Some of these manage their plantations with the help of overseers, and
live here only in the winter; others manage their own places. As you
pass up a bayou on the steamboat, the whitewashed cottages and
neater culture generally tell you that here a Northern man has settled
with capital enough to carry on his business to advantage. Many of
the plantations are still in the hands of the old planters, and often
these have a dilapidated look, which shows that their owners are in
embarrassed circumstances.

The bad condition of the levees has brought serious loss to many planters, especially in the Atchafalaya and Teche country; and there is a general complaint of high taxation and wasteful expenditure of public money.

The planters, without exception, so far as I have heard them speak, are thoroughly satisfied with the colored man as a laborer. I do not mean to say that they have no fault to find; but they say that the negroes are orderly, docile, faithful to their engagements, steady laborers in the field, readily submitting to directions and instructions, and easily managed and made contented. This applies to cotton as well as sugar planters, and all is summed up in the phrase I most frequently heard used, "We have the best laboring class in the world."

Their faults are mainly of carelessness with such property as mules and farming-implements, and killing cattle and hogs. As to the first, several planters told me they had found it useful to give the charge of animals entirely to a special person, who fed and cared for them. But it appears to make no difference whether the mules belong to the planter or to the laborer; the latter is as conscientiously careless of his own as of another's property. It is part of the heedlessness bred of slavery, and it will take time to be bred out, as it was bred in.

As to killing cattle and hogs, this is a custom which arises, in part, out of a slovenly way of letting animals run half wild in the woods without that care which marks special ownership. It is matter which the planters are meeting gradually by letting the laborers keep stock of their own, and thus making it to their interest to put down the indiscriminate theft. A Northern man, a planter, told me that he had brought from the North thirty-four cows, and all had been killed but two, which, for safety, he now kept within the door-yard of his dwelling. I asked if his laborers were generally dishonest, and he replied emphatically, no; he would trust any one of them, he said, with ten thousand dollars to carry to town, without fear of loss; he had never missed any articles from his house, where he had colored servants, and where the women from the quarters often came. But he could keep chickens and turkeys only with the utmost difficulty and care; and as for cows and hogs, it was entirely out of the question.

The laborers on the sugar-plantations receive from thirteen to fifteen dollars per month; a cottage, usually of two rooms, and a garden patch near it; a ration of pork and corn-meal, rather more than enough for a hearty man; and a corn patch, which the laborer culti-vates for himself on Saturday afternoon with the planters' teams. About their cottages they can keep chickens and pigs, if they like; and often they have a horse, a cow, and even an old carriage of some kind, in which they drive out on Sunday with great satisfaction, crowding in wife and children.

The planter usually has on his place a store where necessaries and luxuries are sold, and among the former whisky is reckoned, I am sorry to say. They tell me the blacks will have it, and it is better to sell it in moderation on the place than to compel them to go to a dis-tance for it. As the sugar-plantations are all situated upon navigable streams, they are exposed to a serious nuisance in the shape of ped-dling boats, which sail up and down with a license from the State to sell various matters, among which whisky is prominent. These anchor opposite a plantation for a day or two, and carry away, not only all the spare cash, but chickens and other "truck" which the colored people may have raised.

The negro is fond of credit. Few of them, I find, are sufficiently forehanded to deal for cash. They have credit at the store; and it is the planter's object to so manage the laborer's account that he shall have a pretty little sum at Christmas, which he thereupon mostly spends during Christmas-week with very great satisfaction. If he has been allowed to draw out all of his account beforehand he is dissatis-fied, and likes to remove, thinking that he has not done well—no mat-ter how clearly he is shown that he was wasteful during the year. Only a very few lay by money; but occasionally a negro was pointed out to me who had several hundred dollars ahead.

One thing greatly pleased me: the black man pays his debts. All the petty shopkeepers, of whom the country is full, are ready to give credit to the negroes. It was a question I asked very often, and always received the same reply, "They always pay up." Among the rice-planters, where the blacks work by the day, they frequently hire cot-tages, and the owner of some of these told me he would rather have negroes than whites for tenants, because they paid more promptly. A country store-keeper said to me, "Ninety per cent of my sales are to colored people, and ninety percent of my bad debts are owed by whites."

I had read somewhere in the North a complaint that the planters refused to sell land to the negroes. The case I found stands thus: In the sugar country the negro does not aim to buy twenty or forty acres, and plant cane for himself. He would need to have the cane ground; and the business is too hurried at the close of the season to get this done with certainty and at the proper time. But they like to own an acre or two, on which they place a cabin; and this homestead makes them contented. Unluckily, they do not improve their places; invariably I have found them in the roughest and most disorderly condition. Now, naturally, no man likes to sell a corner of his estate to such purchasers; and the planters very justly and very generally refuse to sell such little patches to negroes. Some would divide their estates into hundred-acre tracts, but there are few purchasers for such parcels. Many others hold on to their large estates, even when they have not capital enough to work them; and I have seen some plantations which were not worked at all, but on which the owners paid the taxes, and waited for better times. For my part, I do not much blame them. Nobody, except a land-speculator, likes to sell land; especially where it has been his home. And these people are not land-speculators.

It is not uncommon, however, for a speculator to buy a hundred acres near a town, and divide it into two-acre tracts, which are readily sold to colored people at a great advance. I have seen several such villages, and certainly the regular rows of neatly whitewashed cabins on the plantation look, and are, far more comfortable.

In the cotton country it is not very uncommon to find negroes owning twenty or forty acres; and they can always buy land if they want to. The great majority, however, as yet, prefer to cultivate the land on shares, either furnishing their own teams or only their labor; and in the rich Louisiana bottoms they make handsome returns in this way.

The sugar-planter lies, in all countries where he is found, under a practical disadvantage, because he combines two callings very different in their nature—he is both a farmer and a manufacturer. I found this recognized in the Sandwich Islands, where one or two of the shrewdest planters have tried the experiment of inducing the natives to raise cane and bring it to their mills to be ground. In this way the risk of the crop is divided; and this is so great that a large sugar-planter may be fatally embarrassed by the loss of a single crop, or by a trifling fall in the price of sugar. There are undoubtedly some difficulties in the way of dividing the business; but in several of the sugar counties of Louisiana planters are making the attempt to turn the mere raising of cane over to laborers and small farmers, and with a promise of success.

In Plaquemine, Mr. Dymond, of New York, has begun to buy cane and grind it at his mill, and with profit to himself and to those who raise the cane. One farmer told me that the experiment last year, which he made only because his own sugar-house had burned down, was so far successful that this year he was putting a part of his land in rice and over two hundred acres in cane. He sold last year one hundred and seventy-five acres of cane for five dollars a ton—he cutting it, and loading it on the barge which carried it to the mill; and he thought the returns satisfactory.

In Terre Bonne I found an intelligent young planter, a Louisianian, who was trying a different plan, and, as he thought with the promise of success. He has made a contract for five years with his laborers, under which they take of him on an average ten acres per hand, he furnishing seed-cane, cane land, houses, fire-wood, fences, and land for a corn patch; they supplying teams, tools, labor, and feeding themselves, and taking half the crop. The men work in squads of half a dozen. When the cane is ready to cut, the planter takes charge, and uses all the teams and men for the common purpose of getting the cane in and the sugar made. At this time also he hires extra hands, and the tenants pay half the cost of these. The planter advances all the money needed, and, in fact, makes advances of food and other supplies also to the tenants, which is the evil custom of the country. The cost of taking the cane from the field and turning it into sugar is about twenty dollars an acre.

Under this system this planter told me that the men worked more zealously than ever before. He had even sold them teams on a credit of three years; and the result of the first year was that the tenants lived, and paid one-third the cost of their teams; and of eleven squads, the members of seven came out at the close of the season one hundred dollars per man ahead. As for himself, he said he had lost money for several years; but last year he made money, and he attributed it largely to the new system. I ought to add that most of his tenants were white men, but a squad of colored men did as well and made as much money as any of the others.

I found a Southern man in charge as superintendent of a railroad which employs a large colored force as track layers and menders, etc. The men receive one dollar and fifty-cents a day, and pay sixty cents a day to their foreman, a colored man also, for food. They are "the very best of laborers, always willing, zealous, and faithful, and will work very hard and in the most disagreeable labor for any one who treats them well." So said the superintendent. One large gang was pointed out to me, which for some years had labored in the swamps through which a part of the road runs. They composed a little independent community, having a justice of the peace of their own, who maintains order and decides disputes.

Where sugar-planters keep no store for their hands, it is customary to pay the hands half their wages at the end of the month and the balance at the close of the year; and I imagine those who make advances in goods try to keep their men to about the same limit.

Very few cotton-planters in Louisiana pay wages. The colored man prefers to take the land on shares, and it is by far the best way. Where they rent land in the rich bottoms, they pay from six to ten dollars per acre, or, which is more usual, eighty pounds of clean cotton. In some cases the planter furnishes land, house, fuel, a corn patch, teams, tools, and feed for the animals, and takes half the crop. If the colored tenant wants to undertake corn as well as cotton, that, too, is planted at halves. They usually work in squads, and undertake about fifteen acres of cotton and ten of corn to the hand.

Cotton will average three-quarters of a bale to the acre, and I judge that the laborer with a fair crop may live through the year, and have one hundred and fifty dollars in cash at the close of the season, neither he nor his family having suffered for any thing in the mean time. The returns are very satisfactory to the laborer, and Northern farmers, who save as well as work, could easily grow rich on the Mississippi and Red River bottom-lands.

Every body tells me that the colored men save but little. In one cotton-parish a Republican who has taken great interest in the welfare of the negroes said, in answer to my question, "They are not worth a dollar a head of the population to-day." "That man had one hundred and fifty dollars due him last Christmas for his cotton," said another planter to me: "he spent it all in ten days, and bought the greatest lot of trash you ever saw; but he and his wife and children were satisfied and happy, and when I reproached him, he said, 'What's the use of living if a man can't have the good of his labor?'"

New Orleans has a considerable number of colored mechanics, who are spoken of as skillful and competent men. Elsewhere in the State I have seen colored men working as masons and carpenters, and occasionally shoe-makers, and they are skillful blacksmiths. I am told, in the towns a considerable proportion of the colored people own the houses in which they live, and they all have a strong desire, as I have said, to own small lots of land. But in a parish which has a negro population of over twelve thousand, a planter who has taken much interest in the colored people told me he knew not more than twenty men who owned farms, and some of these he thought would not make their payments on the price, by reason of improvidence. This was in the cotton country, where the colored people can readily buy land, and at a reasonable rate.

The women do not regularly work in the fields. They receive from eight dollars to ten dollars a month as field-hands, and in the cotton-picking time women and children turn in to this work. In the sugar country, too, the planters employ women in the fields at certain seasons. If the colored laborer is forehanded, he prefers that his wife shall not work in the field.

Of schools most of the parishes have a sufficient number, and the colored people are generally better supplied than the whites with free schools. This arises in part from the fact that school-teachers are made use of as politicians.

The notion that the negro race is dying out is absurd, and one never hears it mentioned here. The whole country is full of hearty, shiny little pickaninnies, fat, quiet, generally nicely dressed; and in the towns and villages the larger children look very neat and happy as they go to and from school or Sunday-school.

The colored people are almost universally, I am told, anxious to send their children to school, and in my conversation with them the most frequent complaint I heard was of the mismanagement or inefficiency of schools. I never heard any complaint of a lack of schools, though some outlying parishes are not well supplied. In a country parish on a Sunday, I fell into conversation with three colored men whom I met in my walk. One had his little children with him. He complained that the school was not kept open—"not more than one day in the week. It was a shame, when they had a good schoolhouse; but the teacher was of no account." I said they ought to cure that by choosing good officers at elections, and one replied that they always got cheated. The Republican office-holders were as bad as Conservatives, and he would just as soon trust one as the other. "And if we put our own color in, somebody comes along and shoves money in their pockets, and makes them forget their own people."

As to churches, in the cotton country the colored people are mostly either Methodists or Baptists, and they have their own churches and preachers of their own color. The meeting is a curiosity. The preacher is almost always so far illiterate that he uses large words in a wrong sense; but he freely denounces the sins of the congregation. Then come screams, violent contortions, jumping, dancing, and shouting—but not more violent or ghastly than I have seen in Western camp-meetings among white people, in my younger days, I must own.

You hear it commonly said that the preachers are not good men, and do not live up to their calling, but I doubt it. They are politicians —as preachers, lawyers, and doctors are commonly among white men. But even though the form which Christianity takes among these people is repugnant to my colder nature, I found no upright, thoughtful planter who did not acknowledge that the Church is a restraining influence upon them; and in one case where I put the question the planter told me that he had noticed that almost all the crime, lawsuits, and troubles generally, in his parish, which came before the courts, originated on those plantations where there was no meeting-house.

"As for me," he said, "I think it an economy to support both church and Sunday-school among the colored people on my plantations." In Southern Louisiana a large part of the colored population are Catholics, and have not separate churches.

The colored people are the main working force of the State. It is not fair to say that they are the only workers, as is sometimes rashly asserted, for there is a considerable population of white farmers scattered over the State. In the Acadian country these people, who are called "Cadians," are industrious and prosperous. They speak French, and retain many of their old French customs. They live a good deal among themselves, and do not even care to trade with the Americans, whom, though they have occupied the country ever since the acquisition of Louisiana, the Acadian still regards as interlopers. In other parts of the State there is a population of white farmers who cultivate the thin uplands. They have been much neglected, and are not very highly thought of by their neighbors in the lowlands.

To conclude, the industrial prospects of the colored people in Louisiana are satisfactory. They work, and they receive a fair and even handsome return for their labor; and working so largely on shares, they have incentives to faithful work which day-laborers in the North are often without. Louisiana is an extraordinarily rich State; millions of acres of the most fertile soil lie uncultivated, and may be obtained at a price so low that an industrious man may pay for a farm from the savings of two cotton crops. These lands are open to the colored people, and when time and a longer experience of liberty have taught them self-denial, economy, and business habits, they will more largely become independent farmers.

It is my belief that they ought now to be finally—in this State—left to themselves, so far as the political interference of the Federal Government is concerned. They know how to help themselves, and it is, in the opinion of the best Republicans I met in the State, a danger to social order that the negroes, preyed upon as they are by demagogues of both colors, shall any longer have cause to believe that the Federal power stands behind them to protect them against the results of their misconduct, or to maintain them in places for which they are, by lack of education and of training and experience, unfit.

. . . For the present year the school-tax will yield only $270,000. Last year there were 135,000 children in the public schools—an increase of 50,000 over 1873. In 1873 there were actually attending school only 63,922 white, and 19,755 colored children; in 1874 the numbers stood 93,167 white and 42,374 colored children. This was out of a total of 218,733 white, and 175,304 colored children within the school ages.

There is still in many counties some prejudice against colored schools, but it constantly decreases; and you will notice that more than twice as many colored children attended schools in 1874 as in 1873. Atlanta has a colored university, and the Legislature appropriates yearly toward its support $8000—the same amount which is given to the old State University. The governor and superintendent of schools both desire that this appropriation shall be diverted to a colored normal school; and there is some ignorant prejudice in Atlanta against the teachers in the university, on the ground of their sitting at table with the colored students, which is thought to promote "social equality." It is not denied, however, that the school does good work; and I imagine the teachers can best instruct the pupils in the minor morals by eating at the same table with them.

One can not help feeling a little contempt for the people who here in the South make themselves needlessly unhappy about "social equality." I was amused at a sensible planter—a Democrat, and a native Georgian—who said to me, "It is absurd in us to make such a fuss. There is scarcely a man of us whose children are not suckled by negro nurses; our playmates were negro boys; all our relations in the old times were of the most intimate; and, for my part, I would as soon ride in a car with a cleanly dressed negro as with a white man. It is all stupid nonsense, and makes us absurd in the eyes of sensible people."

The feeling takes the most ridiculous forms, too: for instance, in Atlanta and Augusta colored people are allowed to ride in street-cars;

in Savannah they are forbidden. Why the difference? Is a Savannah negro less clean, or is a Savannah white man a more noble being, than those in the other two cities?

As showing the relations of the two races, I found on a wall in Augusta a poster giving notice of a colored railroad-excursion to Port Royal, stating price of passage and time required, and at the end a notice that a special car would be provided for such of the white citizens as would like to take advantage of this opportunity to see Port Royal, and special accommodations for their comfort would be at hand. The whole affair was under the conduct of colored men.

The superintendent of schools told me that there was less prejudice against colored schools in the southern counties, where the negroes are the most numerous, than in the northern part of the State.

The negroes in and near the cities and towns are usually prosperous. There are many colored mechanics, and they receive full wages where they are skillful. Near Atlanta and other places they own small "truck-farms," and supply the market with vegetables. There are fewer black than white beggars in the cities; and a missionary clergyman surprised me by the remark that the blackberry crop, which was ripening, was "a blessing to dozens of poor white families whom he knew," who lived half the year, he said, in a condition of semi-starvation. He explained that these people would not only sell blackberries, but that in the season they largely lived on this fruit. These are the kind of people to whom factories would be a blessing.

In the cotton country the planter usually pays his hands ten dollars a month, by the year, with a house and ration. The ration consists of three pounds of bacon, a peck of meal, and a pint of molasses per week. The laborer has also a "patch" of land for a garden, and Saturday afternoon for himself, with the use of the planter's mules and tools to work the garden. They work from sunrise to sunset, and in the summer have two and a half hours for dinner. The cotton-pickers receive fifty cents per one hundred pounds in the seed, and are fed; or sixty-five cents per one hundred pounds, if they feed themselves. The ration costs about fifteen cents a day.

Most planters keep a small store, and sell their laborers meat, bread, and tobacco on credit, the general settlement being made once a year. The women receive for field work six dollars a month and a ration; and I was told that they insist on receiving their own wages, and will not let their husbands use their money. They form an important extra force for pressing work.

One of the most intelligent planters I met in the State told me that his laborers cost him about fifteen dollars a month—wages and ration. He added (what surprised me) that the best planters prefer to pay wages rather than let their land on shares, and that the wages system was growing in favor also with the negroes. I found this confirmed by other testimony. It is very different in the other States I have seen, except, indeed, North Carolina; and I imagine the poverty of the soil is a main reason for it. In Mississippi, Louisiana, and Arkansas, the planters told me it would be poor policy to pay wages. Certainly, it is the poorest system for the negro.

Where the negroes plant on shares, the planter furnishes the land and mules, and feeds the mules. The negro furnishes labor and feeds it, and gets one-third of the crop. He pays for one-third of the fertilizers. The planter gins the whole crop. Where negroes rent land, they pay seven hundred and fifty pounds of lint or ginned cotton for thirty-five to forty acres of land—as much as they can cultivate with one mule—and they keep up the fences, and pay for the fertilizers. "On this day," said a planter to me, "I know one man who made two hundred and fifty dollars clear in a year over and above his support, and another who lost one hundred and fifty dollars." He added that the negroes, on the whole, preferred the wages system; and this is mainly, I imagine, because the artificial manures are costly, and an uncertain element in making the crop. This means really, of course, that it costs more money to make cotton in Georgia than in the other States I have named. A third of a bale to the acre is the average crop in Georgia, but in Mississippi they expect to get from three-quarters to a bale per acre without manure.

A planter from one of the "black counties," where the negroes are most numerous, told me they were a most quiet and docile population. "I live in the midst of several hundred," he said, "with no white family within several miles of me, and my people are never in the least alarmed. I have not a fire-arm in the house half the time. Treat them honestly," he said, "and they are all right."

This man amused me with some stories of how the blacks were deceived by a set of white rascals for some years after the war. Among other things, these fellows brought red and blue sticks, which they sold for one dollar each to the negroes, wherewith to "stake off" the land which the Government was to give them. The blacks used also, when they went to the polls to vote, to bring halters with them, for the mule which General Grant was to give them. I would like to know what graceless wretch it was who spread all over the South, among the blacks, the story of "forty acres and a mule," which has caused bitter disappointment to many thousands of credulous negroes, and appears to have been used mainly to induce them to vote the Republican ticket. In Louisiana, several negroes told me that General Butler, they understood, would make them this gift; but usually it is from General Grant that they expect it, and they are very ready to vote for him.

The planter of whom I speak told me that the young negroes who had grown up since the war worked less steadily than the old hands. He added that, in his county, some blacks owned as much as two hundred and fifty acres of land, and many were doing well on their own farms. "If it were not for petit larceny, they would all do well." He kept a colored school on his own plantation. The black people liked it, he said. They are fond of hoarding coin, especially since the Freedmen's Bank failed, which caused loss to many of them, and they are quite ready to buy gold and silver coins at a premium.

The negroes in Georgia have some, but slight and lessening, causes for dissatisfaction. The fact that they will pay taxes on over seven millions of dollars this year, all acquired since 1866, and by a class notoriously unthrifty, shows that they have suffered no serious wrong or injustice. The fact that over twenty-five thousand negroes have emigrated from the State, shows also that they know how to better their condition.

But their dissatisfaction does not arise from wrongs; for the whites also are dissatisfied, and an equal number of them have removed to other States. The chief difficulty in Georgia is that it is in an old State, with worn lands, whose near neighbors, Mississippi, Arkansas, and Louisiana, invite its people to come and take possession of new and fertile soils, where they need no manures, and can get greater returns for their labor.

Georgia and North Carolina differ from the other Southern States I have seen in this: that much of their land is thin and worn, and will not produce a crop, even in the cotton region, without the use of expensive manures. This, of course, makes cotton-planting less remunerative than it is in the rich bottom-lands of Mississippi, Arkansas, and Louisiana. Moreover, judging from appearances, I should say that even in the old times, before the war, Georgia must have been a less wealthy State than those west of it.

One evidence of a general lack of prosperity in this State I came upon even before I entered Georgia, is the considerable number of emigrants of both colors, who are leaving the State for Arkansas, Texas, and Mississippi, and parties of whom I frequently spoke with at railroad stations. Georgia has lost in this way, since the conclusion of the war, I have been told by good authorities, Democratic citizens, at least fifty thousand people—half of each color.

The fact is that Georgia, though it is still essentially an agricultural State, has its greatest future as a manufacturing region. It has a great deal of valuable water-power; also coal, iron, and other mineral wealth; it has a great deal of land better fitted for small farms and varied agriculture than for either cotton or corn; and it has ready to the hands of manufacturing capitalists a numerous population of "poor whites," whose daughters make excellent factory operatives, and to whom the offer of this species of labor is a real rise in the scale of civilization.

The cotton-planters are not, as a class, either wealthy or prosperous; but the few cotton-factories are, even in this day of general depression, very remunerative. The iron and coal works are in a good condition, and the farmers of Northern Georgia are said to be doing well in all respects. I have been surprised by the unbroken prosperity of the cotton-mills in Georgia. The Augusta mills have paid a yearly dividend of not less than twenty per cent, since 1865, and the stock is quoted at 168 to-day, and none is for sale. The product is 275,000

yards per week. The Eagle and Phoenix mills of Columbus, built since
the war, with a capital of $1,000,000 and 25,000 spindles, have paid
an average dividend of over eighteen per cent, and have a considerable
surplus. No stock can be bought. The Graniteville cotton-mills, which
lie in South Carolina, just across the border-line of Georgia, were not
fairly started until 1867; and since then, I am told, have paid off a
debt of $75,000, increased their capacity from 15,000 to 23,000 spin-
dles, built over forty houses for operatives, and have meantime paid
an average dividend of over twelve per cent.

But all these mills have done a more important work besides; for
all of them give employment to the girls and women of the poor white
class, to whom such labor is, as I have said, a real and very important
step in civilization. They make excellent operatives, I am told, and the
factory life not only improves their own condition in a remarkable
degree, but adds greatly to the comfort of their parents; and is, perhaps, the only means of redeeming this large population from a somewhat abject and degraded condition.

I think I can see that the cotton-manufacturer has several important advantages in this State over his rivals in the Northern States. He
needs no such solid and costly dwellings for the work-people; land is
still cheap; lumber for building is cheap; fuel is unusually cheap; the
operative class is, I suspect, more manageable, and more easily made
intelligent, than the rude, imported labor now used in the North; food
is, and must long remain, cheaper; the mildness of the winter is certainly an advantage, and there is an air of comfort and contentment
about these Southern factories which is very pleasing. The operatives
are usually very nicely lodged in cottages, and are evidently happy
and pleased with their life.

It is among the factory workers and the small farmers of Georgia
that one finds the chief prosperity of the State. Here there is little or
no debt; money circulates rapidly; improvements are seen; and there
are patient, hopeful labor, thrift, and enterprise, which affect, as it
seems to me, the whole population. I heard here and there of instances
of poor young mechanics working steadily and earnestly, in a New
England way, at their trades, making labor respectable, accumulating
property, and taking honorable places in their communities; and some

such men talked to me of their past and their future, of the hopeful change which the extinction of slavery had produced in the prospects of their class, in language which showed me that there is a new-born hope of better things in the poor white people of the State.

When you strike the cotton region, affairs are not so happy. In the first place, the cotton farmers and planters—the large land-owners, less energetic than the population I have spoken above—have suffered from two bad laws which fostered their lack of business capacity and love of ease. The Homestead Law reserves to a land-owner a homestead of the value of three thousand dollars in gold, exempting this from seizure by creditors. Of course, in an agricultural region, so large an exemption can be easily made to cover a very considerable amount of property. To this was added a lien law—fortunately repealed by the last Legislature—which enabled the planter to borrow on or mortgage his unplanted crop; the factor who furnished him tools, manures, food, and clothing having, by this law, the first claim on the crop. Of course, he also secured the handling of it. I have seen the evil operation of such a law in Louisiana in the slavery times, and in the Sandwich Islands more recently. It is ruinous, for it offers a prize to incapacity and unthrift, enables men to undertake planting with insufficient capital, and deranges the whole industry. In Georgia the Homestead Law doubtless increased the evils of the Lien Law; and between the two it resulted that many of the planters fell over head and ears in debt. These were regularly a year or more behindhand; and if the crop—which is more precarious in this State than in some others—failed, or fell short, the factor took all; and the laborers, employed to a great extent on wages, sometimes lost all their pay, except what they had consumed during the year.

I do not doubt that in some cases such loss and wrong fell upon the negro laborer through the recklessness or dishonesty of the planter; but I am satisfied also that much oftener the planter would have honestly paid if he could, and that he, as well as his workman, was the victim of a bad business system and of his lack of capital and of business thrift. It was one of the incidents of the reorganization of labor on a new basis in a State where the culture of cotton is less certainly remunerative than in more fertile regions.

To show you how the Lien Law worked, here is a statement made to me by a planter of the charges which he had known to be paid for advances made by a factor. He instanced to me the case of a planter who required from his factor a loan or advance of five thousand dollars to make his crop. For this he paid one per cent per month, to which I was assured seven per cent per annum were sometimes added, making really nineteen per cent. Then the arrangement was that the factor should buy all the planter's supplies for him; and for this service he charged him two and a half per cent, and billed the goods to him at "time prices," which added eight or ten per cent to their cost. Then the factor sold the planter's crop, and charged for this two and a half per cent again.

I should not have believed such a system possible, had I not seen precisely the same thing regularly done by the sugar-planters in the Sandwich Islands two or three years ago. Of course, no business except the slave-trade could bear such a drain. Some planters complained to me that they could never get advances from the banks, which preferred to lend to the factors; but this will hardly surprise any businessman. The profits were great enough for the bank and the factors to divide.

One of the natural results of this system has been discontent among the negroes—the laborers—who sometimes lost their wages. At least twenty-five thousand of them have left the State; and this emigration, which last year already began to alarm the planters, has not ceased. It has been increased by other causes; but I am satisfied, from conversation with leading colored men, that the lack of prosperity here, and the well-founded belief that they could do better elsewhere, have been one of its main causes.

The repeal of the Lien Law has, of course, left the poor and improvident among the planters without credit, and they are naturally in poor spirits. But they will presently see that it is their salvation. Already they are planting more corn than ever before. They see that to raise bread and meat enough for their laborers will keep them out of the hands of the factors. More corn will be harvested in the cotton region of Georgia this year than in any year since the war.

I have given this statement of the industrial condition of Georgia because it is certain that many of the incidents of Georgia society grow mainly out of the fact that the planting region is less prosperous than the cotton region of Arkansas, Louisiana, or Mississippi; and is so mainly for the reasons I have given—the poverty of the soil, the precariousness of the crop in the far southern countries, where it is peculiarly exposed to the attacks of insects, and the poverty and unthrift of the planters. That you may not think I have overstated this lack of prosperity, I give you here some figures from a mercantile report, which I find in an Augusta journal. The business failures in the State amounted in the last six months to the sum of $2,956,215. This is a greater loss by far than is reported from any other Southern State; greater even than in South Carolina, as the following figures show:

Alabama	$523,000
Arkansas	211,000
Florida	235,000
Georgia	2,956,000
Louisiana	630,000
Mississippi	1,045,000
North Carolina	263,000
South Carolina	2,042,000
Tennessee	325,000
Texas	1,153,000
Virginia and West Virginia	1,383,000
Total	$10,766,000

The liabilities of Georgia amount to nearly one-third of the liabilities of the twelve States; the liabilities of Georgia and South Carolina together amount to nearly half the liabilities of the entire South. Georgia compares as follows with other larger and wealthier States:

Indiana	$1,860,000
Iowa	436,000
Kentucky	2,456,000
Missouri	2,328,000
Ohio	2,594,000
Georgia	2,956,000

Now, you must remember that, unlike Ohio, Indiana, or Missouri, Georgia is almost entirely an agricultural State, and that her factories and other purely business enterprises have been, almost without exception, prosperous. These figures show the condition mainly of the planting interest and of those businesses intimately related to it.

I conclude my account of Georgia with a few remarks about the political condition of the State.

There is no Republican party worthy of the name in the State. There is but one Republican newspaper, and that is a weekly. One of the most zealous Republicans in the State said to me, "The Republican party, so far as its white members are concerned, consists mainly of Federal office-holders and men seeking office—mostly natives of the State." He added, "There are not more than a hundred active white Republicans in Georgia who are honest, and out of office." Another zealous Republican said to me, "The white Republicans of Georgia are made up almost entirely of Federal office-holders whose aim is to keep their places, and of men who are trying to get these places. There is substantially nobody else, white, in the party." Another said, "White men put themselves forward for Congress on the Republican ticket, knowing they will be beaten, with the sole object of rushing to Washington as soon as the election is over to set up a claim for a Federal office on the ground of their defeat." "The Civil Rights Bill killed the Republican party in this State," said a Federal officer to me; "it put us back to 1867."

Less than five thousand whites voted the Republican ticket at the election of 1874. In 1872, a Republican told me, at least ten thousand blacks voted the Greeley ticket, and "more and more negroes vote Democratic all the time." I notice that among the grievances of the blacks mentioned in discussions of the so-called insurrection, is one that they are disfranchised if they do not pay their poll and road taxes. This is perfectly true, and, I think, perfectly just. Poll and road tax is all that the greater part of them pay toward the support of the Government; and if they evade this, they do not deserve to vote. The same law applies to the whites.

In the Georgia Congressional delegation there is not now a single Republican. One reason for this is, that in some cases the party

RECONSTRUCTION IN THE SOUTH · 300

nominates men who can not get the support of honest Republicans. One such man I was told of, who was repudiated by the honest Republicans of his district, but was no sooner beaten than he proceeded to Washington and set up a claim to all the Federal patronage of the district. Nor are claims of this kind always disallowed at Washington. For instance, not long ago a man was appointed collector of internal revenue in a Georgia district who, according to general Republican testimony, had been a Ku-klux in Ku-klux times, and who actually could not take the office because he then stood charged with offering a bribe.

One of the most prominent Federal officers in the State, a native and a zealous Republican, and bitter opponent of the Democratic party, said to me, "I don't know that there is any Republican party in the State. The negroes will not vote in general, because they have no white vote back of them. The blacks are almost totally disfranchised by their neglect to pay their taxes. At least two-thirds of the colored voters are thus disfranchised. Then, again, in some counties where there are large negro majorities half a dozen black demagogues insist on running for the same office, and then Democrats run in between them. Wherever independent tickets have been put up in counties the supporters of these strove for the negro vote, and in such cases the election was always peaceable and full, because there two parties were anxious for this vote. I do not think that for a year or two past there has been much cheating in wages; the people have learned to do better."

Georgia has been longer and more continuously than any other cotton State, since the war, under the rule of the Democratic party. Bullock, the Republican governor, chosen at the adoption of the constitution, in 1868, for a term of four years, abandoned his office and the State in October, 1871; Smith, Democrat, was elected to fill his unexpired term; was re-elected in 1872, and is still governor. The Legislature, which is elected every two years, was Republican by a small majority in 1868; but the body which assembled in November, 1871, was strongly Democratic, and both houses, and all the executive officers, have been Democratic ever since.

It follows that, since the winter of 1871, the State government has been entirely in Democratic hands; and the county governments have also, with but few exceptions, fallen under the same control. The Legislature has been overwhelmingly Democratic in both branches.

It would be strange, considering the circumstances and the party strength, if the ruling party had been always wise; but it must be said that they have done very few wicked or very foolish things. They have been fortunate in the possession of a few wise and Conservative men, with courage enough to make their sentiments known. For instance, in the last Legislature a stupid old Bourbon introduced a bill to make a breach of contract by a negro a penal offense. But Mr. Furlow, a strong Democrat, but a sensible man, rose at once, and declared that he would oppose such a measure as long as he lived; that, in his experience, if you pay a negro and treat him honestly, he will work fairly and stick to his contract. Furlow is a popular man, and has the courage of his opinions; and the result was that, in a house of one hundred and thirty members, only twelve votes were cast for the bill.

In like manner, the Toombs men, who are the Bourbons in Georgia, have tried, on different occasions, to get a constitutional convention, but have always failed, the constitution being a sufficiently good instrument. So, too, in his last message, Governor Smith . . . urged the Legislature to stop the appropriation of eight thousand dollars per annum for the colored university; and the superintendent of public instruction supported him, believing, as he told me, that a normal school for colored teachers was more necessary than a university. But, in spite of a foolish prejudice against the teachers in the university, the Legislature refused to do the governor's bidding.

It is but just to add that, if the dread of "social equality" were likely to die out, this would be skillfully prevented by some leading Republicans, chief of whom is the Northern Methodist Bishop Haven, who has on several occasions openly declared himself in favor of "social equality," and who appears to me to have quite a genius for keeping alive a subject which naturally stirs up rancorous feelings, and which is best left to settle itself.

The prostration of the Republican party has given the Democrats such great power that they are now on the verge of a quarrel among themselves. In two Congressional districts, in 1874, Democrats ran against Democrats; in many counties independent candidates were put forward, and, where the Republicans were wise enough to support them, were elected. There are at this time eight or ten candidates for governor. By the way, Governor Smith is a candidate for re-election, and, in view of this fact, his firm and just course during the "insurrection" excitement shows that he at least believes that the white people, whose votes he would like to get, are in favor of justice to the negroes.

Georgia has some able and many influential public men. Unfortunately for the Republicans, they are all in the Democratic party. Governor Brown, who is reputed the ablest and most popular man in the State, was a Republican in 1868; but he is one no longer. He is a man of moderate views, a lover of justice. Of Mr. Stephens I need not speak. He is deeply repected by all Georgians, who forgive him all his vagaries, and will support him for whatever place he desires, conscious that he will serve them honestly. General Toombs is a man of but little influence. He has a small and decreasing following, composed of a few extremists.

Thomas Nelson Page, Virginia Novelist of the Plantation Tradition, Hails the Collapse of Reconstruction and the Withdrawal of Federal Troops

Among the literary exponents of Virginia's aristocratic myth was Thomas Nelson Page (1853-1922), leader of the sentimental "local-color school" of novelists and short-story writers. Page revived the romantic symbols of a ravished South crushed by war and Reconstruction: the feudal-minded, courageous Anglo-Saxon, the ever-loyal Negro (a compound of Uncle Tom, Uncle Remus, and primitive African), and other idealized characters. He reflected the aristocratic memories of his own Virginian plantation birth and his relationship to the aristocratic families—the Pendletons, the Randolphs, the Carters, and the Lees.

As this essay shows, Page remembers well his student days at Washington College where he revered its president, Robert E. Lee. Later he was to attend the University of Virginia Law School, ever popular among planters. He was a lawyer when Reconstruction ended, but soon turned toward a literary career. He is best remembered for his sketches and Negro-dialect stories, such as "In Ole Virginia" (1887), and the novel *Red Rock* (1897). In 1913 this champion of the old Cotton Kingdom and its haloed past was chosen as ambassador to Italy by a Virginia-born President whose internationalism tempered his own conservative racial inheritance.

The reader of Page's article will find a detailed Southern interpretation of Reconstruction which has won both academic and general popularity in the North as well as in the Old Confederacy. Reconstruction appeared a violation of Southern sensibilities and a tragic misunderstanding of the Negro's innate inferiority. Together with the rascality of the Carpetbaggers, the Radical fanatics insured the failure of their experiment. Or so it seemed to Page.

From "The Southern People During Reconstruction," *The Atlantic Monthly,* LXXXVIII (1901), 289-304.

. . . It was a veteran soldiery that repeopled the plantations and the homesteads of the South, and withstood the forces thrown against them during the period of reconstruction. In addition to such racial traits as personal pride, self-reliance, and physical courage, they possessed also race pride, which is inestimable in a great popular struggle. This race pride the war had only increased. However beaten and broken they were, the people of the South came out of the war with their spirit unquenched, and a belief that they were unconquerable.

A story used to be told of an old Confederate soldier who was trudging home, after the war, broken and ragged and worn. He was asked what he would do if the Yankees got after him when he reached home.

"Oh, they ain't goin' to trouble me," he said. "If they do, I'll just whip 'em agin."

The South, after the war, was ready for peace. Its leaders accepted the terms of capitulation without a single mental reservation.

The terms had been equally honorable to both the victors and the vanquished; and the troops returned home fully prepared to abide by those terms in every particular. They were sustained by the consciousness of having been animated by the highest of motives,—love of country and of home,—of having made an unsurpassed struggle, and of being able to meet and endure every fortune that could befall. Their idolized general refused all proffers of aid and tenders of attention, and retired to the little college town of Lexington, Virginia, to devote the rest of his life to educating the young men of the South. George Washington had given the first endowment to the college there, and the next greatest Virginian now endowed it with his presence and his spirit. Here the sons of his old soldiers flocked to be under the command of the man who had led their fathers in battle, and to learn from his life the high lesson of devotion to duty.

The writer can speak from personal knowledge when he records that his teaching was the purest patriotism. . . .

The example of General Lee was inestimable. It possibly did as much as the garrisons that filled the South to prevent the lawlessness that almost always follows the close of war and the disbandment of armies.

The worst that the people of the South anticipated was being brought back into the Union with their property gone and their wounds yet smarting. The sense of defeat, together with the loss of property by force of arms, which left them almost universally impoverished, and the disruption of their social system, was no little burden for them to bear; but it was assumed bravely enough, and they went to work with energy and courage, and even with a certain high-heartedness. They started in on the plantations, where by reason of the disorganization of all labor they were needed, as wagoners or ploughmen or blacksmiths. They went to the cities, and became breakmen or street-car drivers, or watchmen or porters. Or they sought employment on public works in any capacity, men who had been generals even taking places as axemen or teamsters till they could rise to be superintendents and presidents. But they had peace and hope.

On the 18th of December, 1865, General Grant, who had been sent through the South by the President to inspect and make a report on its condition, in his report said:—

"I am satisfied the mass of thinking men in the South accept the present situation of affairs in good faith. The questions which have hitherto divided the sentiment of the people of the two sections—slavery and state rights, or the right of the state to secede from the Union —they regard as having been settled forever by the highest tribunal, that of arms, that man can resort to."

He also made the wise suggestion that negro troops should not be employed in garrisoning the Southern states, as they tended to excite the people and intensify their animosity.

It is possible that but for the race questions that existed, the South would have been pacified within a few years; the process of reconstruction, if it was tried at all, would have been carried out in a wiser and less disastrous way; the South would have resumed its normal place in the Union with the net results of the war,—an indissoluble

Union and a homogeneous people, freed from the canker of Slavery and bound together by ever closer ties.

The whites numbered, roughly, about 8,000,000, and the other class, the negroes, about 4,000,000. A relationship too singular to be understood by the outside world existed between the races. It bore on the side of the masters a sort of feudal coloring—the right to demand duty, and the duty to give protection; on the part of the slaves it had a tinge that has been well said to resemble a sort of tribal instinct. The outside world, including the North, saw only a relation of brute power and of enforced subservience. The examples which came to their attention were, in the main, only the worst cases. The proportion of negroes who, during the war, availed themselves of the opportunity to escape from Slavery and seek asylum within the Union lines was by no means a large one. Doubtless they comprised many who were ambitious and enterprising; but, speaking generally, they were the idle and the vicious. Others went because of the scarcity on the plantations, caused by war, or of the new hardship, due to the absenteeism of their masters, and the rumors of gilded rewards awaiting them,—rewards beyond freedom—which reached them in their homes. Many Confederate officers had their colored servants with them in the field. It was almost unheard of for one to desert. It was not unknown for them to avail themselves of their color to forage within the enemy's lines for their masters' mess.

The negroes had, as slaves, indeed, have often done during wars, borne themselves admirably all during the war—a fact which speaks with equal force for their loyalty and for their knowledge of the resolution of their masters. Even those who, under the temptation of freedom and bounties, had gone into the Union army had never been charged with exceptional violence. Emancipation had brought no outbreak. They had generally gone off from their old homes—perhaps as a practical proof of freedom,—most of them slipping away in the night; but the first taste of freedom over, and the first pinch of poverty experienced, they had come straggling back with a certain shamefacedness, and had been received with cordiality.

The writer can recall now the return of some of these prodigals, and the welcome they received.

In many cases they had their old cabins assigned them; in others, at their option, they were given a lodgment on a piece of land on some part of the plantation more or less removed from the mansion, where they could build and live independent whilst they worked as laborers for hire. Almost universally, the relation reëstablished after the first break was one of friendship and good will. Their return was marked by a revival of the old plantation life, and in a short time the old régime appeared to have begun again, with every prospect of continuing. Land, the only property which had survived the war, rose in value, until it was as high as it had ever been. Loans were negotiated on it to repair the ravages of war and restock the plantations; cotton, wheat, and tobacco were at prices that promised well for the agricultural interest; and the people of the South began to experience the awakening of hope.

Unhappily, the work of a madman cut down, in the very hour of success, the leader who had brought the country safely through the war, and who might, with his calm foresight and his gift for conciliation, have guided it through the troubled times that were to follow. The assassination of President Lincoln, with the murderous attack on his advisers, filled the North with consternation and rage, and gave the chief haters of the South an opportunity to vent their wrath which they were not slow to use.

Under a plan devised by Mr. Lincoln, the recently seceded states had set to work to reorganize themselves, and their civil governments were in full operation a few months after the close of the war. The next step was the election of representatives in Congress. In the main, men known nationally to be of conservative views, many of them old Union men, were selected. It was, however, to be long before Southern representatives were to be admitted.

Now, in its struggle, the South had no such potent friend as Lincoln might have been. The first official act of Secretary Stanton after Mr. Lincoln's death had been to reverse one of his decisions, and issue an order for the arrest of a member of the late Confederate Cabinet who was on his way to Canada. On Lincoln's death, Andrew Johnson, who had come into note as the war governor of the newly reconstructed state of Tennessee, had begun by breathing threatenings and slaughter against the South. His first measures had been so severe that Mr. Seward had felt it necessary to restrain him. His proposed action had been so violative of the terms accorded by Grant at Appomattox to Lee and his army that Grant, always magnanimous and courageous, had felt himself compelled to threaten him with the surrender of his command. In a short time, however, a contention had arisen between Johnson and the Congress, growing, on his side, partly out of his attempt to exercise the power claimed for the Executive by Mr. Lincoln, partly out of his ambition to be reëlected, and the necessity he was under to secure the votes of the Southern states as a part of his electoral machinery; on the other side, out of the wish of the Congress to control the reorganization of the South, and the determination of its ablest leaders to secure at all cost perpetual control of the government. Johnson, who had been among the most virulent enemies of the South, and assuredly not the least hated, was thrown by this contest into the anomalous position of its advocate, and the Congress was hurried along, with its passions inflamed by its most radical leaders, until reason was lost, moderation was thrown to the winds, and it found itself paramount, indeed—with the South prostrate, the Constitution a thing to be tinkered with or overridden as partisan expediency suggested, and "the party of the Union" burdened in the South with the most ignorant, venal, and debauched representatives that ever cursed a land. The white race of the South, the constituent part of the great race that had made the country and was to help hold it in the coming years against the world, were outraged almost beyond cure. With every divergence of opinion forgot, every possibility of wholesome division on economic or other public questions buried, they were consolidated in the passionate desire to hold their homes and save their race.

The blacks had not been less injured by the political debauchery into which they had been wiled. Withdrawn from the field of activity in which they had been trained, and in which they might have attained continued success, the close of the reconstruction period found them estranged from the whites, their habits of industry impaired, their vision obscured, their aims turned in directions in which they have shown neither the genius nor the training to compete successfully. They were legislated into a position where they did only harm to themselves and others, and in which they could be maintained only by outside power.

It was the South's misfortune that the new problems could not be worked out on their own merits. The negro question, "the direful spring of woes unnumbered," almost at once became the paramount issue, and from that time to the present has tinged nearly every measure in which the South has been concerned. Emancipation had been accepted readily enough; but emancipation brought new problems. The proper solution of the new questions, which would have been a delicate and difficult task under any circumstances, was rendered impossible by the ignorance of the elements to be handled, and the passion infused into every act touching them.

The institution known as the Freedmen's Bureau, and its work in the South, played a not inconsiderable part in the trouble that arose. The motive for its origin was, no doubt, a good one, and, no doubt, a part of its work was beneficial to one of the races. It had the "supervision and management of all abandoned lands, and the control of all subjects relating to refugees and freedmen." It issued rations to freedmen; regulated all matters of labor and contract in which the freedmen were interested; administered justice wherever they were concerned; and had power to take charge of all "abandoned lands" and parcel them out to negroes as homes, and generally to administrate the negro and his affairs. Incident to these duties was the power to arrest and imprison. The Bureau began its work with an idea which was fatal to its success: that the negro was a poor oppressed creature who was to be treated as the nation's ward, and that the white was a hardened tyrant who had to be restrained.

The officials of the Bureau were of various kinds: honest men, more or less fair-minded and wise; honest men, hopelessly prejudiced and bigoted; and men without honesty, wisdom, or any other qualification. All were absolutely ignorant of the true relation between the old masters and slaves; all had a bigoted people behind them, and a bigoted people before them. Unhappily, the largest, or at least the most active element among the officials were the last class: sutlers, skulkers, and other refuse of a great army, who had no sooner found the dangers of war over than they had begun to look about them to see what spoil they could appropriate, and, recognizing in the newly freed negroes the most promising instrument at hand for their purposes, had ingratiated themselves with the Freedmen's Bureau. One of the first evidences of their malign influence was the idea disseminated among the negroes, which grew out of the provision relating to abandoned lands, that every freedman was to be given by the government, out of the lands of his old master, forty acres and a mule—a teaching which was productive of much danger to the whites, and of much evil to the blacks. Among other things, it prevented the former from settling the negroes on the old plantations, as they would otherwise have done very generally.

The Freedmen's Bureau and its work soon had the whole South in a ferment. The distribution of rations relieved the slaves, but misled them into thinking that the government would support them, whether they worked or not. The officials began inquisitorial investigations. They summoned the best and the most stately of the old gentry before them, as if they had been schoolboys. If the officials were of the last class mentioned above, they hectored them before crowds of gaping negroes, which taught another lesson. They interfered with the administration of courts that had begun to work again, even taking convicted prisoners out of the hands of the officers of the law. As an illustration: In Virginia, an old magistrate, who had tried and sentenced a negro for some crime, was peremptorily ordered by the military authority to release the prisoner, and appear himself before the provost to explain his action. He replied that the prisoner had been tried fairly, convicted justly, and sentenced legally; and though he might be released by the military power, it would only be after he had summoned the whole power of the county to resist it. Naturally, such action tended to excite the negroes and embitter the whites.

The negroes in some places began to hold night meetings, and parcel out the lands of their former masters.

On one of the finest plantations in Virginia this nocturnal partition went along amicably enough until the mill was reached. Here trouble arose at once. The idea of being able to sit and watch the meal spurt down from under the hopper, with nothing to do but to take the tithe, was so attractive that there were too many claimants to agree to its disposal to any one of them, and the meeting broke up in a row. Knowledge of what was going on thus reached the master, who sent at once to the court house for the Federal officer stationed there, who then represented law and order in the county; and the officer soon settled the matter, and disposed of all apprehension of further trouble on that plantation.

No one would say that army officers make generally ideal rulers; for, after all, military rule subjects government to the will of one man. In the pacification of a people, the questions are so difficult and delicate that only wisdom, firmness, singleness of purpose, and an inherent sense of equity avail. These did not always exist. But a dispassionate reading of the records shows that the army officers in the South endeavored, in the main, to perform their duties with wisdom, equity, and moderation. Conditions, however, were to grow worse. The army officers were soon to be supplanted by worse rulers.

The carcass was recognized, and the eagles gathered together. The sutlers, skulkers, and refuse, who had been given a chance, under the working of the Bureau, to ingratiate themselves with the negroes, soon were chosen as the political leaders. The ignorance and the credulity of the negro became the capital of these creatures, and with it they traded to their own enrichment and the impoverishment of every one else. The misapprehension on the part of the Southern people of the changed conditions played into their hands.

The laboring population had been withdrawn from the fields, but were still present in the community, while the fields were untilled and the plantations were going to waste. History had shown that such an element might change from a useless to a dangerous one. The legislatures of the various states, assuming that, after a successful war to preserve the Union, the Union still existed, and unable to recognize the completeness of their overthrow, began to pass labor laws directed at the negro, some of which certainly were calculated to impair his freedom of action. Similar laws existed in some of the Northern states, such as Maine, Rhode Island, and Connecticut. But these new statutes were frankly aimed to control the newly emancipated slaves. An impression of profound distrust was created throughout the North, the

people of which, with their sympathies quickened for an entire race
turned adrift, without homes or property, had almost begun to consider that the war had been fought for the emancipation of the blacks.
Unhappily, at the same time state representatives were chosen whose
votes might have a decisive influence on the fortunes of those leaders
who now esteemed themselves the saviors of the country. It was determined by these leaders to perpetuate their power at every hazard,
even if it were found necessary to overthrow the white race altogether,
and put the black over them. The South was intractable and uncom-
promising. The North was blinded by passion, and led by partisan
leaders bent on domination and without scruple in their exercise of
power. A large element of the people of the North believed that they
were doing God and man service in supporting them, and putting
down a rancorous people who were, they thought, still ready to destroy the Union, and were trying to effect by shift what they had failed
to do by force. But so far as the leaders were concerned it would appear that along with other motives was an implacable resentment
against the white people of the South, and a deliberate determination
to humiliate them and render them forever powerless. The result was
one of the mistakes that constitute what in the life of a nation is worse
than a national crime,—a national blunder. Those who had been the
masters, and had given proof by their works that they were behind no
people in the highest fruits of civilization,—who had just shown by
their constancy, if by no other virtue, that they were worthy of being
treated with consideration,—were disfranchised and shut out from
participation in the government, while their former slaves were put
over them.

For instance, in the county that had produced Patrick Henry and
Henry Clay, one of the most noted of the old gentlemen stood as a
conservative candidate for the first General Assembly held in Virginia
after the war. He was a man of remarkable intelligence and culture.
He had traveled abroad—a rare thing in those days,—and had trans-
lated the poems of Ariosto. He was one of the largest property owners
in the state; had been a Union man, and one of the stoutest opponents
of Secession. He was the head of one of the few old families in Virginia who, immediately after the war, announced their determination

to accept the new conditions and act with the Republican party. This gentleman was beaten for the General Assembly by the brother of his negro carriage-driver. This was early in the period following the war. Later on, when "ironclad oaths" had been devised, and the full work of disfranchisement had been effected, no whites but those who had had their disabilities specially removed could hold office or vote. For a time, only the negroes, the carpet-baggers, and those who disregarded perjury voted.

The white race were disfranchised, and were not allowed the franchise again until they had assented to giving the black race absolute equality in all matters of civil right. This the leaders of the other side vainly imagined would perpetuate their power, and for a time it almost promised to do so.

The result of the new régime thus established in the South was such a riot of rapine and rascality as had never been known in the history of this country, and hardly ever in the history of the world. It would seem incredible to any but those who have investigated it for themselves. The states were given over to pillage at the hands of former slaves, led largely by adventurers whose only aim was to gratify their vengeance or their cupidity. The measure of their peculation and damage, as gauged by figures alone, staggers belief.

The cost to the state of Louisiana of four years and five months of carpet-bag rule amounted to $106,020,337. Taxation went up in proportion. The wealth of New Orleans during the eight years of carpet-bag rule, instead of increasing, fell from $146,718,790 to $88,613,930. The governor himself, who, when he stood for the governorship, had a mite chest placed beside the ballot box, to receive contributions from the negroes to pay his expenses to Washington, had been in office only a year when it was estimated that he was worth $225,000. When he retired, he was said to have one of the largest fortunes in Louisiana.

In Mississippi, the state levy for 1871 was four times what it was in 1869. For 1873 it was eight and one half times as great. For 1874 it was fourteen times as great, and 640,000 acres of land, comprising twenty per cent of all the land in the state, had been forfeited for non-payment of these extraordinary taxes.

In South Carolina, the taxable values in 1860 amounted to about

$490,000,000, and the tax to a little less than $400,000. In 1871 the taxable values had been reduced to $184,000,000, and the tax had been increased to $2,000,000. A large percentage of the lands of the state were sold for unpaid taxes, and a land commission was established to take them and distribute them among the freedmen, and their friends on terms that substantially placed them at the disposal of the commission.

But as extraordinary as the mere figures would appear, and as strong as they are to show the extent of the robbery to which the people of the South were subjected, they give little idea of the bitterness of the degradation that they underwent. The true measure of injury to the people of the South was the humiliation to which they were subjected during the progress of this system of rapine. Some states were subjected to greater damage and, if possible, deeper humiliation than others. The people of South Carolina, Mississippi, Louisiana, and Arkansas, perhaps, suffered the most; but all underwent the humiliation of seeing their states given over to pillage by miscreants and malefactors, of having their slaves put over them and kept over them by armed power, whilst they themselves were forced to stand bound, helpless witnesses of their destruction.

Virginia escaped in a measure some of the most extreme consequences. For instance, there were no continued incitements to riot and no wholesale arrests of an entire community, as took place in South Carolina; there was no general subjection to an armed and insolent militia of former slaves who terrorized the country, as happened in the most southerly states. Virginia never had a governor, as Arkansas had, who issued to his adjutant-general proscription lists of leading citizens, accompanied by a notification that he had marked with asterisks the names of the most obnoxious persons, and that if they could be tried by court-martial and executed while the writ of habeas corpus was suspended, the finding would be approved by the governor. The Ku Klux Klan, with its swath of outrage and terrorism, never obtained the footing in Virginia that it had in states farther south, where life had been made more unendurable. But the people of Virginia, like those of the other Southern states, drank from the same cup of bitterness in seeing their civilization overthrown,—intelligence, culture, and refinement put under the heel of ignorance and venality, and a third of the people, who had comprised most of the laboring population and all the domestic servants, and had lived in the past in amity and affection with their masters, turned for a time into violent enemies.

Unhappily, the credulity and ignorance of the negroes threw them into the hands of the worst element among the adventurers who were vying to become their leaders. The man who was bold enough to bid the highest outstripped the others. Under the teaching and with the aid of these leaders, the negroes showed signs of rendering considerable parts of the Southern states uninhabitable by the whites. Had the latter given the slightest sign of being cowed or of yielding, they probably would have been lost forever; but, fortunately for the South, they never yielded.

Unable to resist openly the power of the National government that stood behind the carpet-bag governments of the states, the people of the South resorted to other means which proved for a time more or less effective. Secret societies were formed, which, under such titles as the "Ku Klux Klan," the "Knights of the White Camellia," the "White Brotherhood," etc., played a potent and, at first, it would seem, a beneficial part in restraining the excesses of the newly exalted leaders and their excited levies.

Wherever masked and ghostly riders appeared, the frightened negroes kept under cover. The idea spread with great rapidity over nearly all the South, and the secret organizations, known among themselves as the "Invisible Empire," were found to be so dangerous to the continued power of the carpet-bag governments, and in places so menacing to their representatives personally, that the aid of the National government was called in to suppress them.

In a short time every power of the government was in motion, or ready to be set in motion, against them. "Ku Klux Acts" were passed; presidential proclamations were issued; the entire machinery of the United States courts was put in operation; the writ of habeas corpus was suspended in those sections where the Ku Klux were most in evidence, and Federal troops were employed.

The testimony taken before what was known as the "Ku Klux Committee," with the reports made by that committee, is contained in thirteen volumes, and makes interesting reading for the student of history. The investigation covered every state in the South.

One who studies those reports is likely to find his confidence in human nature somewhat shaken. It will appear to him that gross and palpable perjury was almost common before that committee, and that the story contained in those reports is so dreadful that if published now it would not be believed. It serves to illustrate, at least, the violence of party feeling at that time, that, under the stress of passion which then prevailed, the Republican members of the Committee of Investigation all signed one report laying the entire blame on the Southern people, and the Democratic members all signed a minority report charging the blame wholly on the other side.

With Congress passing penal acts against all connected with the secret societies, the army of the United States at hand to put them down, and the United States courts ready to push through the convictions of all participants in their work, the constituency and purposes of the secret societies soon changed. The more law-abiding and self-respecting element dropped out, and such organizations as remained were composed only of the most disorderly and reckless element. Under conduct of such a class, the societies, whatever their original design, soon degenerated into mere bands of masked ruffians, who used their organization and their disguises for the private purposes of robbery and revenge. As might have been foreseen, they became a general pest in the regions which they infested, and the better element of native Southerners were as concerned to put a stop to their action as was the government. This class, later on, found it necessary to keep themselves banded together; but it was no longer in a secret association. During the later phases of the struggle the meetings of the whites were open. Fortunately for them, by this time the debauchery of those who had formerly been sustained by the government had become so openly infamous that it began to be known at the North for what it really was, and the people of the North began to revolt against its continuance. The indorsement of the government leaders at Washington became more and more half-hearted; and as this was recognized, the white people of the South began to be reanimated with hope.

The action of the other side at the South generally played into their hands. The leaders lacked the first element of wisdom; their moderation was only the limit to their power.

The women and children of the Southern states, during the utmost excitement of war, had slept as secure with their slaves about them as if they had been guarded by their husbands and fathers, but under the new teaching the torch became a weapon. A distinguished leader of the colored race, a native white man in South Carolina, said, in a public speech to his constituents, that the barns had been built by them, and their contents belonged to them; and if they were refused the distribution of those contents, matches were only five cents a box. Is it to be wondered at that, with such suggestions, the burning of houses became more or less frequent in the belts subject to the domination of the excited race? This man, who had many crimes to answer for, after passing through numberless dangers, became the victim of a foul assassination. A story is told that some years ago two men were sitting together in a well-known restaurant in Washington. One of them, who was from a Northern state, said to the other, who was from South Carolina, "Tell me, now that it is so long past, who murdered So-and-So," mentioning the name of the leader who has been spoken of. "Well," said the other quietly, "I was tried for it."

Amiable and orderly as the colored race were when the whites were in control, as soon as an election approached they showed every sign of excitement. When they were in power, life became intolerable, and a clash was imminent at every meeting; men and women went armed; many families, unable to endure the strain, abandoned their homes, and moved to other communities or other states. The distinguished pastor of a large church in the North, one of the godliest of men, who had a church during this period in one of the Southern states, has said that when he went to his night services he as regularly put a pistol in his pocket as he took his Bible. Even funerals were liable to be interrupted by the half-maddened creatures, and instances occurred when the hearse had to be driven at full speed to outstrip a mob bent on the last extremity of insult.

It was notable that even during the periods of greatest excitement, when the negroes were stirred almost to frenzy, the old family servants ever stood ready to prevent personal harm to their former masters and mistresses; and that when the excitement had passed, the entire race were ready to resume, and even to seek, friendly relations with the whites. . . .

It is not probable that any wholly sane man of any section or race, who knows the facts, would ever wish its repetition. The last governor of South Carolina under that régime (who has recently written a paper in this series)* stated, during his incumbency, that when, in May, 1875, he entered on his duties as governor, two hundred trial justices were holding office by executive appointment (of his predecessor) who could neither read nor write. No wonder that he should have declared, as he did, in writing to the New England Society, that the civilization of the Puritan and Cavalier, of the Roundhead and Huguenot, was in peril.

In the last stages of their existence, these governments were sustained solely by the bayonet. As soon as the United States troops were removed they melted away. As an illustration: In South Carolina, in 1876, after the extraordinary Wade Hampton campaign, in which the whites had won a signal victory, two distinct state governments performed their functions in the State House; a small guard of United States soldiers marched their beats back and forth, representing the power that alone sustained one of those governments. An order was issued by the President of the United States removing the troops, and in twenty-four hours, without a drop of blood shed, without a single clash, the government of the carpet-bagger and the negro had disappeared, and the government of the native South Carolinian and of the white man had quietly, after a lapse of years, resumed control. But during those years the people of the South had seen their most cherished traditions traversed, their civilization overthrown. . . .

* Governor D. H. Chamberlain's article; see p. 255.

DATE DUE